Glasgow's Hidden Walks

by Stephen Millar

Glasgow's Hidden Walks

by Stephen Millar

Glasgow's Hidden Walks

Written by Stephen Millar
Photography by Stephen Millar
Edited by Eve Kershman
Book design by Lesley Gilmour and Susi Koch
Illustrations by Lesley Gilmour and Hannah Kershman

All rights reserved. No part of this publication may be reproduced, stored in a retrieval system or transmitted in any form or by any means electronic, mechanical, photocopying, recording or otherwise without the prior consent of the publishers and copyright owners. Every effort has been made to ensure the accuracy of this book; however, due to the nature of the subject the publishers cannot accept responsibility for any errors which occur, or their consequences.

First published in 2025

Metro® is a registered trade mark of Associated Newspapers Limited. The METRO mark is under licence from Associated Newspapers Limited.

Printed and bound in China. This book is produced using paper from registered sustainable and managed sources.

© Stephen Millar
British Library Cataloguing in Publication Data.
A catalogue record for this book is available from the British Library.

ISBN 978-1-902910-81-9

In memory of my father, Bill Millar

Acknowledgements

When researching this, my seventh urban walking book, I took an unconventional approach by creating a walking group through meetup.com. I invited people to join me as I explored new routes promising only possible dead ends, wrong turns and a bit of fun. This decision transformed my experience entirely. Our group grew to over 2,500 members, and I walked with people from every corner of the earth: Saudi Arabia, Indonesia, Iran, Japan, Ukraine, Nigeria, Bolivia, Italy, and more – all eager to discover Glasgow. Many Weegies also came, and I learnt a lot from them as they contributed their own memories of places we were walking through.

Some walks had over forty people and so were not without their challenges: we once huddled under a lone tree in Anderston during a downpour, street democracy in evidence as we voted on whether we could continue or not (we didn't...). On another occasion, we were stopped in the Gorbals by the police who thought we were a splinter group from a political demo taking place in the city centre (we weren't). And then there was the time we stopped in the Govan Arms during a Celtic match and some walkers tried to order cappuccinos (the Govan Arms doesn't serve coffee..).

I would therefore like to extend my gratitude to all who joined these walks and donated to charities such as Maggie's Cancer Trust. Special thanks particularly to regulars who turned up in all weather conditions, including Roy Strong, Sheila Muir, Sandie Gilchrist, Mary Nicholson, Linda Conway, Patricia Burnett, Stuart Dobbie, Amitashuri, and Ann Carrigan. My thanks also to Marie Fleming and Caroline Whyteside who have chased me for years to get this book published.

Thanks also to Neil Gateley who helped me take photographs for the book. Glasgow is a difficult place to photograph given light conditions, so persistence is required.

Finally, I'm grateful to Andrew, Susi, and Lesley at Metro for their continued support.

Contents

Introduction 1
Area Map.. 2-3
1. Partick Walk 5-37
2. Anderston & Finnieston Walk 38-73
3. Garnethill Walk 74-107
4. Gorbals Walk 108-143
5. Miss Cranston Walk.......................... 144-165
6. Pollokshields, Crosshill
   & Govanhill Walk 166-199
7. Medieval Glasgow, Townhead
   & Merchant City Walk.......................200-235
8. City Centre Architects Walk 236-265
9. West End Walk................................266-293
10. Dennistoun Walk 294-319
11. Kelvin River & Canal Walk 320-345
12. Ibrox into Govan Walk.....................346-381
Index 382-389

The 'Sixty Steps', see p.328

Introduction

Glasgow is a fascinating and often underappreciated city. As someone who lived here as a boy, and considers it my spiritual home, it has been a pleasure to rediscover its charms.

This book explores beyond the city centre, venturing into areas like the Gorbals and Govanhill that rarely make it onto the radar of visitors or indeed many Glaswegians. I have also been surprised to meet many residents of Edinburgh who barely know their neighbour, and I hope this book encourages them to journey west and explore.

During the walks you will learn about the city's rapid growth from a mere dozen streets in the early 1700s to becoming the Second City of the Empire. You will also explore the impact of deindustrialisation, and how the city has continued to change and evolve in the 21st century. Throughout your walks, you will see great architecture, an astonishing amount produced by a relatively small number of Victorian and Edwardian era-architects such as James Miller, the Burnets, and Salmons, whose contributions rival those of the more famous 'Greek' Thomson and Charles Rennie Mackintosh.

Along the way you will visit abandoned railway stations, vibrant community gardens, a stretch of the mythical Molendinar Burn, and learn about old shipbuilding yards, infamous murders, and how local activists saved many tenement streets. Glasgow has long been a place that has attracted immigrants and you will see how they have shaped the character of the city as it is today. You will also discover pubs that are at the heart of their community, but also offer a warm welcome to strangers.

Glasgow is a friendly place, so I encourage you to talk to people. You may think that being Glasgow-born I am biased, but the city was voted the UK's friendliest city (in 2024) by *Condé Nast Traveller* readers.

I always enjoy hearing from walkers' experiences of using my books – you can email at stephenwmillar@hotmail.com. I also offer walks (stephenmillarwalks.com).

Stephen Millar

AREA MAP

1. Partick Walk 5-37
2. Anderston & Finnieston Walk 38-73
3. Garnethill Walk 74-107
4. Gorbals Walk 108-143
5. Miss Cranston Walk 144-165
6. Pollokshields, Crosshill & Govanhill Walk 166-199
7. Medieval Glasgow, Townhead & Merchant City Walk 200-235
8. City Centre Architects Walk 236-265
9. West End Walk 266-293
10. Dennistoun Walk 294-319
11. Kelvin River & Canal Walk 320-345
12. Ibrox into Govan Walk 346-381

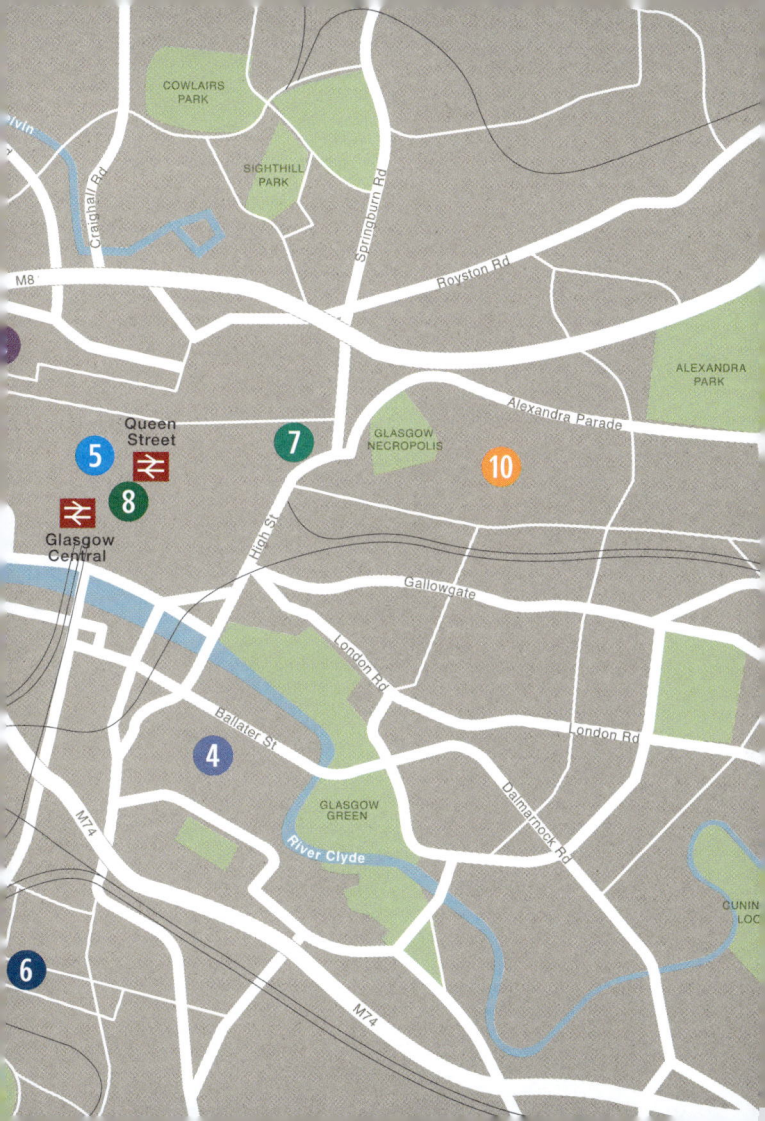

Kelvin River

1 Partick Walk

Partick Walk

Partick Walk
Start/Finish: Kelvinhall subway
Distance: 3.5 miles

Partick Walk

The walk starts at Kelvinhall subway, originally named Partick Cross when it opened in 1896 and renamed after nearby Kelvin Hall in 1977. This is one of many stations mentioned on this walk that have disappeared or changed their names over time. Above the entrance is a hook or 'rosette' holder that once held overhead lines used by electric trams. Glasgow's tram system was one of the most extensive in Europe before it ceased operations in 1962. Keep an eye out for further rosettes.

Opposite is ❶ **The Dolphin**, one of several traditional boozers that line Dumbarton Road, the spine of Partick. In 2015 a man was murdered and two were injured in the flat above. It is known as a Celtic pub and has served locals since 1888.

Walk along Dumbarton Road through Partick Cross – one of several junctions called 'Cross' in Glasgow, which typically signifies the historical heart of a district. Look up for ❷ **Partick Cross Mansions** block on the corner of Byres Road.

Until the 19th century, Partick was a quiet village outside Glasgow, lying mainly to the south of here. It was known for its flour mills powered by the River Kelvin and the location of a ford. It served as a stopping point for Highland drovers bringing livestock into the city's market, who often stayed at local inns.

Before the Industrial Revolution changed Partick forever, the village was known for its fat ducks, which were nourished on grain lying by the mills and considered very tasty. Glaswegians came for countryside strolls. As the area became an industrialised suburb, village streets, and cottages were replaced by hundreds of tenement buildings. Most red sandstone examples you see today were built from the 1890s up until the World War I.

Partick Walk

Turn left up Byres Road and then take the next right onto Torness Street. On the left is the shell of the old ❸ **Church Street School building**, dating from 1903. This was the site of the gymnasium, swimming pool, and janitor's office. Look for signs for 'Govan Parish' (north side), and (along Torness Road) 'Boys' and 'Girls'. Next door is the old school itself – it is worth taking a brief detour to admire the building.

This is a reminder that Govan was once more than just a district on the south side of the Clyde facing Partick. For centuries, it was a large parish that covered villages both south and north of the river, including the burgh of Partick. Before Partick had its own churches, locals might take the ferry to attend services in Govan parish church. The school once had over 1,300 pupils but closed in 1976. It was preceded on this site by Partick Academy, which operated from 1850.

Continue down Torness Street and turn down Church Street to rejoin Dumbarton Road. The street is named for the ❹ **'Old' Partick Parish church** – located here from the 1830s until it was torn down after fire damage in 2002. The restaurant, Málà Project stands on the site today. As late as the 1850s, there were open fields to the east of here and two quarries. Within a few years, these were swept away by newly laid out tenement streets and other buildings.

Turn right on Dumbarton Road, stopping outside number 92 and the sign for ❺ **'Partick St Marys – No 117 – Masonic Lodge'**. Look for Masonic symbols such as

Partick Walk

the 'G', square, and compass (above the 1st-floor level). This Lodge is one of the oldest in the city, having received its charter in 1769. It is amazing to think that predecessors of current-day Freemasons participated in ceremonies in Partick when America was still a British colony. Inside is a Masonic Temple, usually hidden away from the public, but you can often see inside on Glasgow Doors Open Days. Lodge No 117 has been based here since 1908.

Retrace your steps and head along Dumbarton Road. Stop outside an Italian Renaissance-style building on the corner. This was originally ❻ **Anderson's College Medical School**, completed around 1889 by John Keppie. The original architect James Sellars died in 1888 of blood-poisoning after standing on a rusty nail, and Keppie took over. The College was founded in 1796 by John Anderson (1726-96), a professor of natural philosophy at

8 *Old Partick Bridge 'Snow Bridge'*

Glasgow University whose temper earned him the nickname 'JollyJack Phosphorus'. Anderson's College (or Institution) would later morph into Strathclyde University. Keppie (1862-1945) was a noted architect of his day but is mainly remembered today as the boss of Charles Rennie Mackintosh.

Continue over ❼ **Partick Bridge**, dating from 1878. There are great views of the University of Glasgow (left) and the River Kelvin (right).

At the end on the left visit ❽ **Old Partick bridge** (today it's pedestrian only). This bridge was known as the 'Snow Bridge' because railings (still visible) opened to allow snow to be swept off into the river. Before it was built in 1800, people had to cross the Kelvin using an older bridge to the south of here, or a ford or stepping stones (the sites of which can be seen later). Dumbarton Road once had a different route to what you see today, bearing north of the Kelvin slightly before turning back along the Snow Bridge. Imagine the old bridge full of cattle and sheep, their Highland drovers driving them on to market.

Cross over Bunhouse Road (with Kelvin Hall to your left) and head down to the car park by the river's edge to get a different view of Partick Bridge. Look for Partick's coat of arms along the side.

Partick became an independent burgh in 1852. By then, only older residents would remember its days as a village. The people of Partick were proud of this burgh status, symbolised by the burgh hall, the coat of arms, a civic motto, a police force, fire brigade, and other features of independence. However, the authorities of Glasgow wanted to consolidate their power, and Partick was annexed by the city in 1912. The coat of arms is a ghostly reminder of this former status. It features symbols important in the mid-19th

Partick Walk

View from Partick Bridge towards site of Bunhouse Flour Mills

century: a galley representing shipbuilding, a millstone, and a wheatsheaf representing local flour mills, as well as the bishop's mitre and castle for Partick castle.

Today the paths by the River Kelvin are quiet, dominated by walkers and joggers. However, in the past, the riverbank was a busy place and played a crucial role in the livelihoods of thousands of local people. Since medieval times the river provided power for several local flour mills. If you stood here in the 1850s, you would see ❾ **Bunhouse Flour Mills** (where Kelvin Hall car park is today – later called the Regent Mills), and across the river ❿ **Scotstoun Grain Mills**. Regent Mills was owned from 1903 by the Scottish Co-Operative Wholesale Society and produced the once famous 'Lofty Peak' flour.

Over the centuries, the mills had various owners, including the Bishops of Glasgow and the Catholic church (before the Reformation), the Incorporation of Bakers (essentially a trade guild), and later the co-operative movement and companies such as Hovis.

Partick Walk

Retrace your steps over the bridge, turning left down Thurso Street. On the left once stood a tram depot. As you reach the bend in the road, you will see a 'Reception' sign at a student accommodation block called Dunaskin Mill. The proximity of Glasgow University has changed the demographics of Partick significantly. Around a quarter of students come from Asia, their resources helping drive the construction of high-end student accommodation blocks and the founding of local Asian restaurants. It has certainly changed the atmosphere in Partick compared to past decades.

Walk into the new complex and straight ahead on the path to reach the riverside. The student accommodation occupies the site of the **Scotstoun Mills** mentioned earlier.

The first mill was built here in 1507 to produce cloth and was later adapted to mill flour when it was bought by William Walkinshaw of Scotstoun in 1711 (hence the name). The complex was rebuilt in 1877 and was owned for over a century by the White family. The Whites were important people in Partick, and two – both John White – served as provosts of Partick when it was a burgh. In the 20th century, the mill became part of Rank Hovis and operated until 2013 before being demolished. In the late 1980s, 700 tons of bread flour was produced here each week, often made into bread at the Hovis bakery on Duke Street.

Look through the metal fence to see a **⑪ derelict railway bridge** covered in vegetation. This bridge was part of a railway line opened in the 1890s by the Lanarkshire and Dunbartonshire Railway. If you had travelled east along the line, you would have first reached Stobcross station, and heading west would lead to Partick Central station, remains of which you will soon see.

Retrace your steps to the reception office, and walk left

Partick Walk

12

14

Railway line remnants

along Dunaskin Street to reach ⑫ **the former Church of St Simon**, which was the third oldest Roman Catholic place of worship in Glasgow. It was originally St Peter's when it opened in 1858, and its first congregation comprised many Irish immigrants who settled in Partick. However, after World War II, it became known as the Polish church in Glasgow after Polish soldiers stationed in Yorkhill barracks came to worship here.

Many Poles stayed after the war and continued to worship here and were joined more recently by new arrivals from Poland. Sadly in 2021, the interior of the church was gutted by a local arsonist. The cost of rebuilding the church was prohibitive, and the entire site has since been sold to a housing association for redevelopment.

Head down Castle Street, turning left onto Benalder Street. On the left is ⑬ **number 15**, a modern block standing on the site of an iconic nightclub. *The Volcano* (also called at different times Cinder's and Raffles) appeared in the film *Trainspotting* (1996) and is where Renton (Ewan McGregor) meets schoolgirl Diane (Kelly Macdonald).

Continue walking towards the bridge. Before crossing, walk over to the right-hand side and descend down some steps to reach the bank of the Kelvin. If you look through a fence under the bridge, you can see the ghostly remains of a ⑭ **platform from the old Partick Central Station**. The station opened in 1896 and closed to passengers in 1964 (it was then called Kelvin Hall Station). The station building was finally

View from Benalder Street Bridge of ⑪ derelict railway bridge, and ⑯ old ford & stepping stones

Partick Walk

demolished in 2007. It is one of three 'lost' stations that served Partick in the great age of the private railway companies. Cross over Benalder Street Bridge, which dates from 1895 and replaced a nearby bridge built in 1601. As you cross, look down on the left for remnants of the railway line that once ran parallel to the river.

Once over the river, turn left onto Old Dumbarton Road. You have entered Yorkhill and bear left to find the **⑮ Bishop Mills** (or Old Mill). This is the only original mill structure to survive in the area and has been converted into flats. The structure dates from 1839, though mills have existed on this site since medieval times. Its name reflects church ownership of land in Partick up until the Reformation. The mill continued to be used as recently as the 1960s. Look for the sculpted wheatsheaf at the top of the building. Taking care, you can go down behind the mill along a path to the river's edge to get a view of the railway bridge and possibly a heron if you are lucky.

Retrace your steps to return to the end of Benalder Street. Instead of turning onto it, take the left down Ferry Street (named after the Govan Ferry). Long ago, people travelled along Old Dumbarton Road to a ferry that ran to Govan. The old Partick village was established here, and was then part of Govan parish. On your right, you'll pass the location of a **⑯ ford and stepping stones** used before any bridges were built. Further ahead on the left is Centurion Way, where **⑰ Yorkhill Station** once stood. It closed in 1921 and was originally part of the Stobcross Railway. A train from here heading east would have arrived next at Finnieston Station (also now demolished).

Partick Walk

Walk under the still-functioning railway line and bridge, with the horrendous Clydeside Expressway ahead. Turn right, and shortly after, take the path leading under the Expressway through an underpass and follow the sign for Riverside Museum. On the other side, you can see the Kelvin River flowing a few hundred metres before reaching the Clyde.

Path under Expressway

In the 19th century, Partick became known for its shipbuilding industry. Below you here, by the river edge, once stood a long ⑱ **slip dock for Pointhouse Shipyard**. It was founded by Anthony and John Inglis in 1862 and specialised in building ship hulls. The company also produced marine engines in Anderston and employed 2,000 workers. The slip dock stretched for 260 metres, and you can see remnants of its infrastructure by the water's edge.

The company built many paddle steamers, including the original *Waverley*, constructed in 1899. *Waverley* was requisitioned by the Navy in both World Wars and was sunk by German bombers with 600 troops on board in May 1940, during the evacuation of Dunkirk. The shipyard was later bought by Harland & Wolff and closed in 1962, during a period of great decline in Glasgow's shipbuilding industry.

Author and sailor Joseph Conrad, best known for *Heart of Darkness*, served as third mate on a ship called *Loch Etive*, which was built at this yard. He wrote of the *Etive*: 'She was built for hard driving, and undoubtedly she received all the hard driving she could stand'. Conrad spent time in Glasgow seeking employment as a ship captain when book sales were poor. Ironically, his growing reputation as an author counted against him and he wrote to a friend: 'This confounded literature has ruined me entirely'.

Partick Walk

19

Ahead is ⑲ **the Riverside Museum** – worth a detour if you have time. It occupies part of the site of the old shipyard and gives a sense of how big the operations at Pointhouse Yard were. Shipbuilding on this scale was possible because, from the late 1700s, the river authorities organised the dredging of the previously shallow Clyde, allowing the creation of yards for the largest vessels. Dredging was crucial to the development of shipyards at Anderston, Govan and other areas, leading to the foundation of factories, warehouses, and mills close to shipping lines. This is also the site of a new pedestrian footbridge – opened in 2024– that now links Partick to Govan.

The new Govan-Partick bridge that opened here in September 2024 beside the museum, has reinstated ancient transport connections between this part of Glasgow and Govan across the Clyde. In the past there was a ford here until the Clyde was deepened, and also regular ferries. If you walk a short way out onto the bridge and look to your right (north-west), look for the crumbling remains by the water's edge of the old Meadowside shipyard (that features shorty as the walk continues).

When finished, follow the map on the path to the busy road and turn left, heading over the Kelvin. To your right is West View

Student Accommodation. This occupies the ⑳ **site of Partick Castle**, constructed in around 1611 for George Hutcheson, a well-known figure in Glasgow and a significant benefactor of worthy causes (Hutchesons Hospital, Hutchesons Grammar School). An earlier fortification on the same site is believed to have been used as a residence by the Bishop of Glasgow. The original castle may even date back to the 7th century AD, when it was used by the King of Strathclyde. The ruins of Hutcheson's house had disappeared by the 1830s, but substantial foundations of a 12th-century castle were rediscovered by archaeologists in 2016. The castle appears on Partick's coat of arms.

Partick's origins go back a long way. The lands of 'Perdyc' – the old name for Partick – were recorded as far back as 1136 when they were given by King David I to the Bishop of Glasgow. The Catholic church had a major influence over the area up until the Reformation of the 1560s, owning flour mills and benefiting from rights that required farmers to get their wheat processed in church mills. 'Perdyc' is thought to be derived from an ancient Cymro-Celtic word meaning place of orchards or fair fruit trees.

Continue along the pavement and walk for a few minutes. The area to your left on the west bank of the Kelvin was once dominated by ㉑ **the Meadowside shipyard**. It was owned by the partnership of David Tod and John McGregor, described as the 'fathers of iron shipbuilding on the Clyde'. They moved their shipbuilding and repair business here in the 1840s, building Kelvin Dry Dock – the first dry dock on the upper part of the Clyde.

The need for workers at the two shipyards you have walked past helped transform Partick from a village into a working-class urban district. By the mid-1880s, the two shipyards employed around 5,000 workers. Highlanders fleeing the Clearances and Irish men (the majority from Ulster) escaping

Meadowside Shipyard viewed from bridge

View of Govan and last shipyard from Meadowside Quay Walk

the Great Famine, provided a steady stream of workers. As they and their families settled in Partick, the character of the old village changed. Tenement buildings, churches, bridges, and later schools sprang up to cope with the expanding population, while rural paths were built over and widened.

The influence of Partick's industrialists on local life is hard to imagine today. They wielded political power, and several mill and shipyard owners served as provosts of Partick when it was a burgh. When John McGregor died in 1858, Partick came to a standstill, and thousands came out to watch his funeral procession.

The Tod & McGregor shipyard built ships used to break the Union blockade of Southern ports such as Charleston during the American Civil War (1861-65). The shipyard is even mentioned in Jules Verne's short story *The Blockade Runners* (published in 1871). The story centres around a specially built ship called the *Dolphin*, built by Tod & McGregor for a cynical Glaswegian businessman hoping to make a fortune out of the blockade of the Confederate States.

Why were many Glaswegians willing to help the pro-slavery South? Much of it is explained by economic dependency. Thousands of people – from mill owners to factory workers – were part of the cotton processing industry.

Verne explains the issue well in his story: 'The most important material was failing at Glasgow, the cotton famine became

everyday more threatening, thousands of workmen were reduced to living upon public charity. Glasgow possessed 25,000 looms, by which 625,000 yards of cotton were spun daily; that is to say, 50 million pounds yearly. From these numbers, it may be guessed what disturbances were caused in the commercial part of the town when the raw material failed altogether. Failures were hourly taking place, the manufactories were closed, and the workmen were dying of starvation'.

By selling guns and munitions to the Confederate government, and buying cotton in return, the blockade runners helped keep cotton mills in Glasgow running. For many ordinary people, this meant avoiding the workhouse, whilst capitalists kept their mansions. However, it remains a dark chapter in Glasgow's history.

In the 1870s, Tod & McGregor were taken over by the Henderson brothers of the Anchor Line. The company produced ocean liners, whaling ships, sleek yachts, and other types of ships over the following decades. The business was taken over by Harland & Wolff in 1917 and production stopped in 1935. The dry dock was later filled in, and the site cleared. Try to imagine the scale of the yard – the dry dock alone stretched from where you are standing right down to the Clyde. At the time of writing, this area is being transformed by the Glasgow Harbour Lifestyle Outlet, promising a large retail and residential complex.

Partick Walk

Follow the map bearing left down Meadowside Quay Walk and along the edge of the Clyde. On the other side you can see Govan, also once renowned for its shipbuilding industry (some still in operation). The housing complex (part of the Glasgow Harbour Development) partly occupies the site of a ㉒ **football stadium** used by the 'Jags' (Partick Thistle F.C.) from 1897 for around a decade. Founded in 1876, the club was based here and several other locations before settling at Firhill Stadium in Maryhill in 1909.

The stadium site was later home to the Meadowside Granary, initially run by the Clyde Navigation Trust. The granary complex was built in phases between 1911-1967. It was Europe's largest brick-built building and the biggest grain storage complex in Britain. With flour mills nearby, and being by the river, the location of the granary made a lot of sense. However, a decline in shipping on the Clyde contributed to the its closure in 1988. The enormous complex was demolished in 2002, significantly changing the appearance of this part of Partick.

This now tranquil area is known as Thornhill and would have been a much busier place for much of the 20th century, with hundreds of people working in the granary, and men helping unload ships full of grain, timber, and animals (large slaughterhouses and saw mills were located nearby).

Take the second opening on the right and walk through Meadowside Quay Square. As you come through the other side, look for ㉓ *Rise* – a sculpture by Andy Scott (b.1964). On a sunny day, it is stunning, and it is a shame many people are unaware of it, tucked away in a quiet part of the city. Unveiled in 2008, it symbolises the modern city emerging from its maritime

Partick Walk

past. Scott is best known for *The Kelpies* in Falkirk and the statue of Charles Rennie Mackintosh in Anderston.

The Lanarkshire & Dunbartonshire Railway ran just to the north of the stadium, and parallel to the Clyde. Another 'lost' railway station – **㉔ Partick West Station** – stood just next to the site of *Rise*. It was open between 1896-1964, but, like the granary and football stadium, was demolished long ago.

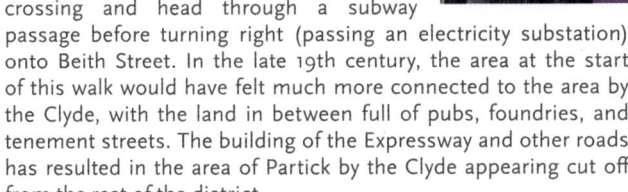

Cross the road via the pedestrian crossing and head through a subway passage before turning right (passing an electricity substation) onto Beith Street. In the late 19th century, the area at the start of this walk would have felt much more connected to the area by the Clyde, with the land in between full of pubs, foundries, and tenement streets. The building of the Expressway and other roads has resulted in the area of Partick by the Clyde appearing cut off from the rest of the district.

Stop outside the former **㉕ Partick Fire Station** building dating from 1906. It was designed by James Miller (1860-1947), one of Glasgow's great architects and best known for his railway stations. At that time engines were horse-drawn, and eight horses were stabled here. They would have emerged from the now-arched ground floor windows. The fire station remained in operation until 1985.

In 1912, Partick was absorbed into Glasgow against the wishes of many local residents. This station became part of the Glasgow Fire Brigade. In 1941 it suffered a direct hit from German bombs and a brave 15-year-old messenger boy named Neil Leitch ignored injuries sustained to continue with his job, however, he died shortly after. Leitch was remembered in a recent work of art by Greg McIndoe entitled *The Boy Messenger*.

Partick Walk

Turn left up Sandy Road, passing a ㉖ **community garden** on the left – one of many that green-fingered Glaswegians have founded in recent years and which uniquely connect local residents.

Shortly you rejoin Dumbarton Road and turn right. On the left is ㉗ **Partick Methodist Church**, a small but fine-looking place of worship built in 1881. As Partick became a densely populated suburb in the 19th century, various religious denominations built churches, hoping to ensure residents did not spend too much time in the local pubs, or fall into the company of rival congregations.

Continue along. On the left, you will see classic late 19th-century and early 20th-century, red sandstone tenements for which Glasgow is well known. Just before you reach the junction with Crow Road, look for older ㉘ **three-storey classical tenement buildings** from the 1860s.

Turn left a short way up Crow Road, passing more churches on your left. This is where Highland drovers brought their livestock into Partick, and 'Crow' is derived from a Gaelic word for cattle. On the right is a retail park on the ㉙ **site of the original Partick Station,** which opened in 1874 and was operated by the North British Railway Company. Renamed Partickhill in 1953, the station closed in 1979, and Partick Station is now located south of Dumbarton Road.

Return to Dumbarton Road and turn left to continue east. On the other side of the road are ㉚ **two traditional local pubs**

– **The Rosevale** (open since the 1920s) and **The Windsor Tavern** – which began as a restaurant in the 1890s. Both establishments have entertained generations of locals and remain popular.

Two doors down from The Windsor, at number 467, is a seemingly unremarkable British Heart Foundation charity shop. This was originally ❸❶ **The Rosevale cinema** that opened in 1920, one of many so-called 'backcourt' cinemas incorporated behind tenement buildings. In its heyday, it could hold 2,100 people and continued as a cinema until 1965. Like many old cinemas, it declined before becoming a bingo hall. The screen was on the right (if you approach the sales desk).

In the mid-19th century, this part of Dumbarton Road was flanked on both sides by substantial detached houses, set back from the road and boasting extensive gardens. All were swept away within a few years by the tenements you see today.

Continue on, passing under the railway bridge where – immediately on the left – is a ❸❷ **disused entrance** to the former Partick (or Partickhill) station. Today, Partick Station is to the south of here.

Further on the right is the ❸❸ **Deoch an Dorus pub**. The name, translated from Gaelic, means 'drink of the door' and refers to the custom of one last drink for a guest before they head home. Many Gaels from the Highland and Islands settled in Partick during the 19th century, often worshipping in their own churches and founding community events and social organisations.

Continue along. One of Scotland's best-known radicals – Stuart Christie (1946-2020) – lived in this area as a child. He later moved to England and became a radical anarchist. Christie is best known for traveling to Spain aged just 18 with a plan to assassinate dictator General Franco. He failed, was imprisoned, and later returned to continue his radical activities and write an excellent autobiography – *Granny Made Me an Anarchist*.

Take a left up Peel Street, looking out for a ❸❹ **ghost advertisement for 'Regalia' Old Highland Whisky**. Some of the modern housing on this street stands on bomb sites resulting from German raids in 1941 that killed several locals. A century before, there was a curling pond and bowling green a little further up on the left-hand side. This was once home to the Partick Curling Club, founded in 1842, and still going today.

Turn right along Burgh Hall Street with the ❸❺ **former Partick Burgh Hall** on the right. The grandest building in Partick, it dates from 1872 when the area was at its zenith – independent from Glasgow, home to expanding industries and run by local people whose confidence is reflected in this impressive structure. It was designed by William Leiper (1839-1916), a respected architect best known for Templeton's carpet factory on Glasgow Green.

Whilst the burgh council was disbanded in 1912 (when Partick was annexed), this remained a community hub hosting everything from weddings to Buddhist festivals. The three relief panels above the entrance refer to the Latin words *Misericordia* (mercy or compassion), *Justicia* (justice) and *Veritas* (truth). They were produced by the Mossman family firm responsible for many fine sculptures in Glasgow.

Opposite is ❸❻ **West of Scotland Cricket club**. Founded in 1862, it has played a leading role in Scottish cricket. Glasgow is known for its football teams but also has a thriving cricket scene. The ground hosted the first official international football match between England and Scotland in November 1872, and W.G Grace played here in 1891. Years ago Rangers fans used to come and watch cricket here when the football season was over.

Take a right down Fortrose Street, returning to Dumbarton Road. You'll see ❸❼ **The Victoria pub** on your left, suitably named as Queen Victoria was on the throne when the pub opened here in the 1880s. In those days it would have been a favourite with shipyard workers.

All around you see tenements constructed using red and blonde sandstone. As a general rule of thumb, the blonde (lighter) sandstone was used on buildings before the 1890s using what was available from quarries in Bishopbriggs and Giffnock. Red sandstone features from the 1890s, when the railway network connected the city to quarries in Dumfries and Ayrshire.

Cross Dumbarton Road and continue onto Anderson Street. Walk for a couple

Partick Walk

of minutes to stop outside a grand building on the corner of Gullane Street. This is the ❸❽ **former Partick police station** that dates from 1853. It was a statement of local pride as Partick had just become a Police Burgh. It served as both the police station and council headquarters before being replaced by the Burgh Hall (seen earlier) in 1872. It was designed with a nod to the architecture of the Italian Renaissance by another famous Glasgow architect – Charles Wilson (1810-63). It was known as Partick Marine because it was home to policemen in the marine division that looked after warehouses and quays beside the Clyde.

Walk along Gullane Street, and turn left up Purdon Street to reach Dumbarton Road. On the left – just before The Smiddy pub (which has stood here since c.1899) – is a ❸❾ **mural by artist Molly Hankinson** inspired by 'Big Rachel' Hamilton. The artist explained 'She was an Irish immigrant who came over and lived in Partick during the 1800s and she was called 'Big Rachel' because she was like 6ft 4in and she was a shipbuilder, which I thought was really cool. And the community agreed that she was a strong character to base the figure off of.'

It is a reminder of Partick's past sectarian tensions. Traditionally an Orange district, many jobs in local shipyards were controlled by Protestant Ulstermen. On 7 August 1875, Irish Catholics gathered in Glasgow Green to celebrate what would have been Daniel O'Connell's 100th birthday. When several hundred headed back, a violent confrontation took place at Partick Cross with members of the Orange Order. This led to a 2-day riot involving hundreds of people,

Partick Walk

and Govan's police force initially struggled to hope. They had to be helped by other city policemen and special constables such as 17-stone 'Big Rachel'.

Years later, in 1915, many local residents, led by women, attacked rent collectors and participated in a rent strike. One protestor's sign explained the issue clearly: 'PARTICK TENANTS STRIKE – Our Husbands, Sons and Brothers are fighting the Prussians of Germany – We are fighting the Prussians of Partick'. Other rent strikes took place in Govan and were caused by unscrupulous landlords raising rents whilst men were away fighting in World War I.

The lack of affordable housing remains an issue in the 21st century. When taking photographs for the book, the author saw posters put up by the Partick branch of the Living Rent organisation. Its website refers to 'organising around issues of urban development, gentrification, hygiene, rats problem, and housing quality in Partick'.

Opposite the mural is ④⓪ **Partick Public Library** which dates from 1925. Scotland's greatest comedian Billy Connolly (b.1942) used to come to this library which he regarded as 'heaven'. He later recalled 'With my aunt making my life hell and Big Rosie beating the shit out of me on a daily basis, I lived in a dark and forbidding world as a kid. But I only had to leave our home and walk over the tramlines to Partick Library and a whole new world opened to me'. One book he read from the library was Jack Kerouac's *On the Road* – and he remembered, 'when I was in my late teens and wanting to go travelling and meet girls and smoke dope and stay up all night, those books spoke to me – they offered me a world of possibility that just didn't seem to exist in Partick'.

Partick Walk

Cross over from the library heading for Gardner Street, opposite the Smiddy Bar that opened in the 1890s. On the corner is a ㊶ **pharmacy** occupying the video shop site that features in the film *Trainspotting*.

Walk up Gardner Street where on the left is a ㊷ **church**, today used by the **Glasgow Reformed Presbyterians**. It was built in 1906 to serve the then-thriving Gaelic-speaking community in the area and was called the Partick United Free Gaelic Church.

Why did Partick become associated with the Gaelic community? It was known to many Gaels because for centuries the village was a stopping point for cattle drovers from the north. As the village turned into an industrialised suburb, it was natural Gaels looking for work moved here, joining friends and relatives who had already arrived. There was safety in numbers as Gaels commonly faced prejudice. In 1846 *The Scotsman* newspaper reflected the views of many Glaswegians when it reported: 'It is a fact that morally and intellectually the Highlanders are an inferior race to the Lowland Saxon.'

The Gaels set up their own institutions. One – the Glasgow Skye Association – is typical of this period. It was founded in 1865 and at the time of writing was holding regular events at the Orange Crawford Hall on Beith Street in Partick. Many Gaels of this era found jobs. Men worked in the shipyards, on Clyde steamers, or the police force; women as domestic servants for the big houses in the West End.

Return to Dumbarton Road and take the next left up Stewartville Street to stop outside the ㊸ **former St Peter's Boys School**. Billy Connolly (b.1942) was a pupil here, living in a flat on this street with his aunts and his abusive father, before moving out to Drumchapel. He later recalled teachers regularly using the strap on him and other children. He was terrified of one teacher called 'Big Rosie' – or Miss McDonald – who he regarded as a psychopath.

Years later, Connolly discovered his jokes about the Catholic church had led to him being removed from the school's records, and he was treated as a non-person. Other pupils were banned from listening to his 'blasphemous' recordings. The harshness of his early life at home and school makes his later achievements as a famous comedian, actor and writer even more remarkable.

Mansfield Park

Surviving this school required a sense of humour. Comedian and writer Armando Iannucci (b.1963) also studied here, and would go on to direct films such as *The Death of Stalin* and television shows *Alan Partridge* and *The Thick of It*. The school, dating from 1890, was one of many needed to serve Partick's rapidly growing population (17,000 in 1871, 27,000 in 1881, 36,000 when the school was completed, and 51,000 in 1901).

Take the next right onto Chancellor Street to reach Hyndland Street and **Mansfield Park**. To see another good example of a ghost sign, turn left and walk uphill where the café ㊸ **Zique's** on the corner has a ghost sign for 'Harga..s Dairy' (originally 'Hargan's Dairy')

Return towards the park, passing ㊺ **St Peter's Catholic Church** on the left. St Simon's seen earlier on (with the Polish connection) was initially called St Peter's when founded in the 1850s. It became too

Partick Walk

small for the local Catholic congregation, and so a new church dedicated to St Peter was opened on this site in 1903.

Continue walking around the edge of Mansfield Park. The park is relatively new, once the site of Victorian residential streets but later cleared to become an open space in the 1970s. As a sign of the area's changing demographics and gentrification, Partick Farmers Market regularly takes place here.

On the left is the substantial building that was once ㊻ **St Peter's RC primary school** (recently turned into flats) and opposite that is the ㊼ **Dowanvale Free Church of Scotland**. The latter dates from 1880 and used to be called the Partick Highland Free Church when its congregation was made up mostly of arrivals from the Highlands and Islands.

Head down Mansfield Street, passing ㊽ **The An Lèanag – Glasgow Gaelic Centre**. In the past speaking Gaelic in Glasgow could be a problem. The 1872 Education (Scotland) Act ruled that only English could be used in schools, and children speaking Gaelic could be punished. This discouraged many Gaels from continuing to use their language or pass it down to their own children. Look up to see the sign for St George Co-Operative Society on a building it constructed in 1907. The Society was founded in 1871 and was just one of several co-operative groups that controlled the production and distribution of foodstuffs and goods to its largely working-class membership.

Walk down to Dumbarton Road, passing the ㊾ **Lismore pub** on the corner. Named after the Isle of Lismore in the Inner Hebrides, it is a popular local pub, boasting a fine whisky selection and a cosy atmosphere. It has stained glass windows depicting events

associated with the Highland Clearances that forced many Gaels to Glasgow and abroad. Those using the gentlemen's toilets, look out for further information on the Clearances above the urinals!

Number 23 Mansfield Street – long demolished – was the location of the 'Partick Poltergeist' that haunted the Hanlon family for two years leading up to the summer of 1961. The residents reported chilling noises, perpetual coldness, and 'constant creepiness' before they cut their losses and fled the house after the poltergeist picked up a lump of coal and dropped it in a bucket.

Cross over, looking for the **50** **Carlton Bingo building**. Whilst it looks modern, it is built around the core of the Star Palace cinema opened in 1910. It later became a dance hall and the rear of the complex contains the old building, despite the modern entrance.

Now take a left onto Keith Street, where you'll see the **51** **Society of Friends (Quakers) burial ground** on your right. This is considered the smallest burial ground in Glasgow and was gifted to the Quakers by an influential local man named John Purdon in 1711. People were buried here until 1857. You walked along Purdon Street earlier, and the first person buried here was John Purdon's

wife nicknamed 'Quaker Meg'. Legend has it that if you came at midnight to Meg's gravestone and asked what she had for her supper she would answer 'naething!'.

This area was once known as The Goat, named after an old term for a burn (small river) that ran through here. The Goat was for centuries the heart of the old village of Partick.

Retrace your steps to Dumbarton Road and Kelvinhall subway is just a short walk further along.

VISIT...

The Riverside Museum
100 Pointhouse Road,
G3 8RS

Partick Farmers' Market
Mansfield Park, G11 6UN

Kelvin Hall Open Collections
1445 Argyle Street, G3 8AW

EAT/DRINK...

The Windsor Tavern
469 Dumbarton Road,
G11 6EJ

Deoch An Dorus
427-429 Dumbarton Road,
G11 6DD

Smiddy Bar
309 Dumbarton Road,
G11 6AL

Zique's
66 Hyndland Street, G11 5PT

The Lismore Pub
206 Dumbarton Road,
G11 6UN

The University Café
87 Byres Road, G11 5HN

Suissi Vegan Kitchen
494 Dumbarton Road,
G11 6SL

St Vincent Crescent

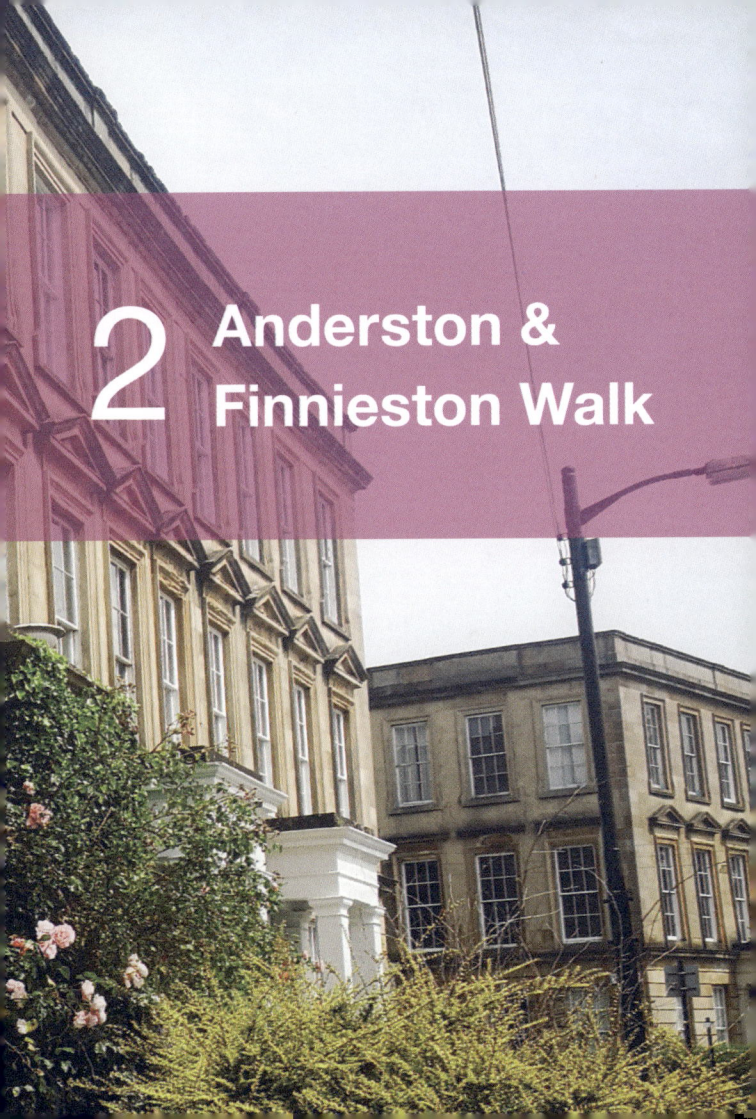

2 Anderston & Finnieston Walk

Anderston & Finnieston Walk

Anderston & Finnieston Walk
Start/Finish: The Mitchell Library North St, G3 7DN
Distance: 3 miles

Anderston & Finnieston Walk

This walk starts at ❶ **the Mitchell Library**. Stop here to admire one of the finest libraries in Scotland. It was initially established in 1877 in Ingram Street, and funded by a bequest from Stephen Mitchell (1789-1874). He was a tobacco tycoon whose great-grandfather (also Stephen Mitchell) established the family business in 1723. Stephen Mitchell & Son would later become part of Imperial Tobacco.

The Mitchell family had connections with the slave trade, and members of the family lived in Colonial Virginia, with links to slave plantations that produced tobacco, cotton and other commodities.

This building was opened in 1911 by Lord Rosebery, a former Prime Minister and then Chancellor of the University of Glasgow. The foundation stone was laid in 1907 by Andrew Carnegie, a multi-millionaire Scots-American industrialist who funded many libraries in Glasgow and elsewhere. If you walk to the rear of the library, you can admire the striking façade that was part of ❷ **St Andrew's Halls**. This concert venue opened in 1877, and the largest of the three halls could hold 4,500 people. In 1962 a fire destroyed the magnificent complex and what remained was incorporated into the Mitchell Library.

Follow the map down North Street (the M8 motorway to your left). It's hard to believe with the traffic roaring past, but in medieval times, the land that became Anderston was covered by a forest belonging to the Bishop of Glasgow. Owned by the wealthy Anderson

Anderston & Finnieston Walk

family since the 1500s, the land here saw the construction of Stobcross House, a grand mansion built around 1700.

In the 1720s, James Anderson founded a village for weavers here, hoping to benefit from rents. So began the slow process of urbanisation, with the founding of a village called 'Anderson's-town' – later Anderston. However, not long after, in 1735, the Andersons sold up to John Orr, their sole legacy being the area's name.

As the community of weavers expanded, fields were built over, and streets, churches, schools and other amenities created. Progress was initially slow. Maps of the early 1800s show a village still surrounded by fields. However, the industrialisation of Glasgow was impacting Anderston. By 1850, the site of the Mitchell Library was occupied by Elmbank iron foundry.

Along North Street you pass ❸ **The Bon Accord**, noted for its whiskies (it has more than 400 on its gantry). A wee dram here might help dull the noise of the M8 as you continue along. There are plans to build a garden over a section of the motorway, so by the time you do the walk the view may have improved. If you had walked here in 1900, the site of the Bon Accord would have

Anderston & Finnieston Walk

been occupied by a biscuit factory and a 'carriage manufactory'. This stretch of the M8 would have contained tenement housing, pubs, schools and hospitals – all demolished to make way for the motorway in the late 1960s.

Cross over St Vincent Street and stop at ❹ **St Patrick's RC church**. It opened in 1898 and represented the growing importance and influence of the local Catholic community, most of whom had Irish roots. By 1831, a quarter of Anderston's residents were Irish. Irish immigration accelerated after the Great Famine of the 1840s. Glaswegians had to cope with a influx of sometimes half-starved, destitute Irish people who brought their own culture and way of life. In just one year – 1857 – 50,000 Irish people arrived, leading to sectarian tensions, the impact of which is still felt in the city today.

The church was designed by ecclesiastical architects Pugin & Pugin (Augustus Pugin designed much of the interior of the Houses of Parliament in London). The church is a rare survivor of 19th-century Anderston before the M8 and other redevelopment changed everything.

In 2006, serial killer Peter Tobin raped and murdered 23-year-old Polish woman Angelika Kluk here and hid her body under the floorboards. Kluk had been working as a cleaner, unaware that handyman Tobin had been previous imprisoned for rape and assault. During Tobin's subsequent trial, a witness living by the church recalled, 'I can only describe what I thought was a loud scream and a short one, within seconds of each other...I have never claimed it to be anything, but when the police came round, I mentioned it. These things do happen where we live, but it was a horrible noise. That is why it stuck in my head'.

The parish was rocked further when it emerged Father Nugent had conducted an affair with Kluk. He was found guilty of contempt of court after failing to tell the truth as a witness during Tobin's murder trial. Tobin (1946-2022) died in prison, serving terms for three murders, including that of Kluk. The police investigated reports that Tobin was responsible for other murders, but nothing came of it. There has been speculation Tobin was the infamous Glasgow serial killer nicknamed 'Bible John'.

Anderston & Finnieston Walk

Follow the map past the church to the ⑤ **Anderston Footbridge** that rises up and over the M8. Take the footbridge, getting a good view of the motorway. If you could go back to 1900, on your left you would see a burial ground, tramway depot and Bishop Street engineering works. On your right, there was a big school, Anderston U.P church, an iron foundry, and Anderston Brewery. All this was swept away, the once vibrant community of Anderston sliced in two by the motorway and now visible only on old maps and nostalgia websites.

St Patrick's from Anderston Footbridge

The footbridge was left unfinished in the 1970s. It was supposed to allow residents in Anderston on the library side of the M8 to access a planned shopping centre on the other side. However, for years nothing happened and it was called the 'Bridge to Nowhere'. It symbolised how cut-off Anderston had become, and how poorly the redevelopment of the area had been carried out. The bridge was completed in 2013, and another 'bridge to nowhere' removed in 2017.

Coming off the footbridge you enter a nondescript no man's land: anonymous hotels, the offices of American banks J.P. Morgan and Morgan Stanley, and little else. At the weekend it feels soulless even though Buchanan Street is only half a mile away.

On the left is ⑥ **Telephone House** – dating from 1937, with a George VI cypher above the entrance. This is part of a BT communication hub, and it is said tunnels stretch from here across the city, constructed decades ago to withstand a nuclear attack

Anderston & Finnieston Walk

during the (first) Cold War. One tunnel runs to the Royal Infirmary. The covers of escape hatches are visible across the city. One such ❼ **escape hatch** is on the road at the junction of Pitt and Bothwell Streets.

Can you guess the link between the offices of JP Morgan, ❽ **Morgan Stanley**, and several Glasgow libraries? Finance titan John Pierpont Morgan Sr. (1837-1913) led the acquisition of Andrew Carnegie's American steel business in 1901. Carnegie spent much of the resulting $225 million he received on philanthropic projects including new public libraries in America, Britain and elsewhere. There are several Carnegie libraries in Glasgow, a remarkable legacy of a man who grew up in poverty in a one-room weaver's cottage in Dunfermline.

John Pierpont Morgan Sr. has his own legacy as his name lives on in the Glasgow branches of JP Morgan, and Morgan Stanley (the latter founded by his grandson – Henry S. Morgan – in 1935).

On your right is the ❾ **Cadogan Square car park and residential area**. This grim development was initially called the Anderston Centre and was completed in 1972. It was designed by Richard Seifert, best known for London's NatWest Tower and Centre Point. A brutalist concrete megastructure, it was intended to put some heart back into Anderston, most of which had been destroyed by the M8. This was as likely as giving a heart transplant to a mummy.

The residential and commercial complex, with a bus station, never succeeded. It gained

Anderston & Finnieston Walk

Anderston & Finnieston Walk

a reputation as a red light area and attracted vandals, a stark contrast to the 1850s, when the site was home to Anderston Free Church. Today, most shops are boarded up, but it is worth walking up the staircase and then bearing right to explore this eerie place that offers unusual views. You can see how the Anderston Centre looked in the mid-1980s in the film *Restless Creatures* (1985).

When finished, follow the map right down Douglas Street to reach Argyle Street. Over the other side is another grim building. ⑩ **Kentigern House** dates from 1986 and was built for the Ministry of Defence. The design was meant to reduce traffic noise and create shade from the sun (had the architect been to Glasgow?). It housed MOD records and was named after St Kentigern, also known as St Mungo, the patron saint of Glasgow.

Continue along Argyle Street, passing dull, modern buildings, including the ⑪ **Marriott Hotel** on the right. The area in front of the hotel was the centre of Anderston Cross, the spiritual heart of the district since Victorian times when Anderston was home to over 30,000 people. Before the Cross, this was the site of Gushet farm.

Continue walking to reach ⑫ **Anderston Station**. Hidden under the road, this is possibly the city's least attractive station. A fine building designed by Sir J.J. Burnet once stood here. Anderston Cross railway station opened in 1896 as part of the Glasgow Central Railway and closed in 1959. Burnett's station, a landmark in old Anderston, was demolished in 1967. The current station dates from 1979.

Anderston & Finnieston Walk

Follow the map to a path that skirts between two elevated roads and down to the ⓭ **19th-century red brick buildings** on your left. Here you can see how the elevated roads almost touch the existing architectural landscape.

What happened to Anderston? Over the previous 200 years, it transformed from a rural hamlet into a densely populated district known for its slum housing and poverty. By the mid-20th century, city authorities, primarily influenced by the Bruce Report, started planning significant changes.

Like several other working-class areas, Anderston was designated a Comprehensive Development Area (CDA). From the 1960s, thousands of local people were moved to the new towns sprouting up on the city's fringes whilst their tenement streets were demolished.

Follow the map to the south side of Argyle Street and turn right down the steps onto Washington Street. This contains relics of old Anderston when it was one of the most industrialised districts in the Second City of the Empire.

On the right is ⓮ **Washington Street School**, built in 1890 during the heyday of a school building programme run by the Glasgow School Board. This resulted from the Scottish Education Act of 1872, which paved the way for free education for children between 5 and 13. The school was designed by H.E. Clifford (1852-1932). In 1901, Clifford won the commission to design the Glasgow Royal Infirmary but internal politics saw him lose the commission. Look for the signs for 'girls' and 'boys' visible at the entrance. You will not see many children on the streets today. When the school was built, thousands lived in tenement residences nearby.

Anderston & Finnieston Walk

Next door is the ⓯ **Pentagon Centre**, home to a wide variety of businesses, but originally James Buchanan's whiskey bond when completed in 1897. H.E. Clifford designed the south part of the structure c.1907. Pause for a moment to take in the scale of the building, once the largest bonded warehouse in the world.

The famous Black & White blended whisky brand was founded by Sir James Buchanan and used to be produced here. Buchanan (1849-1935) worked as a lowly office boy in a Glasgow shipping firm before becoming a multi-millionaire whisky tycoon. One woman who worked here in the 1960s told the author how her secretarial job terminated when she married – a common practice at the time

Why were industry and commerce attracted to Anderston? Proximity to the Clyde was a major factor. Dredging of the river from the 18th century meant big ships could travel up and down through central Glasgow, leading to the foundation of local shipbuilding yards, and new docks. Nearby Broomielaw became one of the busiest areas, particularly with passenger ships.

Good transport links always attract business investors who want to minimise the time and expense of moving goods back and forth. For example, why spend money transporting grain

Anderston & Finnieston Walk

from ships on the Clyde to more distant places when it could be processed in a flour mill nearby in Anderston, with access to a large supply of cheap local workers? Factories, warehouses, shipyards, cotton mills and manufacturing bases sprang up in this area. The textile trade was important in Anderston, whilst later there was more focus on heavy industry, engineering, and warehousing.

If you had walked down Washington Street in the early 1900s, you would pass large warehouses, grain and flour mills, wool stores, tube and oil works, a marine police office and a dozen pubs. It would have been a much busier, smellier and more vibrant place, dominated by working-class men, foreign sailors and new arrivals coming off the ships. By contrast, it's now possible to walk here some days and not passed a single person.

In the 1980s, the site of the Pentagon Centre was home to the Berkeley 2 rehearsal studio space, hosting bands like Simple Minds, Deacon Blue and the Blue Nile. In recent years Berkeley 2 has moved to nearby Lancefield Street, creating Scotland's largest rehearsal space right beside the OVO Hydro. Clients include Grace Jones, Iggy Pop, Beyonce, Slash, and Robert Plant.

On the east side of the street are the remnants of ⓰ **Anderston Rice Mills**, now incorporated into the modern hotel. The remains include part of a steam flour mill from the 1840s. Nearby is Balaclava Street, which – with nearby Crimea Street – is named in memory of Anderston-born William 'Crimea' Simpson.

Simpson (1823-1899) came from a poor family, and his father worked in the shipyards. He became a successful war artist, renowned for his coverage of the Crimean War, the Indian Mutiny, and conflicts in Russia, Egypt, and China. This Anderston boy also knew Queen Victoria and was a regular guest at Buckingham Palace and Balmoral. In the days before photography, radio or television news, the images produced by Simpson appeared in newspapers and had a significant influence on the public.

Anderston & Finnieston Walk

Continue down Washington Street, passing the outer wall of ⑰ **Crown Flour Mills**. The car park, further down on the right, stands on the site of ⑱ **Washington flour mill**. Why Washington Street? The land was owned by a pro-American woman named Mary Read in the early 1800s.

At the bottom, you reach Broomielaw (running to your left) and Anderston Quay (running to your right). Cross over the busy road to reach the footpath by the Clyde. The name Broomielaw comes from a broom or bush growing on a grassy slope called a law. This area was important as it was Glasgow's first harbour. In 1812, Henry Bell's steam-powered paddle ship travelled from Port Glasgow to Broomielaw, the first steam powered passenger service in Europe.

During the 19th century, the riverfront was lined with goods sheds, passenger waiting rooms, cranes, pubs, and the offices of shipping businesses. Not far from here once stood the headquarters of the Clyde Navigation Trust and the Sailor's Home, used by sailors waiting for their next job. Dozens of ships would have been visible whereas today you can stand here and see no river traffic.

The Sailor's Home, four streets to the east of here (corner of Broomielaw and James Watt Street), was the site of a race riot

in January 1919. Hundreds of angry men gathered to protest about jobs on ships being given to foreign sailors (many from India and Africa). A riot broke out on James Watt Street and sailors from Sierra Leone, fearful of being lynched, sought safety in the Sailor's Home. Shots were fired, windows were broken, and the police struggled to control the violence. Luckily no one was killed, but it is a reminder that the era of Red Clydeside was not simply worker versus capitalist, but contained more unsavoury elements.

Anderston & Finnieston Walk

Walk under ⑲ **Kingston Bridge**. Construction began on the bridge in 1967, and it was opened by the Queen Mother in 1970. The bridge is one of the busiest in Europe and is named after the Kingston district south of the Clyde. It is said the foundations of the bridge contain the remains of many unfortunate gangsters.

Look for a memorial to a fire that took place nearby on Cheapside Street. On 28 March 1960, Arbuckle Smith's whisky bond caught fire, and efforts to save the building led to the deaths of 19 people including 14 firefighters. It was Britain's worst peacetime fire services disaster.

On November 30th, 1864, another disaster took place on this stretch of the Clyde. A rowboat ferry departed from Clyde Street, Anderston on its way to Springfield Quay on the other side. It capsized and nineteen people were drowned. Public outrage over the sinking led to the introduction of safer steam-powered ferries.

Follow the map under the M8 and along Piccadilly Street, taking a right on Cheapside Street. This is a grim, post-industrial landscape. In the 1850s, you would pass a cotton spinning mill, Anderston iron foundry, rows of working-class housing, and St Mark's Church and burial ground.

At the end take the pedestrian bridge over Stobcross Street. Below is the Clydeside Expressway, another road that helped cleave old Anderston into smaller, disjointed parts. The street is named after Stobcross House, the country mansion owned by the

Anderston & Finnieston Walk

Anderson family that was located just to the north of the modern-day Scottish Event Campus (SEC Centre, SEC Armadillo etc.) and underneath the Clydeside Expressway.

Just east of Stobcross House stood the Verreville pottery, which, together with the Delftfield pottery by Broomielaw, was an internationally known manufacturer of porcelain and other products. Verreville began as a glass manufacturer in 1777, hence the name – 'glass town'. In 1842 it was converted into a pottery and closed in 1918. Other businesses located in the area include the Stobcross shipbuilding firm of Barclay and Curle, the Hydepark locomotive works, and Saracen Foundry. As many of these businesses became more successful, they needed more space and so moved away. These days there is little to see of this industrial past and so the walk continues to the other side of the bridge and along the path to Argyle Street – originally Main Street. After the first village for weavers was established in this vicinity in the early 18th century, the population of Anderston reached nearly 4,000 by 1790. Most lived around Main Street.

You pass the site of the [20] **Gaiety Theatre** (625 Argyle Street). It opened in 1899 as the Tivoli Variety Theatre and later became a cinema and concert hall before being demolished in 1968. Generations of Anderstonians were entertained here, in the early days enjoying a variety of performers such as Miss Mabel de Vena, Club Swinger and Axe Manipulator. Perhaps the most memorable event took place on Saturday 5 October 1963, when The Beatles arrived.

One local later recalled: 'My mother stood for hours at Cuthbertsons music shop in Sauchiehall St. to get tickets for me and my pal. If I remember correctly they cost six shillings and eight pence, thirty-three pence in decimal coinage. My pal Peter Lannigan and I were in 2nd year of secondary school were 13 and Beatles mad. I don't remember hearing any of the songs cos we were surrounded by screaming girls. Fifty years later the

Anderston & Finnieston Walk

memories are clear, we were the envy of our schoolmates at the height of Beatlemania'.

Continue along Argyle Street (westwards). Only two buildings along this stretch pre-date the redevelopment of the area. Before you reach the first one, stop at ㉑ **640 Argyle Street** to see one of the more recent buildings with the ground-level sign that reads 'Weavers Society Anderston 1738'. In that year 22 villagers signed a document creating the Society and the Society still exists – see www.tradeshouse.org.uk/assoc-weavers-anderston/ for more information on current activities.

Next door is a former pub dating from 1869 and at the time of writing home to the well-known ㉒ **Two Fat Ladies at the Buttery restaurant**. The symbols on the exterior indicate a link with the city's freemasonry movement. The interior contains wood panelling from old church pews and the restaurant is well worth a visit. It is believed to be haunted.

Continue along. A hundred years ago this place would have been crowded with people, many employed in local industries. In 1900 there were around a dozen pubs within 200 yards from here. Today, there is little apart from modern residential housing; you can often walk here alone.

Soon on the left is the ㉓ **Pyramid at Anderston**, originally Anderston Kelvingrove church when completed in 1968, just as the Anderston Comprehensive Development Area (CDA) was being implemented. In recent years this has become a community centre.

Opposite is a second survivor of Victorian Anderston, the ㉔ **old savings bank building** designed by James Salmon Jr. and J.G. Gillespie. Dating from 1900, it was built for the Glasgow Savings Bank and was one of half a dozen bank branches in Anderston. The bust is modelled on the pioneer of community savings banks, Henry Duncan (1774-1846). A remarkable man – church minister, savings bank entrepreneur, soldier and writer. He is depicted holding a money bag and wisely tapping his head

Salmon was close friends with Charles Rennie Mackintosh, and they shared many of the same influences whilst studying at the Glasgow School of Art. However, unlike Mackintosh, Salmon came from a long-established architectural dynasty, and his career was far more successful. Salmon is best known for the 'Hatrack' building in Glasgow.

In recent years, this building has housed recording studios owned by Mogwai and record producer Tony Doogan. Apart from recording bands, the owners have been involved in film and television soundtracks, including films and documentaries such as *Starred Up, Young Adam*, and *Zidane: A 21st Century Portrait*.

In the early 1800s, Glasgow did not stretch much further than this point. A map of 1807 shows the buildings on Argyle Street, called High Street on the map, peter out after the site of today's Pyramid, and fields are visible. The mapmaker did not bother to include any more land to the west.

Continue in the same direction, passing the ㉕ **Salvation Army centre**. When the Sally Army decided to establish a base in Scotland, Glasgow was the obvious starting place, given its reputation for terrible social problems in working-class areas. Anderston must have been bad as the Army set up their headquarters here. When they started holding meetings in 1879 at the nearby Victoria Music Hall, life expectancy was 42 for men and 45 for women.

The Salvation Army is not known today for courting controversy; however, in the 1880s, it was involved in regular confrontations with locals who did not like being told to stop drinking and improve themselves. The Army's history records violent attacks on its workers, barricades being erected to stop marches, and Sunday meetings disrupted by drunken men. It reads like an account from a war zone; clearly, it was not called an Army for nothing.

Today, the Army centre has an excellent café. On a recent visit, a local volunteer recalled that the area was plagued by violent gangs in the 1960s, and how rival hardmen arranged fights in empty warehouses and factories at night, well away from the eyes of the police. Another person remembered foreign sailors coming off ships and leaving chalk messages on walls in Anderston for friends on other berths, explaining where they were staying or which pub to meet at.

Continue up Houldsworth Road, named for another family important in the history of Anderston. Henry Houldsworth arrived from Manchester in 1799 to manage a cotton mill before setting up his own on Cheapside Street. Anderston became an independent burgh in 1824 and Houldsworth – a major employer – served as the first provost. Anderston's independence was short-lived, and his son, John Houldsworth, was the last provost when the area was annexed by Glasgow in 1846. When Anderston was a burgh, it had its own coat of arms and motto. Sadly, unlike some other former burghs annexed by Glasgow, you will not spot any of these on local buildings.

Henry Houldsworth was a tough capitalist and fought attempts by workers to protect the rights of those in his factories. Strikes, violence, and prosecutions of strikers were common in Anderston.

Just to the south of here is Cranston Street, which was the site of the 'Steamie' – public baths and washhouses – that served

Anderston & Finnieston Walk

as a cornerstone of the community when having hot water or indoor toilets at home was uncommon.

There are some visible remnants of the area's industrial past. On the left at ㉖ **69/71 Houldsworth Street** is a fine building from 1877, over the decades occupied by firms making a variety of goods from mangles to tubes. Today it is occupied by the seafood merchants: MacCallum's of Troon.

Carry on to the junction with Elliot Street. On the other side are three more survivors. Take a left down Elliot Street to see the oldest at ㉗ **number 58** – a former iron foundry dating from the 1850s. Next door at ㉘ **number 32** dates from c.1870. It remained in use as a foundry until 1914.

To its right is ㉙ **number 24** – sporting the sign for **W.M. Cook & Sons** and dating from around 1870. William Cook arrived in Glasgow in the 1840s, and this site was home to a saw manufacturing business. The legacy business survives in Sheffield where the William Cook Group is Britain's largest manufacturer of steel castings.

Follow the map to the other side of Elliot Street, passing Andy Scott's ㉚ **statue of Charles Rennie Mackintosh**, Glasgow's most famous architect and designer. Scott is best known for *The Kelpies*, and this statue was unveiled in 2018 by Nicola Sturgeon on the 80th anniversary of the architect's death. It helped celebrate a regeneration of this part of Anderston that saw 1960s residential blocks replaced with the modern flats visible today.

Anderston & Finnieston Walk

30

Subterranean Victorian toilet

Turn left along Argyle Street into Finnieston. The Orr family who bought the estate from the Anderson family decided to develop 20 more acres as a new weaver's village from around 1768. But what to call it? The Orr family had a tutor named the Rev. John Finnie – hence Finnieston.

As you walk along, you will see blonde sandstone tenements on your right. This colour indicates their age, as blonde sandstone was commonly used here from the mid-19th century until around 1890, when red sandstone (cheaper and more durable) began to be transported from quarries in Dumfries and Ayrshire via improved railway routes. Much of what you see dates from the 1850 to 1860s when Finnieston (like Anderston before it) was transformed from a village into a suburb with hundreds of residential dwellings.

Turn left down Minerva Street, passing a subterranean Victorian toilet. The ㉛ **four-storey classical tenement** at number 3 on the corner dates from 1856 and is a superb example of what developers were hoping to achieve in Finnieston. Unlike Anderston, Finnieston never achieved separate burgh status. However, it has long since

Anderston & Finnieston Walk

gone from a run-down post-industrial suburb to being regarded as hipster-central.

Continue down Minerva Street, which becomes St Vincent Crescent — one of the most charming streets in Glasgow. Beneath your feet runs the North Clyde Line. Long ago, this was the Glasgow and City District Railway, and Finnieston Station stood near here (site seen later).

The tenements on the right-hand side — for example, ❷ **number 20 St Vincent Crescent** — are amongst the oldest tenements in Glasgow. These were designed by architect Alexander Kirkland and date from the mid-1850s. Kirkland himself chose to live at number 39 (there is a plaque).

Immediately after number 23 on the left, you will see a break in the housing and a wall. If you are careful and tall enough, you can peek over and see the ❸ **disused line of 'lost' Glasgow Central Railway**. The line opened in 1894 and started in Maryhill. It ran along the side of the River Kelvin and had two stations within the grounds of the Botanic Gardens. It then ran under Great Western Road, headed south under Kelvingrove Park and passed through here before bending eastwards to Central Station and beyond. This stretch carried trains under Finnieston to the old Stobcross station — now the site of the Exhibition Centre station.

Continue along St Vincent Crescent. This area is a great example of the difficulties that urban developers faced in the second half of the 19th century. On one hand, the

St Vincent Crescent

tenements were elegant and very attractive. Middle-class residents could play at the ❸❹ **St Vincent Bowling club**, originally founded as a lawn bowling and curling club in 1859. Almost every new suburb built in Glasgow during this era was blessed with more than one bowling club, and it was often a focal point for local residents.

However, a map from around 1900 illustrates the challenges developers faced. South of the bowling green was St Vincent Pond (or 'Loch') – used for boating and ice skating and long since filled in. Beyond that was a vast railway goods and mineral complex, a number of railway lines, and then – on the Clyde – the Queen's Dock with three huge water basins. On all sides were foundries and other industrial concerns. With the smoke from the steam engines, and noise and smell from other industries, anyone who could afford it might have thought twice about living in these beautiful houses.

Today, the landscape to the south remains a confused mix, featuring railway lines, electricity substations, and the Clyde Expressway, followed by a few isolated modern flats. It then reaches the otherworldly Exhibition Centre that stands atop the filled-in Queen's Dock.

St Vincent Crescent has a connection with the American Civil War of the 1860s. Local resident James Smith proudly flew a Confederate flag from his house here. He had returned to Scotland after living in Jackson, Mississippi, before the Civil War. However, he remained good friends with Confederate

St Vincent Crescent

Anderston & Finnieston Walk

President Jefferson Davis, and James's younger brother died a war hero fighting for the Confederate Army. After the Civil War ended, Davis (having been released from prison) toured Scotland, and the Smith family hosted him for part of the trip.

Many in Scotland welcomed the world's most infamous white supremacist with open arms, a reminder of the dubious role many in Glasgow and beyond played in helping the Confederate States evade the Union blockade of Southern ports. Arguably, the help many in Glasgow gave to the Confederate cause helped extend the Civil War – and delay the abolition of slavery in America – by several months.

Retrace your steps and take the immediate left up Corunna Street, named in memory of Glasgow-born soldier Sir John Moore (1761-1809) who died repulsing a French attack at the Battle of Corunna in Spain. You reach Argyle Street and on your left find the ㉟ **Ben Nevis bar**, occupying a fine building designed by Alexander Kirkland in the mid-1850s.

Turn left to walk a short way up Argyle Street and stop outside an unusual local

Anderston & Finnieston Walk

landmark – the ㊱ **Finnieston ash tree**, thought to be over 150 years old. If you had stood here in the mid-1850s and looked to your left, nothing on the north side of Argyle Street existed yet. Apart from a few scattered houses, there was just open land between here and the River Kelvin.

Nearly opposite the tree is another local landmark and institution – ㊲ **the Park Bar**, famous for its good atmosphere, folk music, and association with those hailing from the Islands and Highlands. Go there on a Saturday night if you want to have a memorable night out. Even better, visit two nearby pubs associated with Gaels – The Islay Inn and the Snaffle Bit (together known as the Teuchter Triangle).

Now follow the map down Argyle Street. In recent years, many of the fairly run-down buildings along this main high street in Finnieston have been redeveloped into trendy restaurants, bars, galleries and shops, with old signs restored.

On the left, on Kelvingrove Street, is ㊳ **The Grove pub**, one of the old-school pubs that is an increasing rarity in this gentrified part of Glasgow.

Continue along Argyle Street, on the right is the ㊴ **Finnieston bar and restaurant**, different from other buildings as it stands only two and a half stories tall. As a rule of thumb, a building of this height means 'old' in Glasgow. This one dates from around 1800 and is the oldest building on the walk so far. When it was built there were still open fields around

Anderston & Finnieston Walk

here, and cattle drovers would stay here (including, it is said, Rob Roy). If you go into the garden at the back of the restaurant and look over the fence, you can see another abandoned stretch of train line from the original Glasgow Central Railway.

Continue on, then turn right down a narrow opening (number 1103) to visit ④⓪ **The Hidden Lane**. This is home to artist studios, creative spaces and small businesses. Old commercial buildings have been imaginatively transformed into this thriving space.

The Hidden Lane Tearoom is a popular spot, along with the Hidden Lane Gallery. There is a recording studio, craft and jewellery businesses, and you can find guitar lessons and a yoga studio here too. The end of the lane, to the right of the Tearoom, is the approximate site of the waiting room for the demolished Finnieston Station.

When finished, continue along Argyle Street, where you'll pass a mix of buildings primarily constructed between the 1850s and 1870s, now housing modern shops. Up above, look for the tram rosettes on the second floor of several buildings. These were once used to hold the connecting cables for the city's extensive tram network (the last tram ran in 1962). When the tram lines were laid here, this was called Dumbarton Road.

Continue past the Tesco on the right, and beyond that is an open section of the railway line. Finnieston Station stood on the right-hand side of the tracks (if you look over the wall just after Tesco). It operated between 1887-1917, and recently there has been discussion about creating a new station here. Further back is ④① **The Hive**, another small business complex part of The Hidden Lane empire.

Anderston & Finnieston Walk

Now turn left up Kent Road, then onto Brechin Street. Further along on the left is ㊷ **The Back Garden** – a volunteer-run community garden developed in an unlikely spot behind residential tenement houses. This hidden gem is a great space for the community, where locals can learn to grow produce together.

At the top turn right onto Berkeley Street and continue straight ahead.

The ㊸ **Tron Church Kelvingrove** on the left dates from 1864 and was designed by John Honeyman, best known today for being Charles Rennie Mackintosh's boss. Originally a church, it was in more recent times Henry Wood Hall, home of the Royal Scottish National Orchestra. It has since returned to its original purpose as a place of worship.

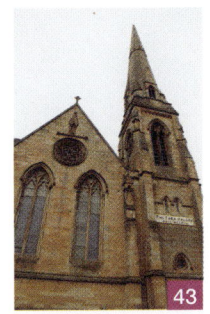

Opposite is the ㊹ **Sgoil Ghàidhlig Ghlaschu** – Glasgow Gaelic School. Whilst the heartland of the Gaelic world is in the islands and highlands of Scotland, the future survival of the language will partly depend on city-based institutions like this. The first Gaelic school opened in Woodlands in 1999 and has since kept expanding due to demand.

Continue along, passing the ㊺ **Glasgow Central Gurdwara** (or 'Singh Sabha). Its origins go back to 1981 when a group of Sikhs bought a building on the street, and then due to growing numbers, an expansion was needed. The first phase of the current building was completed in 2016 adding to the skyline of this area. Once the

Anderston & Finnieston Walk

site of an eye infirmary, today this is the hub of the Sikh community in Scotland.

Keep walking. Running parallel to this street is Dover Street where, at number 69, comedian Billy Connolly was born and grew up. Want to see the house? In Billy's own words: 'I would take you there and show you but they've pulled the building down'. Other local kids who did well include Donovan, in the 1960s touted as Britain's answer to Bob Dylan, and Texas's Sharleen Spiteri (who grew up on Minerva Street).

Shortly on the left, you pass a striking building at ㊻ **number 134**. This was built as a **drill hall**, and during World War I was used by the 1st City of Glasgow Battery, 3rd Lowland Brigade, and Royal Field Artillery. It was later taken over by the Sikh community.

Carry on, passing the modern ㊼ **Berkeley Square development** on the right. Glasgow has changed a lot over time, but sometimes less than you think. Maps of the 1890s show that the exact area of this modern development were horse livery stables. Often buildings are bulldozed only for their plots to be retained by the next developer, creating historical echoes that only maps reveal.

Continue down Berkeley Street. Most buildings on the right are listed, dating from the mid-1850s when the area was first developed.

The left-hand side is home to some of the city's most intriguing institutions, including the Central Association of Spiritualists (number 64) and the Provincial Grand Lodge of Glasgow (number 54). There are around seventy Glasgow lodges listed on the Provincial Grand Lodge of Glasgow's website, all numbered to reflect the chronology of their foundation.

Soon you reach the Mitchell Library again, where this walk ends.

VISIT

The Mitchell Library
201 North Street, G3 7DN
glasgowlife.org.uk

The Hidden Lane
1103 Argyle Street, G3 8ND
thehiddenlaneglasgow.com

Glasgow Central Gurdwara
176 Berkeley Street, G3 7HY

EAT & DRINK

The Bon Accord
153 North Street, G3 7DA
bonaccordpub.com

Two Fat Ladies at the Buttery
652-654 Argyle St, G3 8TB
twofatladiesrestaurant.com

The Ben Nevis Bar
1147 Argyle St, G3 8TE
thebennevisbar.com

The Park Bar
1202 Argyle St. G3 8ND
parkbarglasgow.com

The Hidden Lane Tea Room
Unit 8, 1103 Argyle St, G3 8TE
hiddenlanetearoom.com

The Ottoman Coffee House
73 Berkeley St, G3 7DX
ottomancoffeehouse.co.uk

Sikorski Polish Club
5 Park Grove Terrace, G3 7SD
sikorskipolishclub.org.uk

Wall mural, Garnethill Park, see p.99

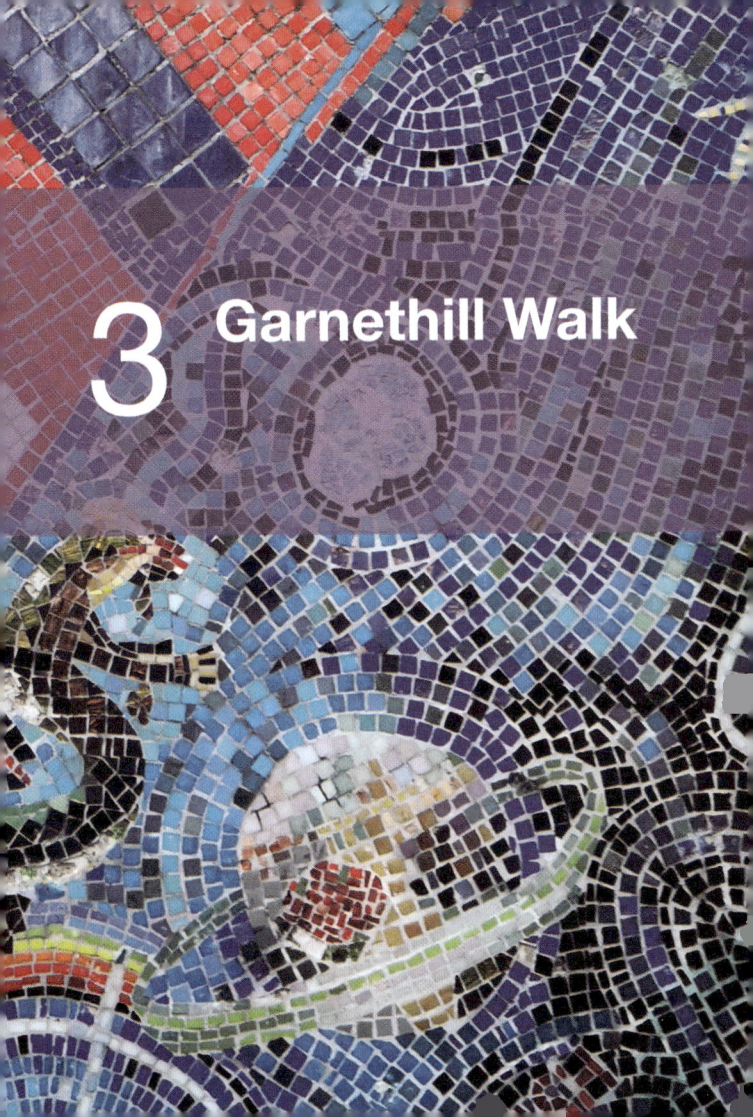

3 Garnethill Walk

Garnethill Walk

1. Dundasvale Court
2. Underpass
3. Dundas Court
4. Former Phoenix Recreation Park
5. Glasgow's mini-Chinatown
6. Glasgow Savings Bank
7. Stow College
8. Light sandstone tenement
9. Red sandstone tenement
10. Street lamp bird sculptures
11. Former Sick Childrens' Hospital Dispensary
12. Buccleuch Lane

13. Ghost sign
14. No. 38
15. Former industrial workshop
16. No. 43
17. Blonde sandstone buildings
18. Former site of the Royal Hospital for Sick Children
19. Mary Macdonald House
20. Grand old school building
21. Tenement House
22. Garnethill Viewpoint
23. Garnethill Synagogue
24. Glasgow Cancer Hospital
25. Wing Hong Chinese Elderly Centre
26. Breadalbane Terrace
27. Peel Terrace
28. Garnethill Community Garden
29. 83 Hill Street
30. Ignatian Spirituality Centre

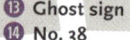

Charing Cross

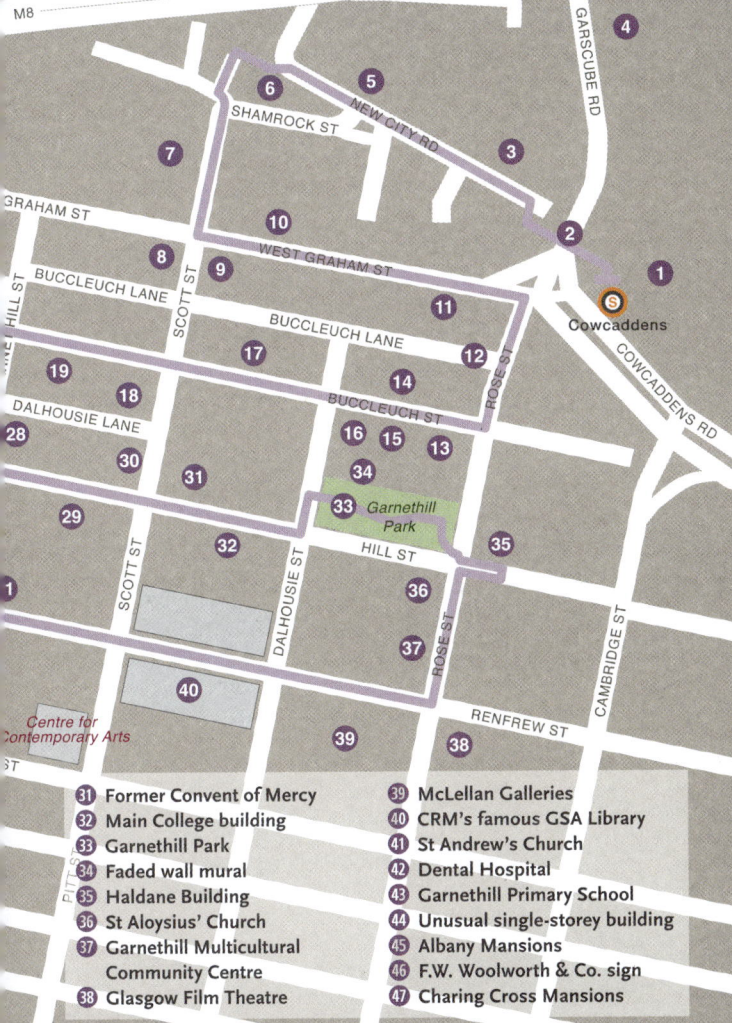

- 31 Former Convent of Mercy
- 32 Main College building
- 33 Garnethill Park
- 34 Faded wall mural
- 35 Haldane Building
- 36 St Aloysius' Church
- 37 Garnethill Multicultural Community Centre
- 38 Glasgow Film Theatre
- 39 McLellan Galleries
- 40 CRM's famous GSA Library
- 41 St Andrew's Church
- 42 Dental Hospital
- 43 Garnethill Primary School
- 44 Unusual single-storey building
- 45 Albany Mansions
- 46 F.W. Woolworth & Co. sign
- 47 Charing Cross Mansions

Garnethill Walk

Start: Cowcaddens subway
Finish: Sauchiehall Street
Distance: 2 miles

Leave the subway via the left exit. Before entering Garnethill, pause to look at the social housing complex to your right ❶ **Dundasvale Court.** The oldest section dates from 1968 and is typical of the urban redevelopment during that period. In the early 2000s, some flats here were sold for as little as £5,000. Over the years, the complex has struggled with issues related to crime and drugs, with the most widely reported incident occurring in 2017 when Zoe Bremner, just shy of her 15th birthday, tragically died in a flat after being sold ecstasy by a drug dealer. There are entrances into the complex if you wish to see the heart of the Court.

Now enter the ❷ **underpass** to your left, where you will see walls adorned with street art. Until recently this included hand-shadow puppet images created by the prominent street artist Rogue.

As you emerge, try and imagine this area in the late 18th century, when it was a hamlet of a few cottages surrounded by cattle. It was rarely included on maps, but that changed with the opening of the nearby Monkland Canal and the Forth & Clyde Canal in 1790. The construction of a branch of the Forth & Clyde down to Port Dundas, just north of here, transformed the area. It attracted workers directly or indirectly involved with the canal, along with industries eager to benefit from transport opportunities.

Garnethill Walk

Change did not happen overnight. A map from 1807 shows Cowcaddens with only a few buildings, still surrounded by gardens and open land. However, a map produced 50 years later reveals that all the open land had disappeared. Within a minute's walk from where you stand now, there was a timber yard, several engine, soap, chemical and dye works, as well as the Phoenix iron foundry.

Dozens of tenement streets, along with pubs, theatres, schools, and churches sprang up here. Hard to imagine now, but outside the subway exit once stood Cowcaddens Cross, home to the Milton Colosseum Concert Hall in the 1860s. This venue was later rebuilt as the Grand Theatre, which held 2,000 people who came to watch plays, pantomimes, operas, boxing matches, and music hall acts. It eventually became the New Grand Picture House before closing in 1959.

As in several other working-class districts, large swathes of Victorian-era Cowcaddens were swept away by post-World War II redevelopment schemes. The construction of the M8 motorway in the 1960s, just to the north of here, further accelerated the transformation.

Garnethill Walk

3

On your right, you'll see the fine-looking ❸ **Dundas Court**, a building dating back to 1837. It is significant for being the first dedicated teacher training facility in Britain. It was both a school (called the Normal School from the French *École Normale*), and a place to train teachers (the Normal Seminary). The institution was the brainchild of educational pioneer David Stow (1793-1864). His 'Glasgow System' of teaching was exported around Britain and colonial territories. The building is one of the oldest to survive in this area and was designed by David Hamilton (1768-1843), regarded as the 'father of the profession' by Glaswegian architects.

A few hundred yards northeast of here stood the ❹ **Phoenix Recreation Park**, created in the 1890s on the former site of the Phoenix Foundry. However, the park was redeveloped in the late 1950s, with the M8 motorway now occupying the space where a bandstand and fountain once stood.

Garnethill Walk

Continue straight on to reach ❺ **Glasgow's mini-Chinatown**, a small but vibrant area with a restaurant, bakery, and other businesses, largely established through the efforts of businessman Maurice Lim in the early 1990s. At the time, *The Herald* (1994) noted: 'Gone are the days when the only Chinese restaurant in the whole of Glasgow was to be found on the Govan shore'. The location made sense as many Chinese people settled in Garnethill in the latter half of the 20th century, and today the Chinese community in the city numbers around 12,000. In recent years, the community's presence in Garnethill has faded a little as the younger generation have begun to move further afield.

Why did the community grow? In 1953 there were thought to be only three Chinese families in Glasgow. However, as demand grew for Chinese food, Cantonese restaurants opened and hired staff from Hong Kong. The Chinese community in Glasgow grew significantly in the 1960s and 70s, establishing its own institutions like the Chinese Community Development Partnership, which includes organisations such as the Glasgow Chinese Badminton Club, Glasgow Chinese School, and Wing Hong Elderly Group.

One member of the community described how his parents had first arrived in England from Hong Kong in the 1950s, but because of the level of racism they faced, decided to try Glasgow. Unfortunately, things were not always easier here.

Garnethill Walk

It was not until the 1860s that maps included the area named Garnethill. By the early 1890s, the site of Glasgow's Chinatown, including the car park, was part of the old Olympia entertainment complex. This venue hosted various attractions, from music hall acts and dancing pavilions to shooting galleries and even a Gypsy show featuring Corlinda Lee, the 'Queen of the Gypsies'. Lee died in 1900 at 42 New City Road, and her gravestone can be found in the Necropolis cemetery.

In recent years interest has grown in the impact of the Wild West legend, 'Buffalo Bill' Cody and his travelling show on Dennistoun during the 1890s. However, this was just one aspect of Glasgow's fascination with the Wild West. 'Mexican Joe', also known as 'Col. Joe Shelley', leased the Olympia site in the early 1890s and brought his own show to the city. It featured Native American tribes, cowboys, sharpshooters, and horses, captivating Glaswegians with the allure of the mythical Wild West.

When Mexican Joe visited another city in England, his tour included, 'Texas Jack, Lasso Mack, California Frank, Suspender Jack, Buckskin, Nevada Fred, Colorado Charlie, and Arizona Pete – and a party of Indian warriors and squaws, under Black Hawk – a Sioux chief famous for his scalping achievements'. Mexican Joe claimed his wife and children had been killed by members of the Apache tribe, but recent research suggests much of his back story was fabricated. If you're intrigued to find out more about this particular moment in Glasgow's history – *Black Elk, Buffalo Bill & Mexican Joe – The Real Story* (2015) by Tom F. Cunningham is a great read.

The Olympia site was also home to Scotland's first permanent zoo, founded by circus and animal menagerie magnate E.H. Bostock (1858-1940). One of his adverts described 'The Greatest Variety of Foreign Beasts & Reptiles Ever Exhibited Under One Roof' and performances involving lions, tigers, leopards, bears, and wolves. The building later became a skating rink,

Garnethill Walk

cinema, and dance hall before being sold and converted into a garage in 1919.

Directly opposite is an Edwardian Baroque red sandstone building, built as a branch of the ❻ **Glasgow Savings Bank** in 1909. Now standing marooned in the shadow of the M8, this architectural gem was designed by Neil C. Duff. It is covered in allegorical figures related to shipbuilding, commerce, and the Royal Arms. The occupants of the flats above benefited from a flat roof used as a drying area for clothes, all invisible to passers-by (the washhouse was under the dome).

Glasgow Savings Bank was a progressive business founded in the 1830s to help poorer people to save. Look for remains of the bank's name — a faded sign for 'Savings' above the ground floor and intertwined 'G', 'S' and 'B'. Duff designed other buildings for the bank and some of the city's earliest cinemas.

Next door is the grim elevated motorway. Its construction destroyed several 19th-century streets, most containing red sandstone tenement buildings. New City Road was a much more prominent thoroughfare

Garnethill Walk

and the location of the Savings Bank made more sense than it does today. Back then, you could have strolled from the bank along New City Road, passing through St George's Cross, and then on up Great Western Road. The motorway development has destroyed this original sense of connectivity.

Follow the map up Scott Street, experiencing the 'hill' in Garnethill. To your right is the former ❼ **Stow College** dating from the 1930s. This institution later became part of Glasgow Kelvin College, whose staff and students founded the Electric Honey record label in 1992. The label gained recognition for releasing records by notable bands like Belle & Sebastian, Snow Patrol, and Biffy Clyro. It was described by one magazine as 'the most successful student-run label in the world'. Scottish musicians who have worked with the College include members of Bay City Rollers, The Associates, and The Bluebells.

Early 19th-century maps reveal few buildings between here and Sauchiehall Street, a third of a mile away, with undeveloped land on all sides and an Observatory standing alone. The city's astronomers picked this area for such a building because it was away from light and smoke pollution. However, urbanisation would soon undermine their stargazing. The Egyptian-style Observatory was demolished in around 1832. Twenty years later, about two-thirds of Garnethill's streets had been developed, and the remaining gaps would soon be filled in.

Why the name Garnethill? It was originally called Summerhill, but developer William Harley (1770-1829) is believed to have renamed it in memory of Thomas Garnett (1766-1802). Garnett studied at the University of Edinburgh during the golden era of the Enlightenment and later became a professor of natural philosophy at Anderson's Institution in Glasgow. His public lectures were particularly popular among women, who were denied the right to pursue university degrees.

Those with insomnia may wish to try Garnett's book, *Observations on a tour through the Highlands and part of the Western isles of Scotland; particularly Staffa and Icolmkill: to which are added, a description of the falls of the Clyde: of the country round Moffat, and an analysis of its mineral waters.*

Continue to reach **West Graham Street** and look for the colour of ❽ **sandstone tenements** on the other side. The lighter, blonde sandstone on the right likely came from quarries in Bishopbriggs and Giffnock that was widely used as Glasgow expanded between the 1850s and 1880s. The ❾ **red sandstone** on the left dates from around 1890, when local quarries had become exhausted, and new railway lines made it cheaper to transport more durable red sandstone from Dumfries and Ayrshire.

Look at the ❿ **street lamps with bird sculptures** on top. The *Chookie Burdies* were created by Glaswegian artist Shona Kinloch in the early 1990s. These sculptures appear on 150 lamp posts, each one unique. Kinloch (b. 1962) studied at the GSA and was one of the first female artists to receive public sculpture commissions in the city. A tram depot once stood near here when Glasgow's tram network was the largest in Europe.

Turn left down West Graham Street, where you'll see the ⓫ **old Sick Childrens' Hospital Dispensary** on the right, with its original sign still visible. This dispensary opened in 1888 as part of the Glasgow Hospital for Sick Children. Funds for the construction were raised through events

Garnethill Walk

organised by prominent women in Glasgow society, led by the Duchess of Montrose. Look for a memorial for the 'Fancy Fair' held by the Duchess and others to raise money in 1884 (at St Andrew's Halls).

In the days before the NHS, thousands of poor, local children were treated here. In around 1900, a quarter of child patients suffered from lung diseases such as bronchitis, pneumonia and pleurisy. Care for children was provided here up until 1953.

Today, the building is part of the GSA. It is one of many GSA buildings that dominate Garnethill these days, almost forming a separate colony. It was designed by the distinguished architect James Sellars (1843–88), whose work you'll encounter later.

Follow the map right up Rose Street, passing ⑫ **Buccleuch Lane** on the right. Don't go down here, but stop to read about the death of four-year-old Betty Alexander in 1952. She lived at 43 Buccleuch Street and disappeared on 7 October. A city-wide search began, sparking intense media coverage. At one point, her mother thought she heard Betty calling from this vicinity and came down to look but could not find her.

On 10 October 1952, a cleaner from the hospital exited to the rear into Buccleuch Lane and found Betty's body, lying on her coat on some steps. The cleaner later recalled: 'It was a terrible sight... I want to forget it as quickly as possible.'

The last sighting of Betty was on Rose Street. Somehow, she ended up in the lane, where she was assaulted and then suffocated. Her death led to an outpouring of public anger and shock. A thousand people gathered at the police cordon around the crime scene, and a mob later arrived outside the home of a local suspect.

The first child murder in 30 years led to a manhunt involving 2,000 police officers and over 100 detectives. However, the culprit was never found. On the day of Betty's funeral 5,000 people lined the streets to pay their respects.

Garnethill Walk

Continue up Rose Street, passing Chinese-Scots-owned businesses before turning right into Buccleuch Street. When Betty lived here in post-war Glasgow, much of Garnethill was run-down. Bedsits, hostels, and other features of a transient community were commonplace. The wealthy classes, attracted to the detached villas on the hill in the 1850s, had long since moved on.

In recent years, Garnethill has come up in the world again, although a description in *The Herald* in 1990, still rings partly true: 'Garnethill sits draped over the shoulders of the city centre like a scruffy overcoat. Its tenements resist the gentrification of the West End and still hold the aura of the older Glasgow that lay around its foothills'.

Continue along Buccleuch Street, noting some of the interesting features on this quiet street . Look for the ⓭ **ghost sign** outside number 29, on the left. This is part of a row of listed tenement buildings dating from the mid-1850s, when Garnethill first developed as a residential area.

Further along, is the mid-19th century villa at ⓮ **number 38** on the right, look for the unique windows with illustrations of buildings. Opposite is a ⓯ **former industrial workshop** from the early 20th century, reminding us that factories were often located in residential areas in a way that would be unthinkable today.

⓰ **Number 43** on the corner is where Betty Alexander lived. There have been other tragedies on this quiet street. In 1996 77-year-old Emily Mutch was brutally

Garnethill Walk

murdered in her flat here. Every male aged over 12 in the area had to provide a DNA sample. A man named Thomas Galloway was eventually convicted of murder.

At the time *The Herald* reported that Garnethill 'had a chequered past. In Betty Alexander's time it was a rooming district for Glasgow's theatreland; seedy, slightly down at heel, with a shifting population of small-time actors and young families. In the years that followed, there were problems with prostitution, drugs, crime, drinking, and gambling'.

Continue along, passing on the right (after Dalhousie Street) another fine ⑰ **row of blonde sandstone buildings** dating from the early 1840s. By the 1890s, Garnethill had been transformed from a semi-rural outpost into the location of several important institutions: the Royal Hospital for Sick Children, a veterinary college, a cancer hospital, a synagogue, several churches, a training home for nurses, a 'House of Shelter for Females', the Convent of Mercy, and so on.

To see just one superb example, stop further on at number 45, the ⑱ **former site of the Royal Hospital for Sick Children**. The first of its kind in Glasgow, it marked a significant milestone in the history of healthcare. At the time, around 30,000 to 40,000 people died each year in Glasgow, around half were children under the age of five. Dating from 1882, it was built around a large villa and designed by James Sellars (who also worked on the dispensary building

Garnethill Walk

seen earlier). Look for the roundel featuring Charity holding a sick child. The hospital moved to Yorkhill in 1914. Today it is owned by St Aloysius' College, another long-established educational institution with several sites in Garnethill.

Take a right onto Buccleuch Street, passing the modern ⓳ **Mary Macdonald House** at number 89 on your left. This stands on the site of a Victorian-era veterinary college that replaced a large water reservoir in the 1850s. The current building accommodates GSA students and is named after artist Mary Macdonald (1864-1933), who studied at the art college in the 1890s. This was when she met her future husband, Charles Rennie Mackintosh.

Passing Garnethill Street, look for the ⓴ **grand old school building** on the left. Constructed in stages from the late 1870s, it was initially Garnethill School before becoming home to the Glasgow High School for Girls, founded in 1894.

Garnethill Walk

Continue to the end of the street until you see ㉑ **The Tenement House**, (number 145) on your left. Managed by the National Trust for Scotland, it is well worth a visit if you have the time and is open daily. Dating from 1892, this was the home of Agnes Toward between 1911-1965, and during this time it barely changed. Preserved as a time capsule, it offers a unique insight into tenement life. About three-quarters of Glaswegians live in flats, whereas in similarly sized cities across Britain, the average is under a quarter, making tenements a significant part of the city's character.

Just past here, take the path on the left leading up to ㉒ **Garnethill Viewpoint**. Try and ignore the traffic noise to enjoy one of the city's best views to the west. If you stood here in 1900, instead of the motorway, you would see a horse livery stable, a tramway, and dozens of red tenement streets, churches, pubs, and other buildings. The construction of the M8 and other roads transformed Garnethill, creating a sense of being hemmed in by traffic on at least two sides.

In the 2018 musical drama film *Wild Rose*, a Glaswegian ex-convict and country and western singer Rose-Lynn (played by Jessie Buckley) is released from prison and soon has sex with Elliot (James Harkness) on the grassy area right beneath this viewpoint (perhaps not what the planners had in mind!). The film partly pays homage to many Glaswegians' love for American country and western music.

Walk up Hill Street. On the right is ㉓ **Garnethill Synagogue**, the first purpose-built synagogue in Scotland. It opened in 1879 and remains an important institution for the Jewish community. Many Jewish refugees fleeing Nazi persecution were housed in Garnethill in accommodation organised by the synagogue. Some remained in Glasgow after World War II to start new lives.

Garnethill Walk

Garnethill Walk

The origins of the Jewish community are often traced back to the late 18th century when craftsmen, merchants, and their families arrived from Holland and Germany. By the 1870s, some members of the community were moving to western parts of the city, which explains why the synagogue was established here. Later, poorer Jewish immigrants tended to settle in the south, particularly in the Gorbals, where a larger mostly working-class community formed. The synagogue is home to The Scottish Jewish Archives Centre and a museum that contains a wide range of information and materials relating to the Jewish community in Scotland (see page 107 for further details).

Opposite is the former ㉔ **Glasgow Cancer Hospital**, another milestone in medical history, as it was the first in Scotland to specialise in cancer treatment. It opened in 1893 and was renamed the Royal Beatson Memorial Hospital in 1948 after Sir George Beatson (1848-1933). Beatson was a pioneer in the field of oncology who served as the hospital's director. The hospital has since relocated, and the site has been converted into flats. A radiographer I met who trained here, was sure that the nurses' quarters were haunted.

Continue up Hill Street. Further up on the left is another important place for the Chinese community – the ㉕ **Wing Hong Elderly Centre**. In 2004, *The Herald* reported: 'The Wing Hong regulars were once the young Cantonese and Hakka-speaking migrants who fled the poverty and overcrowding of Hong Kong and the New Territories in the 1960s and 1970s, many to open restaurants in Scotland'. The centre is located in an impressive villa dating from the early 1800s.

You are also near the site of the Observatory founded by the Glasgow Society for Promoting Astronomical Science. It was founded in 1810 – a map of 1820 shows it was the only substantive building on semi-rural 'Garnet Hill'. Urban expansion brought with it light pollution and the observatory was demolished in 1832.

Continue along Hill Street, arguably the finest street for residential architecture in Garnethill. On the right is ㉖ **Breadalbane Terrace**, a row of blond sandstone buildings considered the work of Charles Wilson (1810-63) and dating from the mid-1840s. Wilson was a prominent architect of his era, involved in everything from building castles to Park Circus.

On the left is the equally attractive ㉗ **Peel Terrace**. Dating from the early 1840s, it was possibly designed by David Hamilton (the 'Father of the profession' mentioned earlier).

27

Garnethill Walk

Next, take a detour down Garnethill Street to visit the quirky ㉘ **Garnethill Community Garden** – one of many in Glasgow that bring local people from all walks of life together.

Return to Hill Street and continue until you reach number ㉙ **83 Hill Street** (on the right). The influence of the GSA on Garnethill is substantial, and not only because of the buildings it owns. Many art students have lived in these streets, including four Turner Prize winners on Hill Street. Among them

were Douglas Gordon and Richard Wright, both of whom lived at number 83. An art exhibition was held at this address in 1997, titled *Wish You Were Here Two*.

Prize winner Martin Boyce lived at number 95 and later recalled life here in the early 2000s: 'We were just in and out of each other's flats all the time. It was an amazing period really, looking back – I remember only one flat had a phone, so the phone would ring and people would be shouting out of the window for someone else'. Other figures in the Glasgow art scene have lived on Hill Street, including those shortlisted for the Turner Prize, serving on the judging panel, writing books about art, or being involved in exhibitions.

This area has featured in Scottish writer Denise Mina's (b.1966) 'Tartan noir' crime novels known as the Garnethill Trilogy: *Garnethill* (1998), *Exile* (2000), *Resolution* (2001)). At the start of the first book, the character Maureen and her neighbourhood is introduced: 'Her flat was at the top of Garnethill, the highest hill in Glasgow, and the craggy North Side lay before her, polka-dotted with cloud shadows'.

There are other artistic connections. Photographer Oscar Marzaroli (1933-88)

Garnethill Walk

moved from Italy to Garnethill as a child and later captured some of the best images of Glasgow and its residents ever taken. Author and journalist Catherine Carswell (1879-1946) was born on Hill Street. She studied at the GSA and wrote two novels about the lives of female characters in Glasgow – *Open the Door* (1920) and *The Camomile* (1922). Carswell has been rediscovered in recent times and is now recognised as an important figure in the development of Scottish literature.

As you may have gathered already, Garnethill has a shady side, and Hill Street is not immune to this. In 2013, the police raided a flat on Hill Street and discovered more than 400 cannabis plants.

Carry on, and on the left, you will find the ㉚ **Ignatian Spirituality Centre**. This is run by the Society of Jesus – better known as the Jesuits. The Jesuits have helped shape this part of Garnethill over the years. They trace their origin back to 1540 when this Catholic religious order was founded by Spanish priest Ignatius of Loyola (1491-1556). Headquartered in Rome, the Jesuits are found in 112 countries. The Jesuits founded nearby St Aloysius' College in 1859, one of the city's best schools.

Continue straight, crossing Scott Street to shortly pass the ㉛ **former Convent of Mercy** building on your left. Home to the Sisters of Mercy from 1861, they were an international Roman Catholic community of women, originally formed in Dublin in 1831. Women from a branch of the Sisters in Limerick, Ireland, were invited over by the Jesuits to establish a presence here in 1849. In recent decades, the Sisters of Mercy have attracted controversy because of their role in running the Magdalene laundries (or asylums) where abuse of young women occurred. The Sisters have branches

Garnethill Walk

worldwide, running schools and hospitals in places such as Australia, Jamaica, the United States and the Philippines. Today the old convent and school building is part of St Aloysius' College.

Continue straight and you will soon pass the ㉜ **main College building** on the right. Founded in 1859 by the Jesuits, the school is named after St Aloysius de Gonzaga (1568-91), a Jesuit born into an aristocratic Italian family. The school was first founded in the city's East End, educating Catholic children of families who had often arrived from Ireland and the Highlands. It moved to Garnethill in 1866. Alumni include Tom Conti, Armando Iannucci, and musicians who have been in Mogwai and Teenage Fanclub.

Walk into ㉝ **Garnethill Park** on the left. This is one of the most interesting spots in the area and was opened in 1991 by Diana, Princess of Wales. The park owes its existence to an unlikely German connection to Garnethill. When Glasgow became the European Capital of Culture in 1990, the German *Goethe Institute* offered to make a permanent contribution to the celebrations.

German environmental artist Dieter Magnus was commissioned to design a new urban park in Glasgow. He recalled: 'As soon as I saw the site in Garnethill, I knew that this derelict wasteland presented an ideal opportunity, a challenge, and I immediately saw it transformed into a playground and recreational area'. He used stones taken from old tenements, dead elms from Pollok Park, and road stones.

34

Look out for ground-level slabs created by artist Ulrike Enslein that contain stories about growing up in the area. By the 1970s, parts of Garnethill had become very run down. However, local community activists working with artists helped begin a slow regeneration. One key figure was 'Battling' Betty Brown, who chaired Garnethill Community Council and played a pivotal role in creating this park. She worked as a cleaner at STV studios, and was famously determined: 'If you don't harass, then things don't get done'. She was awarded an MBE and other honours before she died in 2006.

On one corner of the park, look for a ❸❹ **faded wall mural** dating from the late 1970s. It is an early example of the Glasgow mural tradition, maintained today by artists such as Rogue-One. The mural was part of a project led by John Kraska (b.1948), a local man who studied at the GSA in the late 1960s. He worked with local children and other community members on the piece, which includes 180,000 tiles. One local resident who grew up in Garnethill was less enthusiastic, regretting how he and his young friends missed the football pitches located here before the park was created.

On the other side of the park is the forbidding-looking ❸❺ **Haldane Building**, now part of the GSA but originally the headquarters of the 1st Volunteer Battalion of the Highland Light Infantry, completed in 1897. Soldiers assembled here before going off to fight in World War I. The building is named after 19th-century engraver James

Garnethill Walk

Haldane, who bequeathed money for an arts trust. This money was crucial to the development of the GSA, which was known as the Glasgow School of Art and Haldane Academy until 1891.

Cross over to walk up Rose Street towards the spire of ㊱ **St Aloysius' church**. This Neo-Baroque Jesuit church dates from 1910 and has one of the finest interiors of any church in Glasgow, with decoration reminiscent of Rome. It contains a rare copy of the *Our Lady of Montserrat*, often called the *Black Maddona*, gifted by Spanish visitors in 2008. The building was designed by Belgian Charles Jean Ménart and modelled on the Namur Cathedral in his homeland. This is the only Jesuit-run church in Glasgow.

Continue up Rose Street, passing ㊲ **Garnethill Multicultural Community Centre**. It hosts a wide range of events and classes for – as its name suggests – what is a diverse community.

Walk uphill, and at the junction with Rose Street, look for the art deco ㊳ **Glasgow Film Theatre**. This was Scotland's first arts cinema when it opened as the Cosmo in 1939. It is rare for a cinema from that era still to be operating, especially one with an arts focus, so the GFT holds a special place in many people's hearts. No doubt many GSA students have sat inside, watching a film on a rainy afternoon while dreaming of winning the Turner Prize. Next door, at 6 Rose Street, is an old department store, built around 1925 and now a listed building.

Garnethill Walk

Turn right up Renfrew Street, entering the heart of the GSA campus. On the left you pass the rear of the ㊴ **McLellan Galleries**. Its origins date back to when William Harley began to develop Blythswood Hill, of which the Garnethill area was just a part. The Galleries were constructed in the 1850s and named after Archibald McLellan (1795-1854), a wealthy coachbuilder, civic figure, and patron of the arts. The building later became home to the GSA for three decades from 1869, so figures such as Charles Rennie Mackintosh would have studied here. Since then, the building has been used for a variety of cultural purposes.

Continue up the hill. You will notice some lower-budget hotels and guest houses that give Garnethill a slightly seedy air, despite occupying solid 19th-century buildings. The GSA has around a dozen different buildings in Garnethill, the most famous of which is the Mackintosh Building.

Garnethill Walk

You soon reach ㊵ **Charles Rennie Mackintosh's famous GSA** building. Following devastating fires in 2014 and 2018, little of the original survives. What you will see today will depend on how the restoration is going. Glasgow seems to suffer more mysterious fires than any other similar city, and the damage here resulted in a media frenzy over who was ultimately responsible.

The fire sparked debates about what the destruction of a Glasgow landmark, not once, but twice, meant to locals. Rapper and social commentator Darren McGarvey (Loki) noted in his book *Poverty Safari* that despite condolences and donations from public figures like Brad Pitt, 'most people in Glasgow weren't that bothered' and he and others grew irritated at the 'disproportionate coverage' in the context of a community 'where things burn down all the time'.

The GSA's origins go back to the 1840s when Glasgow's Government School of Design was founded. This became the Glasgow School of Art and in 1896 a competition was held for a new building. Honeyman & Keppie (Mackintosh's employers before he became a partner) won the commission for a new building against competition from the city's best architects. The first part of the construction was completed in the late 1890s, and a further addition followed a decade later.

Mackintosh's career in Glasgow was brief. He left his partnership with Keppie and struck out on his own, however, his business failed. He left the city in 1914 with his wife Mary and never returned. Only decades later was he elevated to his current status as Scotland's greatest architect.

The GSA regularly ranks as one of the top ten art schools in the world. Notable former students include Robbie Coltrane, Peter Capaldi, Fran Healy and several Turner Prize-winning artists.

Opposite is the Reid Building, designed by New York-based practice Steven Holl Architects and completed in 2014. Like all interesting buildings, the design has its critics, but many more regard it as a remarkable contemporary companion to Mackintosh's work and a great addition to Glasgow's architectural heritage.

Garnethill Walk

Continue through the campus along Renfrew Street (if construction work is ongoing, you may need to turn right down Dalhousie Street and take the alleyway on the left).

The next stop on Renfrew Street is ㊶ **St Andrew's Church** to the right, a small church, home to one of Scotland's most unusual Catholic groups. SSPX – or the Society of Saint Pius X – is an international priestly society on Catholicism's ultra-conservative side. SSPX was founded in 1970 by French Archbishop Marcel Lefebvre. The society's refusal to accept reforms by successive Popes has seen it at loggerheads with the Vatican, and some members have been excommunicated. The society has a number of priories, chapels (like this one), and even schools both here and worldwide.

Walk further along to see the ornate ㊷ **Dental Hospital** building, completed in 1931 to a design by Wylie, Wright and Wylie. Its origins go back to 1879, when it was part of Anderson's College. There is an extension facing Sauchiehall Street. One reason it exists today is... football. Local teams took part in a tournament in 1928 to raise money for the construction, and Partick Thistle was the winner.

The houses on the right have a peculiar English connection, originally called Hampton Court Terrace. Most are now cheap hotels. On the left is ㊸ **Garnethill Primary School** and a small janitor's house. Dating from 1905, it bears an original School Board of Glasgow sign high up. It was built during the golden era of school construction following the Education (Scotland) Act of 1872, which, for the first time, provided funding to educate children.

When walking around Garnethill, it's important to remember the lasting impact of William Harley (1770-1829), the visionary developer who laid the groundwork for the area's transformation. Harley, an extraordinary man, owned Sauchy Hall – later renamed Willowbank House – and was instrumental in developing the land around Blythswood Hill. His contributions to Glasgow were manifold: he supplied Willowbank spring water to residents, expanded into bread production, established public baths (giving rise to Bath Street), and even founded a pleasure garden. In Garnethill, he cultivated strawberries and constructed a tower and summer house known as *Harley's Folly*. His pioneering dairy, *Harley's Byres*, became famous throughout Europe. Despite his remarkable achievements, Harley lost much of his fortune late in life and died while on his way to advise the Tsar of Russia on dairy production.

Look for the fine classical villas on the right-hand side, and on the left for the Singl-end café – a great place for lunch.

Further along on the left is an ㊹ **unusual single-storey building** dating from the 1890s. It was initially part of a piano showroom owned by Thomas Ewing. Until recently, a bust of Beethoven stood on top of the building. It mysteriously disappeared and may or may not be there when you visit. The main entrance to the old showroom still exists on Sauchiehall Street.

Next door are ㊺ **Albany Mansions** (c.1896), designed by the renowned Glasgow architect Sir J.J. Burnet (1857-1938). The Charing Cross Mansions (around the corner) is his better known design, but this

Garnethill Walk

dignified, yet understated apartment block is a good example of his work. The well-lit, larger flats within Albany Mansions have made this a favoured residence for artists, including John Cunningham, David Gauld, and John McGhie. It has been visited by actors Jet Li and Morgan Freeman when filming a scene in the film *Unleashed* (2005).

Next door, you can see a vintage **F.W. Woolworth & Co. sign**. This ghost sign is a reminder of the Woolworth store empire that began in the United States when Frank Windfield Woolworth opened a shop in New York in 1878. His stores spread worldwide, and this branch opened on Sauchiehall Street in 1922. It served Glaswegians until the 1970s. Woolworths was one of the first great names of the British High Street to succumb to the disruption wreaked by Amazon and discount stores. In 2015, the last 200 Woolworth stores in the UK closed.

Follow the map to the left, stopping outside **Charing Cross Mansions**, another J.J. Burnet creation, which dates from 1891 and was designed in a French Renaissance style. Charing Cross used to be an impressive part of the city, but the M8 cut through the heart of the area, destroying Victorian-era buildings and much of the atmosphere. In recent years, plans to cover the motorway with a greenspace have been raised.

The clock above is a fantastic creation, surrounded by allegorical figures and signs of the zodiac. The face at the centre represents Father Time and is said to have been modelled on Burnet himself, looking rather forlornly out over the dreary motorway. You are now on Sauchiehall Street where this walk ends. If you wish to return to the start point, head down Sauchiehall Street and turn left up Rose Street (it is a 15-minute walk).

VISIT

Glasgow's mini-Chinatown
42-46 New City Road, G4 9JT

The Tenement House
145 Buccleuch St, G3 6QN
nts.org.uk/visit/places/the-tenement-house

The Scottish Jewish Archives Centre
129 Hill St, G3 6UB
By appointment
sjac.org.uk/

Garnethill Park
Dalhousie St, G3 6PW

St Aloysius' Church
25 Rose St, G3 6RE
staloysiusglasgow.org/

Glasgow Film Theatre
12 Rose St, G3 6RB
glasgowfilm.org

Centre for Contemporary Arts
350 Sauchiehall St, G2 3JD
cca-glasgow.com/

The Glasgow School of Art
167 Renfrew St, G3 6RQ
gsa.ac.uk

EAT & DRINK

Wah Kee Chinese Bakery
42-46 New City Road, G4 9JT

Sylvan
20 Woodlands Rd, G3 6UR
sylvanglasgow.com

Non Viet
263 Renfrew St, G3 6TT
nonviet.co.uk

Singl-end Garnethill
534 Sauchiehall St, G2 3LX
the singl-end.co.uk

SHOPS

Paint and Mortar
Bourdon Building, Scott St, G3 6RQ
paintandmortar.com

Chivas Strathclyde Distillery, see p.125

4 Gorbals Walk

- 22 St Andrew's Suspension Bridge
- 23 Red sandstone tenement buildings
- 24 Hutchesontown Library
- 25 Southern Necropolis
- 26 St Francis Community Centre
- 27 'Gorbals Boys' statues
- 28 Former location of Hutchesontown C
- 29 Gorbals Rose Garden
- 30 Twomax Building
- 31 Benny Lynch Court
- 32 Camden Terrace
- 33 Former Caledonia Road Church
- 34 Former Circus Site
- 35 Gorbals Sound recording studio
- 36 Brazen Head Pub
- 37 Main Street
- 38 Gorbals Station
- 39 Cumberland Street Station
- 40 Former British Linen Bank
- 41 Citizens Theatre
- 42 Gorbals public Bath & Washhouse

Gorbals Walk

Start/Finish: Bridge Street subway
Distance: 3.5 miles

Exit the subway onto ❶ **Eglinton Street**. It's name reflects this area's connections to the 'lost' Glasgow, Paisley, and Ardrossan Canal. Initially conceived by inventor James Watt, the canal project advanced under the patronage of the 12th Earl of Eglinton. It was meant to connect Glasgow, Paisley, and Johnstone to Eglinton's seaport at Ardrossan and the coalfields of Ayrshire.

Construction began in 1807, but the canal was only completed between nearby Port Eglinton and Johnstone, so never reached Ardrossan. The canal closed in the 1880s and was later filled in to make way for a railway line.

Turn right up Eglinton Street, passing the ❷ **Laurieston Bar**. There has been a pub here since 1836, and the current building is famed for its classic 1960s interior. In 2019, actors Saoirse Ronan and Jack Lowden were photographed having a drink here following the release of the film *Mary Queen of Scots* (Ronan played Mary, Queen of Scots, and Lowden her second husband, Lord Darnley). The Laurieston was Glasgow pub of the year in 2018 and has featured in films such as *Young Adam* (2003), starring Ewan McGregor, and *Wild Rose* (2018), starring Jessie Buckley as a country and western singer, as well as music videos by Franz Ferdinand and The Fratellis.

Continue up Bridge Street, passing on the left a building originally part of ❸ **Bridge Street railway station**, the terminus

Gorbals Walk

of the Glasgow & Paisley Joint Railway. The station opened in 1840 and operated until 1905. This building, dating from 1899, was designed by James Miller (1860–1947), a prominent architect of his time, best known for his work with the Caledonian Railway. Look for the lion emblem on the exterior, a symbol of the Caledonian Railway.

If you stood here in 1775, there would have been little to see. A new bridge had recently been completed, the first since medieval times. It connected this area to the heart of Glasgow and symbolised how the city was beginning to expand. On this side of the bridge stood a windmill and washing green surrounded by open land. The village of Gorbals lay half a mile east of here.

By 1850, this area would have looked very different. The fields had gone, replaced by hundreds of tenement homes, factories, churches, pubs, and all manner of industry and entertainment. New districts had sprung up: Tradeston to the west of here, and on the eastern side, Laurieston, Gorbals, Hutchesontown and Oatlands.

Look for three fine buildings on the right-hand side of Bridge Street. The first, a ❹ **corner building**, dates from 1898 and is also by James Miller.

Beside it is the old South Branch of the ❺ **Glasgow Savings Bank**. It dates from the mid-19th century, with later parts attributed to Sir John James ('J.J.') Burnet from 1888. Burnet (1857-1938) and his father (John Burnet) were one of the great architectural dynasties.

Gorbals Walk

Gorbals Walk

Next door (61 Bridge Street) is an ❻ **Art Deco building** originally part of a drapery warehouse. It dates from 1935, and was designed by the architects of the Scottish Co-operative Wholesale Society. Cornelius Horsburgh Armour was involved in this design, as well as that of the better-known Luma Tower in Shieldhall.

Continue along Bridge Street, known as Bloomsbury Street in the early 1800s. Ahead is Glasgow Bridge (or Jamaica Street Bridge). On the left, you will pass a ❼ **former bank building**, dating from 1884, built for the Commercial Bank of Scotland.

Further along, on the right, is Cumbrae House, another ❽ **Art Deco building** from 1938, designed by Launcelot H. Ross. He played a key role in designs for the Glasgow Empire Exhibition of 1938.

Turn right into Carlton Place. On the corner is a ❾ **three-storey building** by John Burnet Senior, father of J.J. Burnet mentioned earlier, and dating from 1857. Carlton Place offers great views over the Clyde and the centre of Glasgow.

The origin of the name 'Gorbals' has been lost over time, but it was recorded about 500 years ago as 'Gorbaldis'. It was then a village in the parish of Govan and owned by the church. After the Reformation, the lands were acquired by the Elphinstone family, and in 1650 transferred to the magistrates of Glasgow for the benefit of the city, Hutchesons Hospital and the Trades House.

Why is this of interest? Because from the late 18th century, the growth of Glasgow led to several new suburbs and commercial districts. In 1771, Gorbals became a parish in its own right, absorbing the lands of Little Govan and Polmadie.

In 1790 Glasgow council apportioned land between Trades House and Hutchesons' Hospital. The Hospital subsequently sold some of this to a developer named James Laurie. James,

Gorbals Walk

and his brother David, then embarked on a new development intended to match anything being built in Regency London. The new district of Laurieston, named after the brothers, was meant to attract wealthy Glaswegians south of the river. Street names were aspirational and inspired by English locations – Carlton, Oxford, Bloomsbury.

Continue along Carlton Place, named after the Prince Regent's mansion in London. Despite being a bit run-down, it is still an impressive street. If anything, the grandeur seems slightly misplaced considering that Laurieston has never attracted the city's elite. Many houses here were designed by Peter Nicholson (1765-1844), also employed by the Earl of Eglinton to design the grid system for the town of Ardrossan.

On the left, you pass the ⑩ **South Portland Street Suspension Bridge**. It was designed by Alexander Kirkland (who ended up as Chicago's Commissioner of Public Buildings) and was completed in the early 1850s and later modified. The bridge is best seen at night when floodlit.

The building of Carlton Place began in 1802. The eastern terrace was completed first, then the western terrace by 1818. Unfortunately for the Laurie brothers, the growth of nearby industrial sites put off potential property buyers. Their venture went bust, although middle-class residents stayed in this part of Laurieston into the 1840s, even as the wider Gorbals district gained a reputation as a working-class slum.

Boot scraper

On the right (50-53 Carlton Place) is the Greek Revival style ⑪ **Laurieston House**, also by Nicholson. When built, it was regarded as one of the finest Georgian houses in Britain and is possibly the last great Glasgow merchant's house to survive largely unaltered in the city. The Laurie brothers had gates installed at the end of Carlton Place to keep the riff-raff out, but it seems they were unsuccessful. Number 40 (on the corner) has a rare Ionic aedicule door (look also for the foot scraper at street level).

Next, you arrive at the ⑫ **Sheriff Court of Glasgow**, a Brutalist building that opened in the 1980s. It stands on the site of the former Gorbals Parish Church, which was designed by renowned architect David Hamilton (1768–1843) and built in 1811. In 1770, this area marked the western edge of Gorbals village, then a small settlement of just a few streets clustered at the southern end of the original bridge over the Clyde.

The Gorbals Parish Church remained a landmark until 1929, when its steeple was struck by lightning, causing 20 tons of masonry to fall, injuring sleeping neighbours. The church stood until 1973, when it was demolished to make room for the court's construction.

The Gorbals was once home to the largest and most vibrant Jewish community in Scotland, and in the early 20th century around 4,700 Jews lived here. At one point, the local school, which stood near here, had the highest percentage of Jewish pupils (around 50%) of any school in the country.

Why did they settle here? A big factor was a mix of antisemitism and poor economic conditions in Russia and other Eastern European countries. Tens of thousands emigrated to America via Scotland, but a small minority decided to try their luck in Glasgow.

Many Jewish immigrants were working-class Yiddish speakers who had to form their own support networks. They opened kosher butchers, bakers, garment shops, and other businesses. Individuals worked in trades ranging from watchmaking and tailoring to hawking and tobacco. The community had its own synagogues, newspapers, social and political clubs, charities, pipe bands, and even football teams. If you had walked here in the early 1900s, you would have noticed Yiddish shop signs and heard Yiddish spoken by passersby.

As the 20th century progressed, many Jews with roots in the Gorbals moved to more affluent parts of the city, and the community gradually faded away.

One notable local was Ralph Glasser (1916-2002), a Jewish boy who won a scholarship to study at Oxford and became a respected psychologist and economist. He would later recall how tough life was in the working-class streets of his youth: 'The streets were slippery with refuse and often with drunken vomit. It was a place of grime and poverty...The Victorian building, in red sandstone blackened by smoke... was in decay. Splintered and broken floorboards sometimes gave way under your feet. Interior walls carried patches of stain from a long succession of burst pipes. Rats and mice moved about freely.'

Now continue along Nicholson Street, named after the architect. Head into Oxford Street and stop outside the ⓭ **pink building** designed by A.B. MacDonald and completed in 1895. This served as a Police Office and Barracks. Look for the figure of Lady Justice, wearing a blindfold to symbolise impartiality. You'll also see the Latin motto *Semper Vigilo* – meaning always alert – which is now incorporated into Police Scotland's logo.

By the early 20th century, much of the Gorbals – by then far larger than the

Gorbals Walk

original village – had become a byword for a dangerous slum. The Industrial Revolution brought mills, foundries, factories, and sweatshops to the area. Poorly paid and often dangerous industrial jobs usually attracted those with few other options. Developers threw up tenement streets to house the factory fodder who had arrived from Ireland, the Highlands and other places.

The mix of Irish Catholic and Protestant residents created sectarian tensions. Even though Glasser was Jewish, he recalled being asked at school 'Wha' are yese – Billy [i.e Protestant – William III] or a Dan [i.e Catholic – Daniel O'Connell]? Billy or Dan! Fists up, they were going to beat us to a pulp if we gave the wrong answer'.

Oxford Street and its surrounding streets were home to several synagogues, all of which have since been demolished as the Jewish population gradually declined in the Gorbals over the 20th century. A sign of changing times was the arrival of Glasgow's first mosque on Oxford Street in 1944.

To your right, you can see the rear of Georgian buildings on Carlton Place. Head left down Oxford Lane to Norfolk Street. On the right, there's a drab red sandstone building that served as the ⓮ **Gorbals Public Library** between 1930-1986. This is a rare survivor from the urban redevelopment of the area that took place in the second half of the 20th century and resulted in most Victorian-era buildings being demolished.

Gorbals Walk

South of here, along South Portland Street, once stood the South Portland Street Synagogue, which operated between 1901-1974, and the Jewish Institute. The latter was the key cultural and social hub of the community between 1935-1970. Both have long been swept away.

Turn left onto Norfolk Street and walk for a few minutes. In the 1770s, this was known as Paisley Lane, but with the development of Laurieston, older names were replaced by more respectable English ones. In 1900, you would have been walking parallel to a tram line, surrounded by tenement streets, with ⑮ **Gorbals Cross** up ahead.

Perhaps no other spot in Glasgow has changed as much as Gorbals Cross. The intersection of roads stood at the centre of Gorbals village, with the original (or 'Old Bridge') across the Clyde standing to your left. In the late 18th century, the road leading up to the bridge was known as High Street.

The Gorbals began as a single-street village on the south side of the medieval bridge. In 1350, a leper colony was established here (approximately where the mosque is today), dedicated to St. Ninian. In 1579, merchant George Elphinstone rented the land from the church, and by the 1650, the City of Glasgow took over the village – then just a few thatched houses that were home to weavers and other tradespeople.

By 1771, the village's population had reached 3,500, but rapid development of new residential streets and industrial sites meant by 1846 the population had surged to 46,000. The old village buildings were either demolished or left to decay, replaced by tenement streets, cotton mills, a distillery, cement works, tube works, a brass foundry, new churches, pubs, and everything else an industrialised, working-class suburb required.

If you stood at Gorbals Cross in 1900, you would have seen a bustling intersection, trams crisscrossing the streets, and a landmark fountain at its heart. It stood here between 1878-1932, before being removed for a road-widening scheme. It had a twin fountain in Basseterre, on the island of Saint Kitts and Nevis in the West Indies. In recent years, a community group sought to recreate the drinking fountain using a 3D laser scan of the structure in Basseterre.

Gorbals Walk

On the northwest side of Gorbals Cross, once stood tenements designed by Alexander 'Greek' Thomson, one of Glasgow's most notable architects. These were demolished in 1975.

This spot also has an American connection. Allan Pinkerton (1819-1884), was born near Muirhead Street (now the site of Glasgow Central Mosque), emigrated to the United States in 1842 and founded the Pinkerton Detective Agency. He provided intelligence services to the Union during the American Civil War and was a close associate of Abraham Lincoln. Pinkerton's work represented the beginning of America's secret intelligence agencies.

Pinkerton's men tried (and failed) to capture the outlaw Jesse James, but they did thwart assassination attempts on President Lincoln. If Lincoln had been killed before the Civil War ended, who knows how history would have unfolded? The Pinkerton Detective Agency's advert featured an eye with the motto 'We Never Sleep', giving rise to the term 'private eye'.

Continue along Ballater Street, passing ⓰ **Glasgow Central Mosque**, Scotland's largest mosque, completed in 1983. Tours of the mosque are available normally Tuesday-Thursday (see page 143). The mosque's construction reflects the demographic changes that have impacted the Gorbals in the mid-20th century, when many Asian people settled here, particularly Muslims from Pakistan, as well as Hindus and Sikhs from India.

The mosque stands on the approximate site of the leper hospital. In medieval times, the village was also known as Brigend, as it stood at the southern end of the bridge. The hospital was still operating in the early 1600s. In the 1890s, the land was the site of the Loch Katrine Distillery.

By the mid-20th century, this area's reputation as a dangerous slum had spread far and wide. The publication of *No Mean City* (1935), with its tales of violent criminals and razor gangs, further popularised this perception of the Gorbals. A *Picture Post* article from 1948 noted: 'Low rent is one reason why people stay in the Gorbals. Another reason may be the liking an Irishman has for an Irishman's company. And anyway, a man seeking to move now is lucky if he can find a place to go. Once the area had a large

Gorbals Walk

immigrant Jewish population, and the district round Gorbals Cross was called 'Little Jerusalem.' But many Jews left as their economic condition improved and nowadays, though you still see Jewish names over the shops, the main landmark at the Cross is Doyle's Irish House'.

Continue straight for about 10 minutes to see the ⑰ **Blessed John Duns Scotus Roman Catholic Church** on the right. This is the site of a Franciscan Friary. St Francis of Assisi sent friars to England in 1224, and by the Reformation, there were about 60 Franciscan friaries across Britain. There is a little-known link between here and Cologne. John Duns Scotus (c.1265-1308) came from Duns in Scotland and was an influential Franciscan philosopher and university teacher. He travelled throughout medieval Europe and died in Cologne, where his sarcophagus can be seen in a Franciscan church today. According to legend, he was (accidentally) buried alive.

This parish results from the merger of five smaller Roman Catholic parishes stretching from Tradeston to Oatlands. They were all formed in the 19th century in response to many Irish and Highland Catholics flocking to this part of the city seeking work. The best-known attraction is the bones of St Valentine, the patron saint of lovers, in a casket just inside the church. The remains were brought to the Gorbals from France by Franciscans in 1868. The shrine outside in the grounds and a bell from the old building are also worth seeing.

Gorbals Walk

Retrace your steps along Ballater Street and take a sharp right onto Florence Street (formerly Rose Street). In the 18th century, this street followed the route of the 'Blind Burn', which had an outflow into the Clyde and ran inland by the village burial ground (seen later). In 1900, this area had many drinking dens and the left side of this street was home to five pubs, with another five on the other side of the block.

Soon, you will arrive at the former ⑱ **Adelphi Terrace School**, built in 1894 during a period of rapid school construction following the Education (Scotland) Act of 1872. This legislation created a new regime for free, compulsory schooling for five to thirteen-year-olds. Now the State was in charge of educating tens of thousands of Glasgow's children, and between 1873-1918 the Glasgow School Board built 75 schools. Most were solid red sandstone giants like this, that could accommodate between 800 to 1000 pupils. Look for the sign for 'Glasgow School Board' and the Egyptian-inspired sculpture.

This was one of three schools in the Gorbals that, between them, had around 1000 Jewish pupils. The name 'Adelphi' is Greek for 'brothers,' referring to George and Thomas Hutcheson, who bequeathed the funds that paid for the foundation of Hutchesons'

hospital in the mid-1600s. As mentioned earlier, the Hospital later acquired land here, hence Hutchesontown. One legacy is the well-known Hutchesons' Grammar school (or 'Hutchie') once based in the Gorbals.

Today you will notice the streets of the Gorbals are often quiet, with few children running around. The area was hollowed out by urban redevelopment in the second half of the 20th century. Try and imagine this place in around 1900 when hundreds of children would have crowded around this school.

Gorbals Walk

Continue on, taking a right onto the pathway beside the Clyde. You will soon pass an odd ⑲ **tidal weir building**, dating from 1901, which helps maintain the water level of the river through Glasgow Green. Downstream from here, the tidal flows have caused flooding, notably in 1941, when many tenements were destroyed.

Keep walking along the slightly higgledy-piggledy path and mind the cycle paths. You are now in Hutchesontown. You pass mostly 20th-century buildings and residential towers. After the World War II, city planners rebuilt much of the Gorbals and particularly Hutchesontown. It was declared a Comprehensive Development Area (CDA) in 1957 and split into areas A to E. You are passing Area B, which still contains tower blocks dating from 1964.

After about 10 minutes walking beside the Clyde, on your right you'll pass a rare reminder of the area's industrial heyday – the ⑳ **Chivas Strathclyde Distillery**. In the 1850s, this was the site of the Albyn cotton and spinning mills. By the 1890s, you would have seen the City tube works, Adelphi Biscuit Factory, Adelphi Hair and Fur Works, Confectionary & Preserve Works and other industries. One can only imagine how polluted the air was.

There are currently three murals by Molly Hankinson, Michael Corr, and Rogue-One. They feature Tom McGuire, frontman of Tom McGuire & the Brassholes, artist Margaret Macdonald, and Mark Coyle, who was diagnosed with Perthes' disease.

Gorbals Walk

Rowers on the Clyde

Next door is the site of the ㉑ **McNeil Street Bakery** – run by The United Co-operative Baking Society. In its heyday, it was the largest baker in the city, employing 1,000 people in 1958 and supplying products to Co-op branches around Glasgow. The first part of the bakery opened in 1886, and it grew to occupy the whole block. Photos show a gorgeously ornate building resembling a French chateau. Sadly it was demolished in 1977.

The next stop is ㉒ **St Andrew's Suspension Bridge** which dates from 1856. It was designed to replace a ferry and enable factory workers to commute back and forth. Notice the 6-metre-high Corinthian columns. If you step onto the bridge, you may spot rowers from nearby clubs.

Head down McNeil Street, passing modern housing that replaced nearly everything built between the 1950s and 1970s as part of the Comprehensive Development Area (CDA) programme. In the early 1800s, this was the Little Govan Nursery.

Turn right onto Ballater Street for a short detour to see another fragment of the area's baking history. Walk towards the ㉓ **red sandstone tenement buildings** on the left, two of the few remaining. On the building, look for the 1903 date and the initials 'UCBS', which stand for United Co-operative Baking Society, along with the emblem of clasping hands. The UCBS was founded in 1869, and vintage biscuit tins proudly portray the bakery building and St Andrew's Bridge.

Gorbals Walk

Co-operative societies played a key role in Glasgow, with one-tenth of all retail sales conducted through Co-op branches in 1950. By 1954, Glasgow's eight co-operative societies had over 200,000 members.

Retrace your steps, and head right down McNeil Street. The area to your right once hosted another 'lost' building by Alexander 'Greek' Thomson – the Chalmers Memorial Free Church, demolished in 1971.

As you walk along McNeil Street, you'll see more modern, low-rise housing. If you want to live in reasonably priced accommodation in a quiet area within walking distance of Glasgow city centre, you could do much worse than here.

The next stop is the ㉔ **Hutchesontown Library** on the right. The library opened in 1906 (you can see the signage if you look carefully). It was funded by the legacy of the Scots-born industrialist Andrew Carnegie and is one of seven libraries in Glasgow designed by James R. Rhind. The library closed in 1964. Look out for the figures of St Mungo with maidens on either side and the figure above of a woman holding a book. It is far more ornate than the first library you visited on the walk.

This library was among those that banned *No Mean City* after its publication in 1935. The book's stark and brutal depiction of street life in the Gorbals was written by unemployed local baker and alcoholic Alexander McArthur, with the help of co-writer and journalist H. Kingley Long. In November 1935, *The Herald* reported that the Glasgow Corporation had banned the book in public libraries, stating it was 'an unfair and inaccurate representation of working-class life in Glasgow'.

The lurid tale centred on gangs and 'Razor King' Johnnie Stark. It became a bestseller but heightened the Gorbals' reputation as a place of crime and deprivation. Author McArthur's tragic life ended in 1947 after a drinking binge when he consumed disinfectant and jumped into the Clyde. Interestingly, the book's title is taken from the New Testament (Acts 21:29, King James Bible).

This was previously the site of Springfield Iron Works, while Todd and Higginbotham's cotton mill stood opposite. In the 1930s, the Gorbals was home to around 85,000 people, many working in local factories. However, by the 1980s, urban redevelopment had drastically reduced the population to about 10,000, erasing swathes of Victorian and Edwardian pubs, churches, shops, community institutions, and tenements.

After passing the former library, the road bends to the right. Instead of following this curve, cut across the pedestrianised strip onto Old Rutherglen Road, continuing towards the tower block. This road becomes Oregon Street. Turn left into Cumberland Street and cross over Caledonia Road to reach the ㉕ **Southern Necropolis**. This grand cemetery opened in 1840 when new public burial grounds were built to replace overcrowded churchyards. An information board near the entrance highlights notable interments, including Alexander 'Greek' Thomson and tea magnate Sir Thomas Lipton.

Alexander 'Greek' Thomson

In September 1954, a rumour spread among local kids that the 'Gorbals Vampire' – standing seven feet tall and with metal teeth – had eaten two children here. Mass hysteria erupted, and hundreds of children gathered, some carrying knives, crucifixes, crosses, and axes. The national and international press reported on the incident, and it even prompted Parliamentary debates on the dangers of sensationalist American comics. A 1953 issue of *Dark Mysteries* included a story called 'The Vampire with the Iron Teeth'. This event later inspired Johnny McKnight's 2016 play, *The Gorbals Vampire*, performed at the nearby Citizens Theatre.

Gorbals Walk

Franciscan Friars' Memorial

For years, the cemetery was a local playground for children. Violent criminal turned sculptor Jimmy Boyle (b.1944) recalled in his autobiography *A Sense of Freedom*, 'The local playing park for our part of the Gorbals was the Caledonia Road graveyard and this was the favourite playground on Saturdays when there was no school'. Outside the cemetery, to the southwest, lay the site of Govan Iron Works, founded by William Dixon in 1839. Its furnaces were so bright they lit up the night sky, earning the nickname 'Dixon's Blazes', and even attracted tourists. It was the last working blast furnace in the city when it closed in 1958.

Other notable features here include the burial monument known as *The White Lady*. Legend has it that the statue's head turns to watch as you pass by. The monument marks the final resting place of John S Smith, his wife Magdalene, and their housekeeper Mary McNaughton. The two women were tragically killed by a tramcar when walking together in 1933. Along the central route from the gatehouse is a memorial to medieval Franciscan friars. Their remains were discovered at the site of their friary in central Glasgow by archaeologists. After a service conducted by Archbishop Conti at St Andrew's Cathedral in 2005, their remains were moved here.

Exit via the gatehouse, which dates from 1848 and was designed by the celebrated architect Charles Wilson (1810-63). Wilson himself is buried here with other members of his family.

Gorbals Walk

Retrace your steps to return to Cumberland Street, following the bend left to reach ㉖ **St Francis Community Centre** – a former church and another survivor of 19th-century Gorbals. The Franciscans were forced out of Glasgow during the Reformation (c.1559) and did not re-establish themselves in the city until 1868. They bought land here and opened the church of St Francis in 1881. The Franciscans later moved to the Blessed John Duns of Scotus site visited earlier.

Sandyfaulds Street, to your right, was home to the notorious local hardman Jimmy Boyle. This area is known as Oatlands – Jimmy Boyle recalled 'The Oatlands had once been a sort of toffy district but now we were in it, and it had changed since those days.' In 1951, his mother couldn't afford electricity: 'St Francis chapel had a poor box and I remember me and my brother...going to see the Franciscan priest there to ask for money to pay for the light' but the poor box was empty and 'Instead they gave us two big candles to use in the house'.

During Boyle's time, Glasgow's large street gangs were at their peak. He recalled two gangs in particular: 'The Big Cumbie' and the 'Wild Young Cumbie', named after Cumberland Street. Despite the violent gangs, social ties between residents were strong. Boyle remembered how 'People stopped and talked in the street after mass to gossip, and there was a very close community feeling at such times'.

Just beyond the centre on the right is the site of the ㉗ **'Gorbals Boys' statues** by Liz Peden, inspired by Oscar Marzaroli's iconic 1963 photograph of three boys playing in their mums' high heels. It captures the innocence of childhood, when the streets would have

been filled with kids at play. Three local boys posed for the statues, and they were unveiled by Nicola Sturgeon (then deputy First Minister) in 2008. Ian Docherty (then 50), one of the boys captured in the original photograph, attended. In 2022, two of the statues were cut off and later found dumped by a train station. Hopefully, by the time you visit, all three will be restored to their original site.

In the past kids played tough street games. Boyle recalled a popular one called ratcatcher (also the name of the acclaimed film set in housing schemes in Glasgow from 1999): 'The first rule of rat-catching was, if you wore long trousers, to tuck the bottoms into your socks in case the scampering rats ran up your trouser-leg, as there were lots of rumours of this having happened'.

Turn right up Queen Elizabeth Gardens. Further along is the ㉘ **former location of the notorious Hutchesontown C**, a 62-acre site within one of the (A-E) Comprehensive Development Areas (CDAs) that did so much to change this area. Architect Sir Basil Spence designed much of the complex, including two Brutalist 20-storey blocks in Queen Elizabeth Square that began to be occupied in the mid-1960s.

Gorbals Walk

While residents initially appreciated the modern conveniences of the 'Hutchie C' development, the combination of harsh weather, damp conditions, and poverty soon made it a cautionary example of failed urban planning. Demolished in 1993, the destruction itself was tragically mishandled, with debris killing onlooker Helen Tinney, and injuring several others.

Turn left into Errol Gardens, you will soon arrive at the ㉙ **Gorbals Rose Garden**. This is an historic burial ground that dates back to around 1715, with headstones from that era still to be seen by the perimeter wall. A map from 1778 shows 'Gorbells Burial Place' amidst open fields, the Blind Burn, and not much else between here and the Clyde.

When this was a village, many locals followed the same trades as their ancestors. They were so central to their identities that symbols of their work were put on their gravestones. Along the perimeter wall you will find examples on headstones including a collier's pick and baker's shovel.

John Mackenzie, the minister of the Gaelic chapel for the Highlanders in the Gorbals, is buried here, along with the Laurie brothers. Look also for the unusual Gorbals Rose war memorial – also by Liz Peden.

Cross right through, coming out onto Old Rutherglen Road on the north side. Ahead is the ㉚ **Twomax Building**, built around 1817. It is the oldest surviving iron-framed fireproof structure in Glasgow. Originally constructed for a cotton merchant, it later

Gorbals Walk

housed the Twomax Clothing Factory (its name reflecting its then owners – McClure and McIntosh). Unlike other mills in the district, it survived demolition. It has a fake smoke figure coming out of the tall chimney in a nod to the building's original use.

Turn left along Old Rutherglen Road and pass ㉛ **Benny Lynch Court**. It is named after local boy and flyweight boxer, Benny Lynch (1912-1946). Born at 17 Florence Street, he became a world champion in 1935 and was so popular that after one win, a crowd of 20,000 came to Central Station to greet him. However, his life was blighted by alcohol and violence. By his late 20s his career was in decline and he died at just 33.

Alcohol's grip on the Gorbals was well-known. As Jimmy Boyle recalled: 'On Friday nights the men came home from their work and went straight into the pub with their mates, as most of them had just been paid, and those who had no jobs were taken for a drink by their pals. The Gorbals must have had more pubs per head than any other district in Glasgow, as there was one at almost every corner. On Friday kids would be at the pub doors, sent there by their mothers to tell their fathers to come home with the wages before they drank most of them. There were occasions when wives went to the pubs to hunt down their men and rescue the income, but on the whole this was considered an affront to the husband'. When the pubs shut, dozens of illicit drinking dens – or shebeens – filled their place.

Continue straight and take a left onto Crown Street. This is one of the few places in the Gorbals which still has a community feel: the Co-op, local library, a café, a butcher, Greggs. A Gorbals resident from the 1930s would likely not recognise the

Gorbals Walk

Crown St (new housing)

scene, and probably ask 'where's everyone gone?'. However, some of the modern buildings around here are as impressive as any new build in central Glasgow.

Continue along Crown Street. In 1780 this was all open land, but by 1857 it had been urbanised, with streets laid out on all sides. Hutcheson's Hospital School stood opposite today's Co-op, and patriotic naming conventions were everywhere – Victoria Place, Albert Place, Palmerston Place, and so on.

To the east of here, ㉜ **Camden Terrace** was once home to one of Britain's most notorious serial killers, Ian Brady (1938-2017). He was known as Dracula to his neighbours due to his obsession with horror films. Brady attended the local Camden Street Primary School but was known to be somewhat of a loner, and even then showed some disturbing signs of anti-social behaviour. He left for Manchester when he was sixteen but would later recall: 'Even to the end I regularly returned to the Gorbals, strolling its alleys and backs after midnight, reliving childhood adventures, remembering air raids and the blackout, etc.'

The adult lives of people like Brady, Lynch, and Boyle – once dubbed 'Scotland's Most Violent Man' – were influenced by the conditions in which they grew up. Brady remembered handling a gun whilst at primary school, and watching men fight outside in the street having exited the seven pubs visible from his home. Lynch was a deeply troubled individual too, convicted of assaulting young children in his final years.

The *Picture Post* article on the Gorbals from 1948 captured the deep-seated problems that blighted the place: 'The air of calm that covers a multitude of horrors. Nearly 40,000 people live in the Gorbals. They live four, six, eight to a room, often thirty to a lavatory, forty to a tap. They live in Britain's most abandoned slum. At first sight, of an early morning, the Gorbals looks like any other poor area. Its flat wide streets are lined with flat-faced tenements.

There is a pub on every corner and an undertaker's (open day and night) in almost every other block'.

Some did thrive after they made it out, Allan Pinkerton and Ralph Glasser being just two. Another was Sir Thomas Lipton (1848-1931) founder of the global Lipton tea brand. Lipton's family, Irish immigrants fleeing the Great Famine, settled on Crown Street, a testament to the area's historical role as a haven for poor, new arrivals. He went on to become a millionaire and a peer of the realm.

Follow the map to see the landmark tower of the ㉝ **former Caledonia Road Church**, strangely marooned by traffic. The nearby Alexander Crescent is named after the architect of this church – Alexander 'Greek' Thomson (1817-75). Carefully cross the road to visit the former church. Built in 1856, the Caledonia Road United Presbyterian Church was where Thomson himself worshipped. Sadly it caught fire in 1965 and has lain in ruins since.

UPSTAIRS TO
DURTY NELLIES

CUMBERLAND ST

the BRAZEN head

36

Gorbals Walk

Other Thomson buildings in this immediate vicinity were demolished in the name of progress. These included buildings on Waverley Terrace near the bottom of Camden Terrace, as well as parts of the church complex at 190-92 Hospital Street and 37-39 Cathcart Road.

Walk down Cathcart Road with the former church to your right. Cross under the railway bridge, which carries an abandoned line overgrown with vegetation. Immediately after the bridge, look to the left for a ㉞ **semi-circular, grass-covered space** that was once the site of a **circus** in the 1890s. Next door to the Go Radio sign, you'll find the ㉟ **Gorbals Sound recording studio**, a high-end facility whose clients include Simple Minds, Eddi Reader, Susan Boyle, Deacon Blue, Texas, and Lewis Capaldi.

Continue along, passing the Celtic-supporting ㊱ **Brazen Head pub**. In 2003, a journalist for *The Sunday Times* came to investigate, as the police were trying to close it down. He wrote under the headline 'Inside the Gorbals' Hardest Pub' and posed the question, 'How hard is the Brazen Head? Well, it advertises one of its souvenir products like this: 'Save your teeth, use a Brazen Head bottle opener.' To the police, it is the epicentre of violence in the Gorbals... Police insiders hint darkly about sectarianism'. Nowadays, the pub has mellowed out a bit, and is more hospitable to strangers, including those researching walking guides with pen and camera in hand.

Gorbals Walk

39

old railway arches

BAT ROOST

40

Opposite the pub is a garage that was the site of the adjoining railway stations – ㊲ **Main Street** and ㊳ **Gorbals Station**. Main Street was built by the City of Glasgow Union Railway and operated between 1872-1900, when it was replaced by Cumberland Street Station. Gorbals Station, part of the Glasgow, Barrhead, and Kilmarnock Joint Railway, operated between 1877-1928, although the line was in use until 1966. You can still see steps leading up to where the station platform once stood.

To see an abandoned station building, head left along Cumberland Street to the junction with Salisbury Street on the left. On the corner is a building with 'Station' still visible on the frontage. This is the former ㊴ **Cumberland Street station**, opened in 1900 and operated by the Glasgow and South Western Railway as a replacement for Main Street Station (mentioned earlier). It closed in 1966.

If the history of the various railway companies that built this maze of lines and stations seems confusing, you're not alone. These companies competed with each other, building unprofitable lines just to stay in the game. Victorian-era railway companies were forced to merged with rivals, and the survivors were nationalised in 1948.

Retrace your steps until you return to the junction, then take a left onto Gorbals Street. Passing under a second railway bridge, you'll see the platform and waiting room of the old Gorbals Main Street station extended to the right. Further along, there's

Gorbals Walk

a sweep of abandoned elevated railway line structures, which some have suggested could become Glasgow's equivalent of New York's High Line – although standing here today, such plans seem very distant.

After a few minutes on the left is the ㊵ **former British Linen Bank building** – the last Victorian tenement of its kind in this part of the Gorbals. It dates from around 1900 and was designed by the well-known architect James Salmon (1873-1924) for the British Linen Bank. Salmon was a friend of Charles Rennie Mackintosh, and both studied at the Glasgow School of Art. Originally established in Edinburgh in 1746 to promote the linen industry, the British Linen Bank soon shifted its focus to finance and eventually became a fully-fledged bank. The building was saved from demolition and won a Scottish Design Award for its restoration. It's also home to the Gorbals Art Project, a backlit gable sculpture made from stacked laser-cut Corten steel plates, inspired by the building's interior stair metalwork. There is a quote from Salmon at its base.

Gorbals Walk

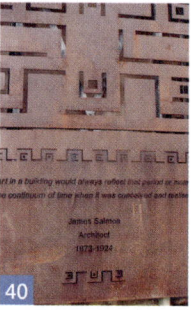

Continue up this long road, dominated on the left by new housing and passing the famous ㊶ **Citizens Theatre** on the right. Founded in 1943, the theatre company moved here two years later. It has long been known for putting on original plays and attracting some of Britain's best actors. It stands on the site of what was originally Her Majesty's Theatre and Opera House when it opened in 1878, although it soon changed its name to the Royal Princess's Theatre.

Next door, to the south, was The Grand National Hall of the Good Templars, which became a music hall known as the Palace Theatre in 1904. Unfortunately, the Victorian-era classical frontage of the Citizens Theatre was demolished in 1977, although much of the original structure was preserved. The Palace Theatre was not so lucky and was totally demolished that same year.

Also long gone is the ㊷ **Gorbals public bath and washhouse** complex, which stood opposite the theatre, founded in 1885. For generations of locals the 'Steamie' was a focal point of the community. As late as 1951, more than half of Glasgow's population (over 500,000 people) had no access to fixed baths, and over a third shared a water closet. On top of that, 44% of houses were officially categorised as overcrowded. So the public baths were essential to provide an affordable hot bath and wash clothes.

From here, continue up Gorbals Street and turn left onto Norfolk Street. After a few minutes' walk, you will return to your starting point.

VISIT

People's Palace
Glasgow Green, G40 1AT

Glasgow Central Mosque
1 Mosque Ave, G5 9TA
centralmosque.co.uk

**Blessed John Duns
Scotus RC Church**
270 Ballater St, G5 0YT
blessedjohndunsscotusparish.org

The Southern Necropolis
300 Caledonia Rd, G5 0TB
southernnecropolis.co.uk

Gorbals Rose Garden
Old Rutherglen Rd, G5 0RS

Citizens Theatre
119 Gorbals St, G5 9DS
citz.co.uk

EAT & DRINK

Laurieston Bar
58 Bridge St, G5 9HU

The Brazen Head Pub
1-3 Cathcart Rd, G42 7BE
brazenhead.net

Mackintosh at the Willow, see p.162

5 Miss Cranston Walk

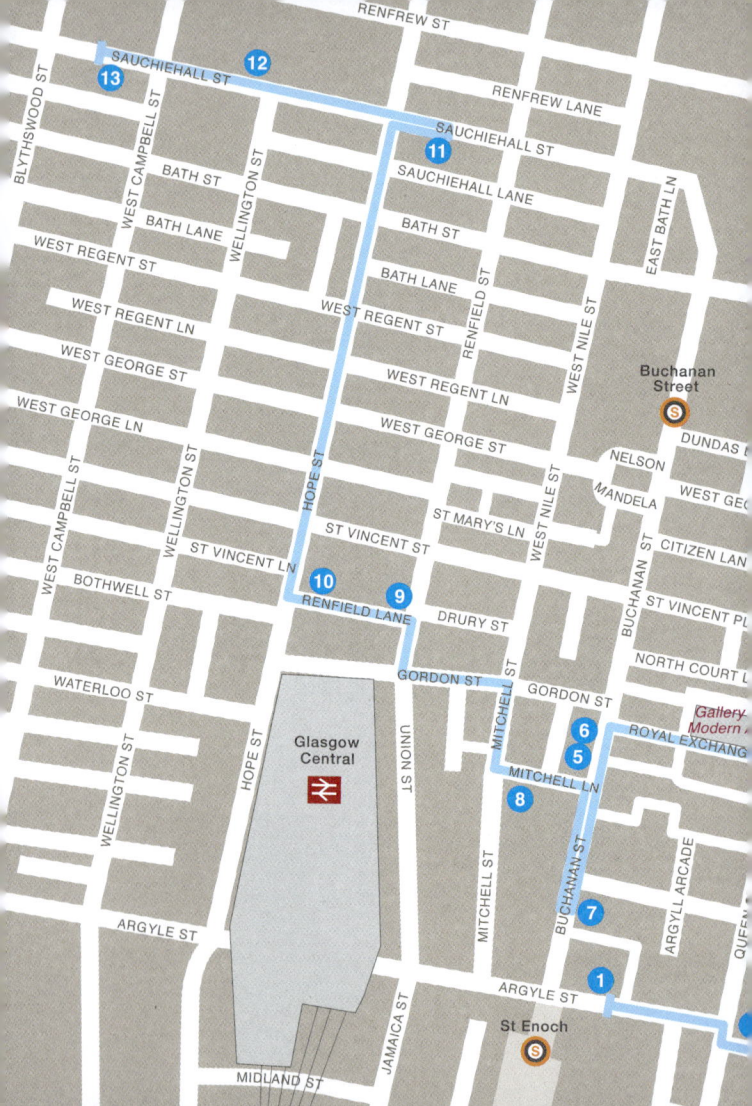

Miss Cranston Walk

1. Cranston House – Kate's first tea room
2. Former site of Stuart Cranston's tea room
3. Location of Kate's second tea room
4. North British Station Hotel
5. 91-93 Buchanan St – Kate's third tea room
6. The Willow Tea Rooms – Kate's fourth tea room
7. Argyll Arcade
8. The Lighthouse
9. 13 Renfield Street
10. *Daily Record* Building
11. 91 Sauchiehall Street
12. Washington Temperance Hotel
13. Original Willow Tea Rooms

Miss Cranston Walk

Miss Cranston Walk
Start: 104/114 Argyle Street
Finish: Willow Tea rooms Sauchiehall Street
Distance: 1.75 miles

Miss Cranston Walk

This walk explores the key Glasgow sites associated with Catherine (or 'Kate') Cranston (1849-1934), a pioneering figure of her era. While she is best known today for her patronage of Charles Rennie Mackintosh (1868-1928) (referred to as 'CRM'), her establishment of a tea room empire from the late 1870s deserves far greater recognition.

Her tea room empire began here on Argyle Street inside ❶ **Cranston House** (number 104/114). In 1878, she founded the Crown Tea and Luncheon Rooms on the ground floor of the building situated above a temperance hotel. At the time, Kate was in her late twenties, and between then and 1903, she went on to establish a total of four tea rooms in the heart of Glasgow. Look out for a sign for Glasgow's oldest restaurant, Sloans, as well.

Why did Kate's tea room empire matter? It is remarkable because it was rare in the mid-19th century for a woman of Kate's social standing to own such a business in Glasgow. When she opened the first tea room here, she was unmarried and is said to have visited her female friends to say goodbye, assuming she would no longer be welcome in respectable circles.

Her tea room empire was also highly innovative. In an era when there was no equivalent of a Starbucks, there were few options available for a respectable woman shopping alone in the city centre. Male-dominated pubs or stand-up lunch counters were not an option. Kate Cranston

and her brother, Stuart, each founded tea rooms that offered an alternative: light lunches and suppers, along with other facilities that were both appealing and socially respectable, particularly for women visiting on their own.

For example, women could congregate in luncheon rooms designed with them in mind, while the men could use the billiard or smoking rooms if they preferred. This tea room concept established by Kate and her brother, soon spread to many other cities.

Everything began for Kate with the Argyle Street premises. She would eventually expand to own the whole building, not just the basement. Whilst the original tea room of 1878 was tastefully decorated, it would be several years before her establishments became associated with innovative artistic design. Kate had a keen eye for talent, first employing the often-overlooked designer and architect George Walton (1867-1933), and later Charles Rennie Mackintosh (CRM), to work on designing rooms, furnishings, and other features.

Now, continue along Argyle Street. The road bends left into Queen Street where on the corner you will find a building that occupies the ❷ **former site of Stuart Cranston's tea rooms** (70-78 Argyle Street). This is where the tea room 'revolution' all began. Stuart, Kate's older brother (born in 1848), grew up learning the trade, in hotels run by their parents in George Square.

In the 1870s, still in his early 20s, Stuart decided to strike out on his own as a tea merchant. At that time, tea was a premium product mostly imported from China. Stuart established his first tea business at 44 St Enoch Square before moving to this location in 1875. Customers would visit to sample the various teas on offer. If you could travel back in time, Stuart's premises would feel more like an upmarket fragrance shop than a place to relax. Stuart even placed newspaper adverts extolling the virtues of a particular batch of imported tea he had secured from an exotic location. It would be some time before cheaper products were introduced from Ceylon (now Sri Lanka) and India, or tea would sell in cheaper, retail-friendly packets.

It was here that Stuart conceived the ground-breaking idea of generating extra income by charging for the sample cups of tea, as well as offering food. Enough space was put aside for a dozen customers to sit down and buy (as advertised) 'A cup of Kaisow 2d, bread and cakes extra'. In 1909, a book titled *The Story of the Glasgow Tea Rooms,* described how Stuart's pioneering tea room concept spread throughout Glasgow, then to London and Europe, and eventually 'to every civilised spot on earth.'

By 1888, 13 years after opening up here, Stuart was clearly aware of its significance. His adverts described it as 'The First Tea Rooms in the City' and how customers could buy 'A cup of 4s. Mandarin Tea for 2d., with Cream and Sugar'. It also referred to separate but 'Superior Accommodation for Ladies at our Branch Tea Rooms' at 46 Queen Street. Clearly, the mixing of the sexes was not to be encouraged. Already on this walk you have stopped at or passed four locations run by Kate and Stuart between them.

Now, continue along Argyle Street, and then turn left up Miller Street. Walk for a few minutes until you reach the junction with Ingram Street, and stop. On the right-hand corner is the ❸ **location of Kate's second tea room**, originally founded at number 205 in 1886.

At this time, Kate was almost 40, unmarried, and increasingly visible as a businesswoman in a male-dominated city. However, in the early years, the Post

Miss Cranston Walk

Office directory only referred to 'C. Cranston', and the announcement of the new Ingram Street establishment was listed as 'C. Cranston – Crown Luncheon Rooms'. By contrast, her brother's adverts all refer to 'Stuart Cranston'. Over time, Kate began to refer to her full name more regularly.

The advert from 1886 announcing the new Ingram Street premises is not targeted at women. Instead, it refers to the fact 'the situation is suitable for gentlemen attending the exchange, courts, banks and warehouses.... smoking room open next week'.

The Industrial Revolution, directly and indirectly, transformed Glasgow and every aspect of society. It spurred the creation of new suburbs, canals, tram and railway lines, as well as new forms of mass entertainment and shopping districts. The growth of suburbs and new department stores in central Glasgow had a ripple effect on other aspects of life. In the early 1800s, many men still worked at offices in the city centre and lived nearby, enabling them to pop home for lunch. By the 1870s, many lived further afield, connected by commuter lines, making lunchtime trips home impractical. This shift created a demand for places offering reasonably priced lunches that were not pubs.

As with her first tea room, Kate Cranston expanded the Ingram Street site multiple times after its opening to meet growing demand. In 1888, the Glasgow International Exhibition helped cement the city's burgeoning reputation and its informal title as the 'Second City of the Empire'. More visitors began flocking to Glasgow, and Kate was determined to modernise her tea rooms to meet new expectations. That same year, she first employed a young designer named George Walton to redesign parts of Argyle Street tea room and this is generally regarded as the start of Cranston's patronage of more innovative and artistic interior design concepts.

Eager to expand on Ingram Street, Kate acquired the lease to the ground floor of number 209 next door and, in 1900, secured the lease for the ground floor of numbers 213-15. By then, George Walton had moved to London, so CRM was commissioned to redesign the interior. He worked closely with his wife Margaret Macdonald, and amongst their collaborations were two panels that faced each other (his was called 'The Wassail' and hers 'The May Queen').

During this period, the White Luncheon Room was created, and a few years later, in 1907, Kate commissioned CRM to undertake further work here after she acquired number 217. By then, Kate's tea room complex on Ingram Street encompassed the ground floor. The Oak Room was preserved and can now be seen in the Scottish Design Galleries at V&A Dundee.

Now walk up Hanover Street (a continuation of Miller Street) until you reach George Square. Kate didn't have a tea room here, but the Square had a very important place at the beginning and end of Kate's life. Her father, George, and mother Grace Lee, moved here just before Kate was born in order to run Edinburgh and Glasgow Chop House and Commercial Lodgings. George Cranston had originally worked as a coachman, and by 1839, when his first wife died, he already had two young sons. He married Grace Lee in 1845 and became a bread, biscuit, and pastry maker on Sauchiehall Street. George and Grace had three children together, including George and Kate.

Kate was born in the first family hotel here, which later dropped its original 'chop house' title to become more clearly a hotel (at one point 'Cranston's Hotel'). At this time, George Square was transitioning from a commercial and residential area into the civic centre it is today, dominated by the City Chambers and statues of the good and great. The Cranston Hotel, which attracted guests arriving at the nearby railway stations, was located at number 39 on the west side of the Square, though it has long since been demolished.

George Cranston managed three hotels over the years in George Square, moving his family next to the Crow Hotel (number 20 George Square) and finally the Crown Hotel (number 54 on the

Miss Cranston Walk

North Side). It must have been a busy place for Kate to grow up, in the heart of a rapidly modernising city, and surrounded by residents of the hotel who came from far and wide. This is where she cut her teeth, learning the hospitality trade and understanding what clients wanted and how to provide it at a profit.

In 1867, when Kate was just eighteen, her mother passed away. Life changed again in 1874 when her father sold the family business and retired, moving with Kate and some of her siblings to a flat on Sauchiehall Street. Kate was then in her mid-twenties, from a respectable but by no means rich family. Her father having closed the family business, the expected path would have been to find a suitable husband and start a family. However, Kate had other ideas.

Kate retained a strong attachment to life in the Square and, many decades later, as an eccentric widow in retirement, she sold her tea room business and took up residence in the ❹ **North British Station Hotel** at 40 George Square, next door to where her father's hotel once stood. The current building on the site, despite numerous later extensions and additions, has a core dating from the early 1800s. It is a rare survivor of the George Square that Kate would have known.

Miss Cranston Walk

Now follow the map to Buchanan Street. This street could almost have been named Cranston Street, as Kate, Stuart and her cousins from Edinburgh had several establishments here.

Your first stop is ❺ **number 91-93 Buchanan Street**, where Kate's third tea room opened in 1897. As you now know, Kate's first two tea rooms on Argyle and Ingram Streets resembled a game of Monopoly, with Kate adding extensions here and there as funds became available. The Buchanan Street enterprise was a major step up for Kate as she bought the site, had the existing building demolished, and commissioned the striking design you see today.

By this time, Kate had been running a successful business for nearly 20 years against growing competition as other tea rooms opened. Her personal life had also changed. 1892, at the age of 43, she married John Cochrane, an engineer who was eight years her junior and ran a successful family-owned boiler-making business. The couple were well-suited to each other and enjoyed a happy, though childless, marriage. In that era, many 'respectable' women were expected to give up careers upon getting married, but John and Kate were comfortable that each would continue largely as they had done before.

They moved to a large house on Carlibar Road in Barrhead. Interestingly, at home, Kate was Mrs Cochrane, but in the world of business, she remained Miss Cranston. By some accounts, John helped fund some of her new ventures, including the acquisition of the entire Argyle Street building seen at the start of this walk. However, there is also evidence that she lent him money at times, suggesting theirs was a very modern marriage.

Miss Cranston Walk

Kate employed architect George Washington Browne to design her new flagship tea room, and he was responsible for most of the interior and furnishings. No expense was spared and Kate had to raise a mortgage of £14,000 – a great sum in the early 1890s – to fund the development.

The Buchanan Street tea room is notable for being the first occasion Kate commissioned the young CRM. It marked the beginning of a working relationship that lasted until her retirement. Here, he decorated the walls over three floors. At the time, CRM was in his mid-twenties and working for the architectural practice of Honeyman & Keppie. It is unclear how Kate met CRM, but – just as with George Walton – she had a keen eye for young talent and may have encountered both men while mingling in the city's artistic circles. What Walton thought of sharing the limelight with CRM is also unknown, but one suspects there was a bit of rivalry between the two young bucks for Kate's patronage.

The Buchanan Street tea room contained a variety of tea and luncheon rooms, a place reserved for women, as well as billiard and smoking rooms for men. The kitchen was located in the basement, and Walton's designs distinguished Kate's premises from the more conventional establishments run by her brother.

Kate's flagship Buchanan Street tea room was widely admired. The book *Glasgow in 1901* reported at the time: 'Glasgow, in truth, is a very Tokio for tea rooms. Nowhere can one have so much for so little, and nowhere are such places more popular or frequented'.

Next door is ❻ **The Willow Tea Rooms** (at 97 Buchanan Street), featuring an interior based on CRM's designs for Kate's tea room on Ingram Street, rather than the original Buchanan Street tea room next door. Inside you'll find a gift shop with various CRM-related items which is well worth a visit.

This blend of pleasure and art, set Kate's tea rooms apart from her rivals,

Miss Cranston Walk

and competition certainly grew during her decades in business. An observer of the time noticed how some architectural features were described as 'quite Kate Cranston-ish! The other tea shops are less ambitious, but all have come under her influence'. Ironically, while Kate herself was known as a local eccentric for walking around Glasgow in outdated dresses, she simultaneously employed CRM to create groundbreaking and contemporary designs for her tea rooms.

When finished, continue down Buchanan Street until you reach the ❼ **Argyll Arcade**. Look up, to see the sign for Argyll Chambers. Kate's brother Stuart was also ambitious, and the growing demand for tea rooms encouraged him to diversify from his dry tea business. In 1889, he opened a tea room at 26-28 Buchanan Street, followed by a second location at 43 Argyll Arcade in 1892. The first tea room was advertised as the largest in Britain and marked a significant departure from Stuart's early career.

Kate's tea rooms would increasingly be distinguished from her brother's through her

Miss Cranston Walk

focus on food and artistic interior design by figures such as Walton and CRM. No up-and-coming designer ever enjoyed Stuart's patronage.

The original building Stuart owned here has long gone, but he expanded into 43 Argyll Arcade, funding the construction of Argyll Chambers (the Edwardian Baroque design dates from 1904). Look for the intertwined letters of 'S' and 'C' – standing for Stuart Cranston. Stuart also acquired a further site at 13 Renfield Street (seen later).

Take a moment to appreciate the impact of the Cranston siblings had on this part of Glasgow. Within a short walk, you can find Kate's flagship tea room on Buchanan Street, Stuart's own premises here, and Kate's original tea room on Argyll Street. If you had been here at lunchtime in the early 1900s, there would be hundreds of people eating and drinking, playing billiards or smoking at a Cranston establishment. Their venues offered hospitality on a grand scale, with surroundings more akin to a boutique hotel of today rather than a Starbucks or Costa. On a typically rainy Glasgow day, the appeal to shoppers on Buchanan Street would have been undeniable.

Miss Cranston Walk

The Edinburgh branch of the Cranston family mentioned earlier was also a major influence on Kate's life. They had their own temperance hotels, under the 'Waverley' brand in Edinburgh's Princes Street and on **185 Buchanan Street** in Glasgow (which no longer exists), and in London's Cheapside.

Kate's career had been launched with an investment from Robert Cranston, her father's cousin. She was also well-acquainted with Robert's wife, Elizabeth, who managed the Buchanan Street hotel, and maintained a lifelong friendship with their daughter Mary. Mary ran her own hotel on Sauchiehall Street (seen later). Between them, the Glasgow and Edinburgh Cranstons owned half a dozen tea rooms or hotels within the half-mile stretch between Argyle and Sauchiehall Streets.

Whilst Stuart and Kate's tea rooms were not temperance establishments, they benefited from the general demand for places to relax that were not dominated by alcohol. After Kate's death, one commentator suggested that she had done more for the temperance movement than those, like her cousins, who ran temperance-branded establishments.

Walk down the narrow Mitchell Lane to reach ❽ **The Lighthouse**. Located in the rear portion of the *Glasgow Herald* newspaper building, it was designed by a team that included CRM and finally completed in 1937. This section of the complex consisted of a warehouse and a water tower, with the main entrance on Buchanan Street.

What was Kate's importance to CRM's career and vice versa? Kate was already a successful entrepreneur before CRM entered the scene. As a young draughtsman at Honeyman & Keppie, CRM accepted what he was given and did not always receive recognition. But his private commissions for Kate allowed him to explore another side of his talents, including decoration, furniture design, and remodelling existing interiors. During this period, he also collaborated closely with his wife, Margaret Macdonald, particularly on the Ingram Street tea room. Unlike his other clients and employers, Kate gave CRM considerable creative freedom, allowing him to fully express his vision.

There is no doubt CRM also learned a great deal from George Walton, and contact was thanks to Kate's patronage of both men. Their work, displayed in Kate's tea rooms, became more visible to the wider public, and the tea rooms acted as informal art galleries for their designs. This stands in sharp contrast to more conventional architectural commissions like the one for *The Herald* building – hidden away in what was clearly not a prestigious site for an ambitious architect like CRM.

After his early success in the 1900s, CRM's career began to decline, particularly after he left (or was sacked from) his partnership with Keppie. He set up his own architectural practice but struggled to secure enough work. In 1914, he left the city of his birth never to return. Over the following years, his morale declined and his drinking increased. However, Kate continued giving him commissions, large and small, for her tea rooms and own home, so she could be credited with slowing his decline.

Follow the map to stop at at the junction with Renfield Lane on the left. The building on the right is ❾ **13 Renfield Street** – once the headquarters of Stuart Cranston's business. He purchased the site in 1898, further evidence that his own footprint in Glasgow was on a par with Kate's.

Stuart was the first of the siblings to retire – aged 67 – in 1915. This was not a good time for tea rooms, as the World War I imposed restrictions on what could be sold to customers, affecting menus. Additionally, young women who had once worked as waitresses now found other job opportunities in industries supporting the war effort. The tearoom boom was also now over, evidenced by the fact Kate and Stuart had stopped opening new establishments years before.

In a sign of the times, Stuart's business was taken over after his retirement by a colleague, and his original building here was replaced in 1916 by Cranston's Cinema De Luxe. By this time around a hundred cinemas had opened in Glasgow, and the new management of Stuart's business wanted to cash in by offering tea rooms alongside the motion picture experience. The architect was James Miller, one of the greatest and most prolific architects

Miss Cranston Walk

of his era in Glasgow. Stuart would not live much longer, passing away in 1921 and leaving a relatively modest estate valued at a little over £3,000.

Now walk down Renfield Lane, passing CRM's **10 CRM's *Daily Record* building** of 1901 on the right. This is even more hidden away than the Glasgow Herald structure seen earlier, but CRM made the best of a challenging location with its poor light and such a narrow angle to appreciate the design.

At the end of Renfield Lane, turn right up Hope Street and walk for a few minutes, bearing towards Sauchiehall Street.

As you cross St Vincent Street, pause for a moment. Less than a mile to the west of here, at the junction of Pitt and St Vincent Streets, Kate had another establishment, though it wasn't open to the public. She acquired the site in 1908, and it served as a horse stable, bakery and laundry. Kate was well-known for walking between her four tea rooms on a regular basis to keep a watchful eye on the manageresses, and quality control was also maintained through this central supply site. St Vincent Street also had a personal significance for Kate, as she married John Cochrane at the nearby Windsor Hotel in 1892.

Continue up to reach Sauchiehall Street and turn right, stopping at the McDonald's. Here stood a long-demolished tenement building at ⓫ **91 Sauchiehall Street**, where Kate moved into a flat with her father, George, after he retired from the hotel business in George Square in around 1874. Perhaps George was reconnecting with a happier past – long before his life as a hotelier. He had started his working life as a coachman and a 'bread, biscuit, and pastry maker,' working nearby and moving from 42 to 88 Sauchiehall Street in 1846.

Now walk up Sauchiehall Street (with McDonalds on your left), and stop on the right outside 172 Sauchiehall Street, once the site of the ⓬ **Washington Temperance Hotel**, later renamed under the Waverley brand, and more recently, an M&S. In Kate's time, this was her older cousin Mary Cranston's temperance hotel. As mentioned earlier, Mary was one of Kate's closest friends, and they no doubt exchanged views on commercial matters that were important to them both. In the Glasgow of this time, there were few other female business owners they could talk openly to, so having Mary (and Mary's mother, Elizabeth Cranston) as trusted mentors must have meant a great deal to Kate.

Now continue on to Kate's best-known establishment and the only surviving Tea Rooms designed by CRM for Miss Kate Cranston – the ⓭ **original Willow Tea Rooms at 215-17 Sauchiehall Street** (now known as Mackintosh at the Willow). It opened in 1903 as the fourth and most daring of Kate's tea rooms. This also marked the peak of Kate's collaboration with CRM. For the first time he was given full rein to design the building, interior, and furnishings – even down to the cutlery. George Walton had left for London, so CRM was Kate's undisputed first-choice designer. The result was a novel, modernist exterior that re-modelled an existing tenement building, and the interior perfectly blended Kate's commercial instincts with her reputation for promoting artistic influences.

This period also marked the beginning of the end for Kate and CRM's respective careers. Kate was devastated by her husband's death in 1917 and soon decided to retire. She began to sell off her tea room empire, and some establishments would continue under new management for several decades. Kate spent time with her wider family, living in the North British Station Hotel for several years before moving down to Terregles Avenue in Pollokshields, Strathbungo. CRM, having lost a major patron, would die of cancer in 1928 at just 60 years old. Kate outlived him by six years. When she passed away aged 85, she left a fortune of around £67,000, much of which was bequeathed to worthy causes – a testament to her success as a businesswoman.

Kate Cranston offers a rare example of a Victorian-era woman who built and managed a highly successful and well-known business, defying societal expectations of settling down into a domestic life. Her patronage of Walton and CRM was significant; in modern parlance, she was a disruptor – willing to take risks, try new approaches, and trust her instincts.

Kate was also a benevolent employer, tough but fair with her staff, ensuring young waitresses received a square meal and some health insurance. Several of her employees went on to manage their own businesses after leaving her employment, a testament to Kate's mentoring of younger women.

The walk ends here, and if you've resisted the temptation for a cup of tea and something sweet so far, this is probably the time to stop. Inside, there's also a small exhibition providing more history about Kate and CRM.

13 *Mackintosh at the Willow*

Miss Cranston Walk

⑬ Mackintosh at the Willow

When the building at 215-17 Sauchiehall Street went up for sale in 2014, it was purchased by The Willow Tea Rooms Trust to save the building and prevent the loss of its contents. Original features were restored or replicated following the original designs. Remarkably, the ironmongers who worked on the original tea room still had some of the original glass in stock! Fortunately, CRM often over-ordered materials (though he was notorious for not paying for the excess).

You can visit the site for tea, a tour, or to explore the permanent exhibition. Now managed by the National Trust for Scotland, its future is secure for generations to come.

VISIT

Cranston House
104-114 Argyle St, G2 8BH

Argyll Arcade
30 Buchanan St, G2 8BA
argyll-arcade.com

The Lighthouse
11 Mitchell Ln, G1 3NU
thelighthouse.co.uk

EAT & DRINK

The Willow Tea Rooms
97 Buchanan St, G1 3HF
willowtearooms.co.uk

Mackintosh At The Willow
215-217 Sauchiehall St, G2 3EX
mackintoshatthewillow.com

The 78
10-14 Kelvinhaugh St, G3 8NU
the78.co.uk

Horseshoe Bar
17-19 Drury St, G2 5AE
thehorseshoebarglasgow.co.uk

Tramway arts venue, see p.197

6 Pollockshields, Crosshill & Govanhill Walk

Pollokshields, Crosshill & Govanhill Walk

Start: Pollokshields West railway station
Finish: Finish Early: Queen's Park station
Distance: 3 miles shorter walk, 3.5 miles longer

This walk begins in Pollokshields at the ❶ **junction of Kenmure Street and Nithsdale Street**, near Pollokshields West railway station.

Walk a short way up Kenmure Street to reach Zia-Ul-Quran Mosque at number 257. On May 13 2021, the road was occupied by hundreds of protestors after Border Force officials mounted a dawn raid on a property to detain two Indian nationals. It sparked a furious reaction from locals and under media scrutiny, the authorities beat a retreat.

There have long been tensions in this multicultural area over immigration and a tradition of social activism. Some saw the Kenmure Street blockade as symbolic of Scotland's approach to social issues. In 2022 Lorna Slater of the Green Party said (at her party conference), 'We can be the Scotland of Kenmure Street, not Downing Street'.

Glasgow's demographic has changed significantly since this area was first laid out as a residential suburb in the Victorian era. The city's first mosque was established as late as 1944 (in Oxford Street, Gorbals), long after most churches or synagogues seen in this walk were constructed.

Kenmure Street was one of 62 streets whose names have been linked to the slave trade. The estate here was owned by Archibald Stirling and later bought by Charles Stirling of Kenmure (1771-1830). Archibald was a planter in Jamaica, and Charles was involved in pro-slavery lobbying. It was the landowning Stirling-Maxwell family who laid out much of the Pollokshields residential area from the mid-1800s.

Pollokshields, Crosshill & Govanhill Walk

Now walk down Kildrostan Street. This stretch of shops and nearby Nithsdale Street is home to a brassiere, espresso bars, restaurants, a florist – all signs of prosperity. This walk is a tale of two cities, as you are only half a mile from some of the most deprived streets in Glasgow.

Turn right along Terregles Avenue to stop outside ❷ **number 34**. This was the last residence of tea-room pioneer Catherine (or 'Kate') Cranston (1849-1934). Raised in a hotel-owning family, she defied Victorian

conventions by pursuing a business career and choosing not to have children. She became famous for her tea room empire but today is mainly remembered for being an important patron of Charles Rennie Mackintosh.

Retrace your steps and turn right on Kildrostan Street, walking towards the ❸ **pedestrian bridge**. To your left, by the road bridge, until recently stood the old booking office for Strathbungo Station. The station was first run by the Glasgow, Barrhead and Kilmarnock Joint Railway, and was in operation from 1877 until 1962. The expansion of Glasgow meant new residential areas such as Pollokshields, Strathbungo, Crosshill and Govanhill sprung up, encouraged by the railway revolution that allowed workers to commute more easily.

After crossing the bridge, turn left into ❹ **Moray Place**, within Strathbungo (or 'Bungo' as it is known). Stop outside number 1. Numbers 1 to 10 were designed by the great Glasgow architect Alexander 'Greek' Thomson (1817-75) and date from around 1860. He liked it so much that he lived here from 1861 until his untimely death at the age of 57. Along this walk, you will see other houses that demonstrate 'Thomsonesque' design.

Pollokshields, Crosshill & Govanhill Walk

Moray Place is a desirable address where houses can sell for more than £800,000. Another well-known architect, Henry (Harry) Edward Clifford, lived at number 12 Moray Place. He was responsible for the design of many streets in Bungo.

No one knows where the name Strathbungo came from (there are lots of theories), but the origins of the village are connected to the Maxwell family, who owned land here for many years. Sir John Maxwell, 8th Baronet of Pollock (1791-1865), sold land here for development, cashing in on growing demand for suburban living as the city's population grew rapidly. Most of what you see today was built from around 1860 by John McIntyre and the quarryman William Stevenson. The village name of Strathbungo was first marked on a map in 1773, although the Maxwell family apparently wanted to call it 'Marchtown' as the village was found near boundaries – or 'marches'.

Even well into the 19th century, Bungo remained a village populated largely by weavers, miners, and crofters. It was residential

Pollokshields, Crosshill & Govanhill Walk

developments such as Thomson's Moray Place that transformed the village into a residential suburb.

Return to the pedestrian bridge and take a left up the pretty Regent Park Square. Charles Rennie Mackintosh (CRM) (1868-1928) lived at two addresses on this street as a young man – ❺ **number 15** (originally 27) and ❻ **number 6** (originally 2). The McIntosh family (as they were called – CRM changed his surname later) moved here from Dennistoun in 1892 and in 1895, he moved again to number 15. CRM and Alexander 'Greek' Thomson are often described as two of Glasgow's greatest architects. It is a happy coincidence their addresses here are so close to one another. In 1890, CRM won the Alexander Thomson Travelling Studentship prize, something that enabled him to go abroad and expand his horizons.

Continue to reach the junction with Pollokshaws Road, home to some nice cafés and other shops where you might want to take a break.

Cross over, continuing down Queen's Drive. As streets were laid out in the second half of the 19th century, different Christian faiths wanted to establish their influence over the new suburban population. As a result new churches appeared at an astonishing rate, as is evident by the three churches in a row to your left. The first is ❼ **Queen's Park Baptist Church** (built in the 1880s), and just past the junction with Niddrie Road are two more – what was originally the ❽ **Seventh Day Adventist** (built in 1880s), and then

further along Queen's Park Govanhill Church of Scotland (built in the 1870s). As Christian churches attendance dropped in later years, many were demolished or repurposed (including as mosques).

To see echoes of the past, turn up Niddrie Road where you will see the former ⑨ **Langside Synagogue** on the right. In the late 19th century and early 20th century, the Jewish community in Glasgow grew due to an influx of people fleeing economic conditions and antisemitism in Eastern Europe. Most settled in the Gorbals, but over time those who could afford it moved to more desirable areas such as this.

Langside Synagogue opened in 1926 and is a rare example of a traditional immigrant shul interior, with similar decorative details to those found during the same era in Poland, Ukraine, and Romania. The date 5686, inscribed on the memorial stone, corresponds to the Hebrew calendar, which counts from the date of Creation.

During the second half of the 20th century, the Jewish population in this area declined, with many community members relocating to suburbs like Newton Mearns. The decline forced the synagogue to close in 2014. A few years later, a Jewish group known as Irn-Ju (whose members described themselves as an 'anarchist diasporist Jewish collective') protested outside the building, advocating for its reestablishment as a synagogue and fearing it would fall victim to developers. Despite these efforts, the synagogue is now permanently closed.

Return to Queen's Drive, stopping outside ⑩ **Queen's Park Govanhill Church of Scotland**. If it is open, look for a stained-glass memorial window to Jane Haining (1897-1944). She lived nearby (Langside Road and Forth Street), and was an active member of this congregation before departing in the early 1930s to undertake missionary work at a Jewish orphanage in Budapest. After World War II broke out she was ordered to return home, but she refused, saying, 'If these children need me in the days of sunshine, how much more do they need me in the days of darkness?'. Haining and some of her wards would die in Auschwitz. If you want to know more about this courageous figure, read Mary Miller's book *Jane Haining: A Life of Love and Courage* (2019).

Pollokshields, Crosshill & Govanhill Walk

9

10

Pollokshields, Crosshill & Govanhill Walk

Queen's Park

Strathbungo and the surrounding areas have other links to the Holocaust. Rosa Sacharin lived in Vennard Gardens (three streets south of here) for around 60 years until her death in 2019 at the age of 93. She was brought up in Berlin, and once found herself standing in front of Hitler at a public rally. In 1938, at the age of 13, Rosa escaped Nazi persecution of Jews in Berlin. She was given a place on a *kindertransport* train, taking her to safety in Britain.

Getting to Glasgow did not end Rosa's problems, and in her book *The Unwanted Jew* (2014), she describes how difficult it was to start again in an unfamiliar country. Rosa went on to have a full life, raising her own children and becoming a much respected nurse.

In recent years, Govanhill has become home to the highest concentration of Roma people in Scotland. It is estimated that as many as 250,000 Roma perished during the Holocaust. Today, the local Roma community participates in events on Roma Holocaust Memorial Day (2 August), a date chosen because nearly 3,000 Roma women, children, and elderly were killed at Auschwitz-Birkenau on that day. Local charity, Romano Lav, planted a tree of remembrance

Pollokshields, Crosshill & Govanhill Walk

View from Queen's Park

in Queen's Park in 2019, but it was later vandalised – a reminder of how evils of the past haunt us to this day. Thankfully, a replacement memorial was erected.

Continue along, with Queen's Park to your right. Named after Mary, Queen of Scots (and not Queen Victoria), the land here was acquired by the council in 1857 and designed by Sir Joseph Paxton (1803-65), best known for designing the Crystal Palace in London. Paxton was also important in the banana world as he spearheaded the cultivation of a type of banana called the 'Cavendish', now the more widely produced variety in the Western world. Nearby, the Battle of Langside took place in 1568, when Queen Mary's army was defeated, forcing her to flee to England to seek protection from her cousin, Queen Elizabeth I (a move that didn't end well).

The park is a focal point for many Southsiders, and its highest point offers one of the best views across Glasgow. Few people are aware that Shieldhall Tunnel runs underneath their feet – a 5-kilometre wastewater tunnel that opened in 2018 and is large enough to drive a double-decker bus through.

Pollokshields, Crosshill & Govanhill Walk

Continue along, passing ⓫ **Wellcroft Bowling Club** on the right. This area becomes Crosshill, another village that transformed into a residential suburb from the mid-19th century. Between 1801-1881, Glasgow's population ballooned from 77,000 to over 700,000, so housing shortages were a major problem. Unlike Strathbungo, Crosshill became an independent burgh in 1871. However, this was short-lived, and Crosshill was annexed by Glasgow 20 years later. Like other burghs, Crosshill had its own coat of arms, civic administration, and services.

Stop outside ⓬ **number 128/130 Queen's Drive** and look for a lamppost on the strip of land facing the park that boasts some extraordinary details. This design has been attributed to Alexander 'Greek' Thomson, and is the only survivor of five similar lamp posts.

Continue along, passing Victoria Road. On your left is a French Renaissance-style Crescent designed by William McNicol Whyte (1854-1930). Dating from around 1884 and originally called Balmoral Crescent, it is one of the finest tenement streets in Glasgow. Looking at it, you might imagine you are in a corner of Paris, but it also reflects American influences – thought to be inspired by Whyte's travels in North America.

On the corner of Victoria Road and Queen's Drive look for the ⓭ **two bearded male sculptures**, thought to represent Whyte (right) and Hugh Miller, his builder. Continue along, looking for other sculptures representing arts, crafts, and the seasons. It

Pollokshields, Crosshill & Govanhill Walk

Queen's Drive

14

is said Whyte exacted revenge on local officials who had objected to his plans by immortalising their features on sculptures here – the 'Crosshill Bailies'.

Walk along the crescent to reach the last house (number 82) and look up to see Whyte's most famous sculpture known as ⓮ **Statue of Liberty** for obvious reasons. America-loving Whyte would have been aware of the French-built statue that became famous from the moment of its construction in 1875 to its unveiling in New York in 1886 – the same time as Whyte's work here was completed.

Now turn left up Langside Road, and after Burton Lane on the left, stop by a ⓯ **modern block of flats**. This stands on the site of a 'lost' church designed by Alexander 'Greek' Thomson. Queen's Park United Presbyterian Church was completed in 1869, the last of four churches Thomson designed. It was destroyed by a German bomb in 1943 and never rebuilt. There is a small plaque with a picture of Thomson's church, and its destruction was a great loss to the area.

Pollokshields, Crosshill & Govanhill Walk

Queen Mary Ave

Queen Mary Ave

Turn up Queen Mary Avenue. Amongst the late 19th-century tenement buildings, look on the left (numbers 3-11) at the ⓰ **older two-storey Georgian houses** dating from the mid-1800s.

As a rule of thumb, blonde sandstone was used in Glasgow up until around 1890, when red sandstone, brought in from Dumfriesshire by train, became the norm. Langside, Queen Mary – all these names recall the Battle of Langside that took place less than half a mile away from there on 13 May 1568.

As you continue along, you will notice this is a prosperous street: large, detached houses, many with distinctive designs that are a welcome relief from rows of identical tenement buildings. You will see a smattering of Mercedes and BMWs and even the odd treehouse. Maps from around 1900 list individual house names – all very aspirational; 'Sutherland Cottage', 'Bell Vue', 'Florence Villa'.

Number 56 on the right-hand side is an example of a ⓱ **late 19th-century 'Thomsonesque' villa** and a listed building. If you are puffing a bit, you will understand the 'hill' in Crosshill.

After a few minutes, you reach Cathcart Road. Stop to look at the ⓲ **iron railway bridge** at the junction. On the wall is a sign for James Goodwin & Co., 'Iron Founders & Bridge Builders' from Motherwell dated 1885. Goodwin's is a reminder of Scotland's industrial heritage and its influence further afield.

Pollokshields, Crosshill & Govanhill Walk

Goodwin's built bridges, boilers, and produced iron and steel. Their products were exported around the world, and they also supplied engineers for infrastructure projects. The firm's advert in 1888 depicts the 'Hooghly Bridge' in West Bengal, for which it had supplied the steel. Goodwin's may no longer exist, but the bridge – today the 'Jubilee Bridge' – still stands over the Hooghly River and was commissioned by the East India Railway. The bridge in Crosshill is therefore linked with one standing 6,000 miles away. Perhaps bridge builders who worked in Crosshill also worked in India and elsewhere.

Turn left on Cathcart Road, passing ⑲ **Crosshill Station**. It opened in 1886 and enabled more people to move out from central Glasgow to live in newly built villas and tenements. When the station was built, most of the land east (right-hand side) of Cathcart Road was undeveloped. Within a few years, all the remaining gaps would be filled with buildings.

Continue up Cathcart Road. Look up to the first floor (for example, above number 697 on the right) for ⑳ **little hooks**. These are 'rosettes' that held connecting wires between the building and the cable that powered trams running along this route.

Carry on to the junction with Dixon Avenue where, on the left, are ㉑ **Dixon Halls**. Before you read about the Halls, there are two interesting places nearby that are not strictly on the route, but near enough to warrant a mention.

21 *Dixon Halls*

Pollokshields, Crosshill & Govanhill Walk

Less than a five-minute walk along Dixon Road is ❷❷ **Holyrood High School**. This is a well-known school, and past pupils include members of Simple Minds (Jim Kerr and Charlie Burchill), Fran Healey of Travis, Johnny McElhone of Texas, Altered Images, and Hipsway, comedian Frankie Boyle, lawyer Baroness Shaw, footballer Alan Brazil, and actor Tony Curran (who has appeared in films as varied as *Shallow Grave*, *Gladiator*, *X-Men*, and – appropriately – *Mary Queen of Scots*).

Near to the school on Boyd Street once stood a ❷❸ **football ground** that was home to Third Lanark football club. Its origins go back to when The Third Lanarkshire Rifle Volunteers drilled on the site, and some volunteers began playing football in their spare time. They went on to form Third Lanark in 1872, based here at what was the original Cathkin Park. Known as the 'Hi-Hi's', the club played top-flight football for years until it had to close due to financial difficulties in 1967.

Stand outside **Dixon Halls** (on old maps, it is called 'Joint Burgh Hall', and 'Dixon Hall'). Why does the name Dixon appear here and in nearby street names? The building dates from 1879 and was gifted by William Smith Dixon (1824-80), an iron and coal magnate. He owned Govan Iron Works and a nearby colliery, amongst other things. He was also the grandson of William Dixon, who left Northumberland in the 1770s to found an empire encompassing collieries and iron works in Scotland.

William Dixon bought the Govanhill estate in 1820 and created Govanhill out of nothing when he founded a village for workers at Little Govan Colliery nearby. The village was known to locals as the 'Fireworks'. The Dixon family is known for founding (in 1839) Govan Iron Works which stood to the north of here. Its furnaces lit up the night sky and were known as 'Dixon's Blazes'. By 1841, 600 people lived at the Fireworks, including 160 miners. As the main landowners, the Dixon family did more than anyone to develop this area.

Dixon Halls was designed by Frank Stirrat in a Scots baronial style. It served as the administrative base for two different burghs – Govanhill and Crosshill. Each burgh had its own administrative and

Pollokshields, Crosshill & Govanhill Walk

court facilities inside, with their own entrance. The coat of arms on the side facing Cathcart Road is of the Dixon family (motto 'Fortes Fortuna Juvat' or fortune favours the brave).

The relationship between the neighbouring burghs was not always easy. The Dixon family kept a watchful eye on things, much like a long-suffering parent overseeing squabbling children. At the opening ceremony of the halls, a speech was read out on behalf of William Dixon, in which he reminded people of 'the many fights I have had with you defending our independence' and how he had seen the area 'changed from green fields to two extensive and populous burghs'. In 1891, the two burghs succumbed to long-standing pressure and were annexed by the city. Dixon Halls has since been used for a variety of purposes.

Head along Dixon Avenue, the southern edge of Govanhill. As the Fireworks village became established, it was clear the area needed a name. For a while nobody could agree, so it was known as 'No-Man's Land'. It was only when the area became a burgh in 1877 that 'Govanhill' was formally adopted.

As new streets were laid out during the 19th century, the area gained a reputation as a respectable working-class district, the sort of place people from the nearby Gorbals aspired to live in. It was densely populated, home to 10,000 people by 1890. In the second half of the 20th century, the area escaped much of the destruction inflicted by urban planners on other working-class districts. As a result, Govanhill is one of the best-preserved Victorian and Edwardian tenement districts in the city. By contrast, go to the Gorbals and you will find it difficult to get a sense of how the area looked a century ago.

After Dixon Halls on the right is the Romanesque-styled **Holy Cross Catholic church**. Dating from 1911, it was designed by Pugin & Pugin, a London-based firm of architects best known for their Gothic church buildings. It was founded by Augustus Pugin, who contributed to the design of the Palace of Westminster.

Opposite, at 106, is the ㉕ **Convent of the Sisters of the Gospel of Life**. When it was founded in 2000, it was the first new female religious community to be established in Scotland since the mid-19th century. It follows a strong pro-life agenda.

Turn right down Belleisle Street, stopping by ㉖ **Govanhill Free Church** on the left. The more modern-looking building on the right was once Crosshill Synagogue, known as the 'cut-price shul' because it was attended by many traders, small businessmen, and craft workers. Alasdair Gray (1934-2019) painted a ceiling mural here in 1959 that is now covered over. Gray's novel *Lanark* (1981) established his reputation as one of Scotland's great writers. As the local Jewish presence declined, the synagogue suffered and finally closed in 1986.

Return to Dixon Avenue and continue along. Govanhill has been described as the Ellis Island of Glasgow. Before the Roma community, the area was home to Gaelic-speaking Highlanders, the Irish, Jews, Pakistanis, and other groups.

Pollokshields, Crosshill & Govanhill Walk

Ramp to coal cellar

As you walk along, look out on the left-hand side (for example at number 60) for unusual little ramps leading down to what were once coal cellars, now converted into basement flats.

Shortly on the left is the ㉗ **Al-Farooq Education and Community Centre**. When built in 1893, this was Hutchesontown Free Church. It ceased being a church in 1971 and later became an arts complex before being converted into a mosque. The Gothic-style building has had all Christian sculptures removed. It was designed by John Bennie Wilson (1848-1923), who worked as a young man for John Honeyman (as did Charles Rennie Mackintosh). Bennie also worked for another eminent architect, John Burnet Senior, became a Colonel in the 3rd Lanarkshire Scottish Rifles volunteer regiment, and was a football enthusiast.

Almost opposite, at number 51, below the first-floor window, is a rare example of old ornamental metalwork. This feature would have been much more common when the buildings were constructed in the late 19th century.

Pollokshields, Crosshill & Govanhill Walk

Further along, at ㉘ **number 28** on the left-hand side, is the so-called 'House of Blood,' where a triple murder took place in the top-floor flat in October 2004. Edith McAlinden, her son John, and his friend Jamie Gray killed three men after an argument erupted between McAlinden and her boyfriend (one of the victims).

During the 2005 murder trial, *The Daily Record* described the video of the crime scene: 'The walls ran blood red and around the room lay a hammer, a golf club, baseball bat, lumps of wood and an electric drill – all smeared red. Now and then the camera zoomed in on one item – a golf club with blood-stained tufts of hair, a knife with fleshy matter sticking to the blade and handle'.

Continue to Victoria Road, an interesting street that, like many city shopping districts, has suffered in recent years. It contains a typical modern-day mix of old-fashioned pubs founded in the late 19th century, nail bars, bookmakers, charity shops, beauty salons, and 'artisan' coffee shops. The variety of shops reflects Govanhill's status as Scotland's most culturally diverse neighbourhood, with over 40% of local residents coming from various ethnic backgrounds.

If you fancy a cultural detour, turn left and cross over to reach ㉙ **Queens Park Station**. The waiting room downstairs is home to a gallery and artist-run space called the Queens Park Railway Club. While some streets in Govanhill are among the most economically deprived in Scotland, the area has a vibrant artistic undercurrent, attracting many artists – hence spaces like this club. The station dates from 1886 and was built by the Caledonian Railway.

Retrace your steps up Victoria Road and take a left onto Prince Edward Street, named

Pollokshields, Crosshill & Govanhill Walk

for the son of Queen Victoria who succeeded her as monarch (King Edward VII) in 1901. Then turn right onto Craigie Street, the view on the right is dominated by a sturdy **30 School Board of Glasgow building**, originally Strathbungo Public School (look for the original sign). Today it is St Bride's Primary School, and it is good to see such a building used for its original purpose. Too many other School Board buildings lie derelict or have been demolished. Dating from 1894, you can see signs for 'Boys' and 'Girls', and the building was constructed with a swimming pool on its lowest level.

Opposite the school are impressive **31 Scottish Renaissance-style buildings** dating from the mid-1890s that were originally home to a police and fire station. You can see the Glasgow coat of arms above the entrance.

At the end, turn right onto Allison Street. Opposite, at **32 number 51**, is another site associated with a murder. In 1969, former policeman turned criminal, Howard Wilson lived in the ground floor. On 30 December, he returned here with two accomplices and a haul of stolen bank cash. Spotted by local police who entered the flat, Wilson shot two officers dead and wounded three more. He was later jailed for what was dubbed the Allison Street Murders. The dead officers were commemorated by a police pipe band and 700 policemen, who marched down Allison Street in January 1970.

Turn right along Allison Street. The area to your left (between Craigie and Chapman Streets) used to be open land and part of

Pollokshields, Crosshill & Govanhill Walk

a large brick field. Topsoil would have been removed, and the clay underneath would have been used for bricks. Maps show many of the surrounding tenements appeared around 1905.

You reach Victoria Cross, one of Glasgow's many crosses that mark the intersection of roads at the heart of a community. There are fewer pubs here than there were in the Victorian age, but traditional bars remain. The ③③ **Victoria Bar** on the corner occupies a site that has been home to licensed premises since 1887. In recent years it was owned by Scotland and Celtic footballer Jim Brogan (1944-2018). The listed building statement describes the pub as being part of a 'Thomsonesque' corner tenement dating from around 1880.

Cross over and continue down Allison Street. Govanhill is one of the most densely populated areas of Scotland, with around 18,000 residents. A survey by Govanhill Housing Association covering 13 tenement blocks identified 52 nationalities and 32 languages spoken.

Pass ③④ **Ryan's Bar**, another traditional Govanhill pub – until recently called **P. J. Neeson's**. This area has had a strong Irish presence since the mid-19th century when Irish colliers came to Glasgow to work in Dixon's coal mine. A pub has stood here since 1877 and was named after former owner Paddy Neeson from 1903 until 2023.

Back in the 1880s, the Glasgow Post Office directory shows that the professions of those living along here included wrights,

Pollokshields, Crosshill & Govanhill Walk

Rosettes

35

36

slaters, builders, masons, joiners, hay and seed merchants, and bank tellers.

As you continue down Allison Street, look out for more tram rosettes. Turn left into Annette Street – named for a member of the Dixon dynasty (as is Daisy Street, seen later).

On the right is ❸❺ **Annette Street Primary School**, the façade displaying the original name – Govanhill Public School. It was designed by sibling architects Hugh and David Barclay, responsible for dozens of churches and schools around Scotland in the late 19th century. It was opened in 1886 by Sir William Pearce, then chairman of the legendary Fairfield shipyard in Govan.

Why are there references to Govan Parish at the front of the school? The old Govan parish boundary encompassed a vast amount of land both north and south of the Clyde, far beyond the limits of the modern-day district of Govan. This school was at the centre of a media storm in 2016 when right-wing press reports dubbed it 'the school with no Scottish pupils'. At the time, around 80 per cent of pupils were from the Roma community, mostly with roots in Romania and Slovakia, while many of the other students were of Asian heritage.

Return to Allison Street and continue to the corner with ❸❻ **Garturk Street**. The last two tenement buildings on the corner (numbers 19 & 21), those along Allison Street (numbers 265-289), and around the corner along Daisy Street (number 34) are the work of Alexander 'Greek' Thomson and date from the mid-1870s.

Pollokshields, Crosshill & Govanhill Walk

Whilst in recent years Govanhill has been tagged as part of the 'cool' Southside that the media have picked up on, it also attracts negative headlines relating to slumlords, crime, and deprivation. In December 2018, *The Herald* ran an article about 'the most demonised neighbourhood in Scotland', describing Govanhill as 'without question the most intensely scrutinised neighbourhood in all of Scotland. It is a place where the ugly issue of race is front and centre every single day'.

In recent years, there has been a problem with landlords exploiting poorer tenants and failing to maintain properties. The council is trying to address this, taking on slumlords and much good work is done by Govanhill Housing Association.

Soon, you will reach Cathcart Road again, where you follow the map, turning left and then right into Bankhall Street. On the left is the **㉗ former Govanhill Picture House**. This Egyptian-styled cinema was designed by Eric A. Sutherland in 1926. It showed films until 1961 when it became a bingo hall. It is a reminder of Glasgow's cinema heyday when the city boasted more cinema seats per capita than possibly anywhere else in the world. The Egyptian design was popular in the 1920s due to the excitement generated by the discovery of Tutankhamun's tomb.

This street is the approximate location of the Fireworks Village mentioned earlier, just a short distance from Govan Colliery. The first local pits were established by 1717 and covered around 180 acres. By the 1840s, many children worked here, including boys as young as nine working down the pit. The Dixon family controlled it all, wielding huge power over the political, economic, and social life of the area.

Retrace your steps, crossing Cathcart Road and continuing down Bankhall Road. At the end is Govanhill Trinity Church, which was closed at the time of writing and dates from around 1880. Turn right up Daisy Street, named after a Dixon family member, and pass the Govanhill Neighbourhood Centre on the corner. Turn left into Calder Street and walk for a few minutes until you reach ㊳ **Govanhill Library**.

It dates from 1906 and is one of the Carnegie libraries funded by Andrew Carnegie (1835-1919), the Scottish-born American multi-millionaire industrialist. It was designed in an Edwardian-Baroque style by James R. Rhind (1854-1918). Rhind was a great beneficiary of Carnegie's fortune, having been commissioned to design seven of the dozen Carnegie libraries in Glasgow, a few of which still exist today. The figures at the top depict a mother reading to children.

After the library, turn right up Ardbeg Street and stop at number 21 to see a ㊴ **blue plaque commorating Ronald David Laing**. Born here in 1927, he later attended Hutchesons'

Pollokshields, Crosshill & Govanhill Walk

Boys Grammar. Better known as R.D. Laing, he became one of the best-known and controversial psychiatrists of his time. His innovative treatments made him a countercultural figure, and numerous films, documentaries, and books have celebrated him.

In 2017, David Tennant played Laing (who died in 1989) in the film *Mad to be Normal*. Laing was a regular visitor to the library and from his bedroom window, he would gaze at the statue on top. He recalled that it had an almost hypnotic effect on him, symbolising the hope of escaping Depression-era Govanhill through the power of learning.

Carry on along Calder Street, associated with another murder. In 1960, 19-year-old Tony Miller lived on Dixon Road with his parents. His friend, 16-year-old James Douglas Denovan, lived on Calder Street. Queen's Park was then (and remains) a meeting area for the gay community, and the teenagers used to attack and rob gay men.

In April 1960, one attack was so severe, the victim died. Miller and Denovan were both convicted, but while Donovan was imprisoned, the older Miller was sentenced to death. The situation led to a public campaign that included a petition of 30,000 signatures. These efforts proved in vain as the sentence was carried out at Barlinnie Prison in December 1960. Miller became the last teenager to be executed in Britain.

The next stop is ④ **Govanhill Baths**. It opened in 1914, offering working-class people not only a swimming pool but a Turkish and Russian bath, shampooing room, cold plunge baths and washhouse. The wash house – or 'steamie' – was where generations of local women met to wash clothes and exchange news. For many locals, this was the only place they could get a wash or hot bath, given the lack of such facilities at home.

In recent years, the baths have become a symbol of community action. It began when the baths were threatened with demolition. A sit-in was organised in 2001 as part of a 'Save Our Pool' campaign. This led to the creation of Govanhill Baths Community Trust, a charity and grassroots community organisation that does good work helping local people. You can find out more about what is going on at the baths on their website (*govanhillbaths.com*). Other connected community-led groups include The People's Pantry (providing locals with food at a subsidised rate) and The Deep End (offering everything from artist studios to pottery courses).

While Govanhill is often in the press for negative reasons, many local organisations contribute to making this one of the most vibrant and interesting areas in Glasgow. Romano Lav, another charity linked to the baths, works with the Roma community.

Continue on to reach Victoria Road again. On the corner is ④ **Locavore Grocery**, which is worth a stop for coffee and look at the produce, much of it organic and sourced from local suppliers.

Turn right up Victoria Road, then right into Kingarth Street, passing the old entrance to the washhouse, which became

Pollokshields, Crosshill & Govanhill Walk

a laundrette in the 1970s. At the end, turn left up Langside Road to reach ㊷ **Govanhill Park**. Walk through the centre of the park, surrounded by fine tenements. On a sunny day, it should be obvious why a century ago working-class people saw moving here as a step up the social ladder. Sadly, the bandstand added in 1903 has long gone. Those interested in Glasgow's 'lost rivers' (or burns) might like to know that the Blind Burn flows beneath the park.

Turn left into Coplaw Street and follow the map. On the right, you pass buildings originally part of ㊸ **The Royal Samaritan Hospital for Women**. The hospital was built in stages from 1896, much of it funded by wealthy women in Glasgow, particularly those within the Ladies Auxiliary Association. Their fundraising bazaar in St Andrews Halls in 1890 included a demonstration of Edison's 'talking machine that is a wonder of the world'. By 1907, the hospital had become the largest gynaecological hospital in Britain. It eventually closed in the early 1990s, and the buildings are now part of the Govanhill Housing Association.

Pollokshields, Crosshill & Govanhill Walk

There is a pleasant and unexpected Samaritan Community Garden here (you can visit via the entrance at 79 Coplaw Street). The various foundation stones visible from the pavement illustrate how the original hospital expanded over the years.

When you reach Victoria Road, you can either turn left and explore Govanhill at your leisure (leaving via Queens Park station), or to see more, cross over and continue down Coplaw Street. This used to be an important street for the Jewish community, home to the Glasgow Jewish Board of Guardians after it moved from the Gorbals in 1970. It played an important role in helping new Jewish arrivals in Glasgow. The Jewish Blind Society, a theatrical group called The Avrom Greenbaum Players, and the *Jewish Echo* newspaper were also based on this street.

Continue down the street where, on the right, is the ㊹ **frontage of an army drill hall** dating from 1884. This served as the headquarters of the 3rd Lanarkshire Rifle Volunteers. Volunteer regiments were formed across Britain in the late 1850s due to concern about a French invasion. Many adopted the motto 'Defence not Defiance' (seen above the entrance). The Volunteers were renamed the Seventh Battalion of the Cameronians in 1907, and the hall continued to be used for military purposes before its conversion into residential flats.

Pollokshields, Crosshill & Govanhill Walk

Volunteers who trained here would go on to fight in the Boer War, on the beaches of Gallipoli, and on the Western Front during World War I.

Opposite is ㊺ **Cuthbertson Primary School**, dating from 1906. It was designed for the Glasgow School Board by James Miller (1860-1947), one of the best and most prolific architects of his era. Like the schools seen earlier, it is great to see such fine buildings still being used for their original purpose. The name on the side – Sir John Neilson Cuthbertson – refers to the chairman of the Glasgow School Board between 1885-1903. R.D. Laing used to walk to attend the primary school from his home seen earlier.

Continue on to the end of the road, with the ㊻ **Scottish Ballet** building directly opposite. This is one of the five leading ballet companies in Britain and has been based in the Tramway Arts Centre since 2009. The original company was founded in Bristol in 1957 before moving to Scotland.

Turn right and then left down Albert Drive, passing ㊼ **Tramway** – one of the best-known cultural centres in the city. As the name suggests, it was originally a tram works and depot built from 1894 onwards. It even contained stables inside for the horse-drawn trams. In the main exhibition room, you can still see the tram lines embedded in the ground. This was just a small part of the city's vast tram system which, at its height, was the largest in any European city. Be sure to visit the Hidden Gardens to the rear.

Pollokshields, Crosshill & Govanhill Walk

Just past Tramway is ④⑧ **The Glasgow Gurdwara**, used by the Sikh community. When this area was first become a suburb in the 19th century, only Christian churches were constructed. In recent years more churches have closed than have been built, and instead, it is the emerging Sikh and Muslim communities that are investing most in new places of worship.

This was the first purpose-built Gurdwara in Scotland when it opened in 2013. The Sikh community raised nearly £4 million to fund the construction. It can accommodate 1,500 worshippers, and the energy invested in the project stands in contrast to the near-empty or former churches and synagogues you have passed today, that were established in a very different time. Just past here is Pollokshields East railway station where this walk ends.

VISIT

Queen's Park
Langside Rd, G42 9QL
friendsofgreenparkglasgow.org

Govanhill Baths
99-126 Calder St, G42 7RA
govanhillbaths.com

Tramway
25 Albert Dr, G41 2PE
tramway.org

The Glasgow Gurdwara
37 Albert Dr, G41 2PE

The Roma Cultural Centre
43 Nithsdale St, G41 2PZ
romanolav.org

EAT & DRINK

The Victoria Bar
400 Victoria Rd, G42 8YS

The Allison Arms
720 Pollokshaws Rd,
G41 2AD

The Bell Jar
21 Dixon Ave, G42 8EB

Ranjit's Kitchen
607 Pollokshaws Rd,
G41 2QG
ranjitskitchen.com

MILK
452 Victoria Rd, G42 8YU
milkcafeglasgow.co.uk

Errol's Hot Pizza
379 Victoria Rd, G42 8RZ

Pakistani Street Food
412 Victoria Rd, G42 8YS

Glasgow Sweet Centre
202 Allison St, G42 8RS

Statue of 'King Billy' & Barony Church, see p.216

7 Medieval Glasgow, Townhead & Merchant City Walk

Medieval Glasgow, Townhead & Merchant City Walk

Start/Finish: High Street Station
Distance: 2.7 miles

The walk begins at High Street station and aims to give a sense of how small medieval Glasgow was. It also explores parts of Townhead and the Merchant City.

Today the High Street feels like a backwater, but for centuries this was the heart of Glasgow. According to folklore the monastic church was founded beside the Molendinar Burn by St Kentigern (also known as St Mungo) in 543 A.D., near the site of today's Cathedral. However, little is known about the original village of Glasgow until the early 12th century, when work began on the Cathedral, which was consecrated in 1136 A.D.

Most inhabitants of the medieval village depended on fishing and farming, but having a Cathedral changed everything. Religious orders wanted to be near the centre of ecclesiastical power, creating a momentum for development. Those within sometimes competing parts of the Catholic church would found hospitals, churches, a school, the university, and so on. This all required in turn; fortifications, builders, workers, merchants, food, wine, blacksmiths and taverns.

Glasgow developed along the one-mile lane linking the heart of religious life around the Cathedral with more commercial interests nearer the Clyde. This lane would become the High Street (with Cathedral Street on the north side and Saltmarket to the south).

If you could time travel to 1500, this immediate vicinity was home to several institutions that shaped Glasgow's development. On the side of the street with the station, look beyond to where the heart of the ❶ **University of Glasgow** once stood. It was inaugurated in 1451 due to the efforts of William Turnbull, Bishop of Glasgow. Pope Nicholas V issued a Papal Bull, allowing the creation of what was then called a 'Studium Generale'.

Medieval Glasgow, Townhead & Merchant City Walk

Initially, lectures were given in the Cathedral's Chapter House before the University moved to a building on the High Street. Later, a larger complex (known as Old College) with two courtyards, occupied several acres to the east of the High Street site. The High Street became more important, and not just a link road.

The University grew over the centuries, but so did Glasgow. Old College became surrounded by slums and factories belching smoke, so plans were developed to move to a more pleasant environment. In 1870, the University sold off Old College and began anew at Gilmorehill. Old College was demolished to make way for a railway goods yard.

Cross to the other side of the street and walk towards the three-storey Neoclassical sandstone building, a ❷ **former British Linen Company Bank building** dating from 1895. It was designed in an Edwardian Renaissance style by William Forrest Salmon (1843-1911), the middle member of a famous Glasgow architectural dynasty founded by his father, James (1805-88), and continued by his son, also James (1873-1924). Look for the 'putti' figures on the arch above the main window. These were common Victorian decorative features inspired by Greco-Roman classical mythological sources and symbolised love.

A plaque records this was the site of poet Thomas Campbell's house. Campbell (1777-1844) had an exciting life, although his poetry is difficult to enjoy today. His father was a Tobacco Lord with interests in

Virginia, before losing most of his fortune in the American Revolutionary War. Campbell rubbed shoulders with literary figures such as Sir Walter Scott, and one of his poems, 'The Soldier's Dream,' was set to music by Ludwig van Beethoven as part of his *25 Irish Songs* in the early 1800s.

Walk up Nicholas Street, which serves as a reminder of the city's Catholic past, named after Pope Nicholas V. He issued the Papal Bull that led to the founding of the University.

Stop at ❸ **Deanside Well Garden**, an open seating area and stone well structure. Its name recalls Deanside (or Meadow) Well, which was located here for centuries. This area was once home to a Franciscan friary. The Franciscans are a Catholic order founded in Italy in 1209 by St. Francis of Assisi. Known as the Grey Friars on account of the colour of their tunics, they established their friary in the mid-1470s on a site granted by Bishop John Laing. For around 80 years the Grey Friars were an essential part of life in Glasgow.

The Reformation upended centuries of Catholic power. From around 1559, Catholic institutions were attacked and forced to close. The Franciscan friary was among the targets, and one member was burnt as a heretic. In the following years, the friary complex (including its kirk) was repurposed until it was eventually demolished and built over. In 2003, archaeologists found the remains of twelve men and three women here. Some were probably Franciscans. They were reburied in the Southern Necropolis, where a memorial can be seen (see Gorbals walk).

Retrace your steps to the High Street and turn left. Before the Reformation, this spot was a few minutes walk from several Catholic institutions, including the Collegiate Church of St Mary of Loreto and St Anne, the Chapel of Little St Mungo or St Kentigern, the Dominican Friary, the Grammar School, St Nicholas Hospital, Blackadder's Hospital and the Church of St Mary. With a population of around 4,500, most of Glasgow's residents would have been connected to the church in some way.

Medieval Glasgow, Townhead & Merchant City Walk

Another change to the fabric of Glasgow took place in the late 19th century – evidenced by ④ **the red sandstone building** on the right-hand corner of High Street and Duke Street. Signage on the building (above the clock) spells out 'City Improvement Trust'.

Glasgow's population quadrupled between 1800-1850, contributing to terrible living conditions for many people. By the mid-1860s, health authorities had established the link between poor housing and sanitation and epidemics such as typhus and cholera. The mortality rate in some areas was 48 per 1,000, compared to a UK rate of around 9 per 1,000 at the time. Inspired by urban planning in Paris, Glasgow Council took on the challenge, leading to the creation of the City Improvement Trust in 1866. With new funds, the Trust bought up several streets and demolished buildings on a scale that surpassed anywhere else in Europe at the time.

Turn right down ⑤ **Duke Street**, said to be named after John Graham, 1st Duke of Montrose (1682-1742). He held high political office and unwisely made an enemy of outlaw folk hero Rob Roy MacGregor over a debt. He also served as Chancellor of Glasgow University and had a house in Drygate. There is still a Duke of Montrose today, with the family seat in Stirlingshire (the Duke is the chief of Clan Graham). Duke Street is said to be the longest in Britain and opened in 1794. A driver for its creation was the Carron Company, which wanted a better route out of Glasgow towards the Carron Iron Works in Falkirk.

On the right, you pass a ⑥ **red brick wall** with modern buildings above. This exterior wall is all that remains of the College Goods Station, built in the 1870s by the City of Glasgow Union Railway Company. The

Medieval Glasgow, Townhead & Merchant City Walk

railway station occupied the site of the old University. It was eventually run by British Rail and closed by 1968, with nearly all the railway buildings later demolished.

Continue along. If you stood here in 1780, Duke Street did not exist, and you would be surrounded by open land. Walking for five minutes past Drygate would have taken you outside Glasgow. This gives a sense of how small the city was until relatively recently. The nearest road was Havannah Street, to the south of here. It opened in 1763 and was named after the British capture of Havana in Cuba the previous year. Up until the 18th century, Glasgow only contained around a dozen streets (today it has close to 6,000).

Carry on, passing the ❼ **former Alexander's Public School**. This was designed by another great city architect, John Burnet Senior (1814-1901). Dating from 1858, it was built for James Alexander, who owned R.F. & J. Alexander's Cotton Thread Mill (seen shortly). Alexander was a hardened capitalist, but he wanted to educate local children. This was before the Education Act of 1872 paved the way for the public funding of school education and the establishment of the School Board of Glasgow. The building later became Ladywell School and, in more recent years, a business park.

Look for sculpted faces on the exterior, the work of John Crawford (1830-61), an artist who trained with the Mossman family firm and produced many sculptures in Glasgow.

They represent Shakespeare, Milton, Michelangelo, Aristotle, and Homer. The identity of the 'Sixth Man' remains unknown, but but it may be Alexander. Glasgow's unsanitary conditions in the 19th century were mentioned earlier, and it was during a typhus outbreak that Crawford and his entire family died.

Directly opposite stood ❽ **Duke Street Prison**. It was originally known as 'The Bridewell' when founded in 1792 and later became a female-only prison before being demolished in 1958. It was replaced by the Ladywell housing scheme, constructed in the early 1960s, representing later efforts by the city's urban planners to continue the work begun by the City Improvement Trust. You will see some remains of the prison shortly.

After the old school, continue walking and shortly stopping at a wall with railings to your right. Look over to see a stretch of murky water – this is part of the fabled ❾ **Molendinar Burn**. Its source is about 4 miles to the northeast, at Frankfield Loch.

It was by this burn that St Mungo founded his monastic church, and so the Molendinar is vital to the city's foundation story

(or legend). As Glasgow grew, the burn became a nuisance – impeding the construction of buildings and roads and becoming a dumping ground for waste. Late 18th-century maps show the burn was still above ground, but that would soon change. This is the only section remaining in central Glasgow.

Next door is a solid-looking building that was originally ❿ **R.F. & J. Alexander's Cotton Thread Mill**. It was designed by another important architect – Charles Wilson (1810-61). Dating from 1848, in the early 1900s it was converted into the Great

Medieval Glasgow, Townhead & Merchant City Walk

Eastern Hotel for homeless working men. It also contained a roller-skating rink 200 yards long. Having a cotton mill (and other industries) so close to the University helps you understand why the latter moved away.

Cross over and turn left into John Knox Street. ⓫ **Tennent's Wellpark Brewery** has dominated the landscape to your right for many years. Robert Tennent established the first brewery in this area in 1556, attracted by the water supply of the Molendinar Burn. Later generations of the Tennent family continued in the beer business, notably Hugh and Robert Tennent, who founded Drygate brewery in 1740. Another Hugh would go on to create the first Tennent's lager in 1885.

Wellpark Brewery offers tours exploring the history of this important site in Glasgow's industrial history. You will also see signs for ⓬ **Drygate Brewing Co.**, a joint venture between Tennents' and craft brewery William Bros. It also offers tours, as well as a beer hall and dining facilities.

Turn left into Drygate and the Ladywell housing scheme. After a short walk, on your right you'll reach a short section of the wall of ⓭ **Duke Street Prison**. At one point, this was the only prison in Glasgow and had a terrible reputation. It held several suffragettes as prisoners, some of whom went on hunger strikes and were forcibly fed. Susan Newell became the last woman in Scotland to be executed when she was hanged here in 1923 (she had strangled a paper boy). Executions by hanging took place at the prison from 1865 to 1928.

Medieval Glasgow, Townhead & Merchant City Walk

Retrace your steps along Drygate to John Knox Street and turn left. Drygate is the oldest street in the city, and 'dry' may derive from an old word meaning a pagan priest or druid. It has long been speculated that the location of today's Necropolis was an ancient spiritual site for pagan worship, and perhaps Druids once approached along this route. The course of Drygate Street has changed significantly in recent times, and much of the old route is now beneath modern buildings.

Next, turn right down Ladywell Street to find remains of the **14 Lady Well** on the left. Medieval Glaswegians and visiting pilgrims drew their water from several burns or springs turned into wells. In the early 18th century there were still 16 wells in Glasgow, but these would soon disappear as the city expanded. This is a rare surviving well, probably dedicated to the Virgin Mary. It was closed in the 1830s after the Necropolis burial ground was opened above, leading to concerns that rotting corpses would contaminate the water. There are many theories about the significance of these wells in prehistory, possibly venerated by pagans and later attributed with miraculous healing powers in the Christian era and dedicated to saints.

Retrace your steps to John Knox Street, named for the man who did more than anyone else to bring the Reformation to Scotland and sweep away all Catholic institutions.

Stop to look down **15 Wishart Street** on the right, named after Bishop Robert Wishart (1271-1316). He was closely involved with King Robert the Bruce and William Wallace in the battle for Scottish independence. His tomb is inside the Cathedral, although it was severely damaged during the Reformation. Alternatively, it has been suggested the street is named after George Wishart, a Protestant reformer who was burnt at the stake.

In the distance on Wishart Street, you can see the so-called Bridge of Sighs, designed by David Hamilton. It connects the Cathedral to the Necropolis burial ground that dominates the view to your right. Old pictures show the Molendinar Burn flowing above ground under the bridge and along the route of Wishart Street towards where you stand today. The Glasgow Necropolis, founded in 1832, has too much history to be covered in this walk.

Medieval Glasgow, Townhead & Merchant City Walk

Glasgow Necropolis

16 *Cathedral House Hotel*

Medieval Glasgow, Townhead & Merchant City Walk

Continue up the curving street. On the corner of Cathedral Square to your left is the Scottish Baronial-style ⑯ **Cathedral House Hotel**. It has a connection to the nearby prison, as it was established in 1877 as a hostel for released prisoners. The building once contained murals (now destroyed) by some of the Glasgow Boys artists. The hotel is reputedly one of Scotland's most haunted places – unsurprising, given the nearby burials and the executions carried out at the prison.

Take a left at the corner of the hotel, and you'll shortly reach a memorial on the wall dedicated to the ⑰ **Townhead Martyrs**. James Nisbet and two others were executed not far from here in 1684 during 'The Killing Time' when Scottish Presbyterian Covenanters were engaged in a struggle with the Stuart regime (under King Charles II) over matters of religious freedom. An estimated 18,000 people died during this grisly period. The memorial's inscription is blunt, referring to 'The British rulers made such laws....Declared 'twas Satan's reign. As Britain lyes in guilt you see, this ask'd, o reader! Art thou free?'. The memorial has been moved several times since it was first erected.

Next door is the Italianate Baroque-style ⑱ **Glasgow Evangelical Church** dating from 1878. It was designed by John Honeyman (1831-1914), a prominent architect best remembered today as the employer of Charles Rennie Mackintosh. This building was originally Barony North Church, named after the Barony Parish, which was formed around 1595. Look for the statues of St Peter (left) and St Paul. Walk to the end of the street, at the edge of the church, to see steps down to Drygate. Don't go down, but note that for centuries the Drygate thoroughfare ran through this space and along the southern side of Cathedral Square.

Medieval Glasgow, Townhead & Merchant City Walk

Cut through Cathedral Square to reach the ⑲ **statue of 'King Billy'** – aka William of Orange (1650-1702), King William III of England and William II of Scotland. He came to power following the religious upheaval that weakened the Stuart monarchy, leading to the expulsion of James II from England in 1688 – an event known as the Glorious Revolution.

James II's Catholicism had created tensions, but it was the birth of a son and the possibility of a Catholic dynasty that triggered the Glorious Revolution, when he was replaced by his protestant daughter Mary and her Dutch husband, William of Orange. William and Mary's reign brought a more tolerant climate for Scottish Presbyterianism and marked the end of the Killing Time. James II tried to reclaim the throne, but was defeated at the Battle of the Boyne in Ireland in 1690. This victory is celebrated by Protestant Orange Order marches in Glasgow to this day.

The Roman-style statue of William of Orange was a gift to the city in 1735 from James Macrae, the Governor of Madras. The horse's tail features a ball and socket joint, allowing it to move in the wind. The statue originally stood for years in Trongate and then at Glasgow

Statue of 'King Billy' & Barony Church

Medieval Glasgow, Townhead & Merchant City Walk

Cross before being moved to its current location in 1926. Given sectarian tensions, the statue of 'King Billy' is not universally admired. In 2020, the police had to protect the statue after it was targeted by Black Lives Matter protesters. William owned shares in the Royal African Company, responsible in the 1680s for the transportation of around 5,000 people a year from Africa to slave markets.

Exit the Square, passing on the other side of Castle Street the ⓴ **former Barony Church,** designed by Sir John James Burnet and John Archibald Campbell, dating from c.1889. This neo-Gothic building is now used as a ceremonial hall for Strathclyde University.

It was in this vicinity that the Battle of Rottenrow took place on 4th May 1921. A member of the IRA named Frank J. Carty was being transported to Duke Street Prison when the police van carrying him was ambushed by men emerging from nearby streets. Shots were fired, and one policeman was killed. The attackers were unable to free Carty as the van doors jammed. The shocking incident stoked sectarian tensions as suspected Republican sympathisers (including priests) were arrested. Riots took place in the Catholic-dominated district of Carlton. No one was ever convicted for the attack, and it remains one of the city's most violent incidents. It is said that bullets marks can still be seen on nearby walls, although they are quite obscured.

Now, passing the old police telephone box, head towards the Glasgow Cathedral. You pass a statue of clothing manufacturer ㉑ **James Arthur** (1819-1885). He owned three factories and employed hundreds of salesmen. Arthur's wife, Jane Glen (1827-1907), was a pioneer for women's rights and the first woman to serve on a Scottish school board, so perhaps merits a statue of her own.

Medieval Glasgow, Townhead & Merchant City Walk

On the left is **㉒ St Mungo Museum of Religious Life & Art**, which is well worth a visit (there is a café, toilet, and Zen garden). Although the museum looks old, it only opened in 1993. If you have time, you may wish to visit the Glasgow Cathedral or Necropolis now. The cathedral is the oldest building in the city, constructed between 1136-1485. Up high, this was an excellent defensive position as well, with the water from the Molendinar Burn nearby.

Follow the map to the ㉓ **memorial stone** that marks the site of Glasgow's 'lost' castle. The origin of the Bishop's Palace, also known as the Bishop's Castle, is unclear, but it was probably first built in the 12th century. The castle was captured by 'Braveheart' William Wallace in 1296 and later garrisoned by English soldiers. It served as the home of the Bishop (and later Archbishop) until 1689. After that, the building fell into disrepair and was demolished in 1789 to make way for the hospital.

Continue to Castle Street, to reach ㉔ **Provand's Lordship**. This dates from 1471, making it the second oldest building in the city. It was initially built as part of St Nicholas's Hospital. In medieval times, there were 32 'prebendal' houses around here, a 'prebend' referring to an income provided by the church – 'Provand' is a corruption of this word. This is the only prebendary house to survive in Glasgow. It is worth a visit as it feels like travelling back in time. The St Nicholas Garden, a herb garden, is a highlight.

24 *Provand's Lordship*

Medieval Glasgow, Townhead & Merchant City Walk

The medieval hospital of St Nicholas housed a dozen poor men who were cared for by a priest. The Blackadder Hospital also stood nearby, founded in 1524 by Roland Blackadder. It survived the Reformation before closing down in the early 1600s.

Continue on Castle Street, then take a slight left to continue onto Glebe Street by the Gatehouse Building. This area is Townhead. In medieval times, the land north of the Cathedral was open, and even in the late 1700s, only a few buildings stood here. That would soon change, and as the 19th century progressed, dozens of new tenement streets were constructed, filling in all the gaps.

Follow the pedestrian path uphill to Parson Street. The road once stretched across this part of Townhead and was one of the few thoroughfares visible on old maps before the area was redeveloped in the 19th century. It is home to the ㉕ **former Martyrs' Public School**, built in the late 1890s by Honeyman & Keppie, and bearing the influence of their young employee Charles Rennie Mackintosh (1868–1928). This was a place he knew well as he was born and raised at the family home at 70 Parson Street (later demolished). His family, called McIntosh, would later move to Dennistoun.

The reference to Martyrs is linked to the memorial stone you saw earlier on Cathedral Square. In 1684, Covenanters James Nisbet, James Lawson, and Alexander Wood were executed at a spot near here called ㉖ **the Howgate**. This old execution site was located where the slip road at junction 15 merges into the M8.

Opposite is ㉗ **St Mungo's RC Church**, a relic of 19th-century Townhead. It was built in 1841 and altered in 1877. It is associated with the Passionists, a Catholic order founded in Italy in 1720. An Irish branch of this order came to Townhead in 1865. Mackintosh would have been familiar with this church, and perhaps it influenced his own interest in architecture.

Follow the map along St Mungo Avenue to enter the western part of Townhead. If you travelled back in time to 1900, you would struggle to get your bearings. This part of Townhead would look completely different: tenement streets, pubs, churches, factories, foundries, and warehouses. You would be near the Monkland Canal, the Sun Foundry, the Fever Hospital, the City Poorhouse, St Rollox Chemical Works, Grafton Square, a bowling green, and Townhead Public Baths and Washhouse. All this has gone, except for some isolated survivors.

Townhead was designated as a Comprehensive Development Area (CDA) by urban planners, leading to sweeping changes in the 1960s as streets were demolished and thousands of residents were moved to housing schemes on the city's outskirts. Today, it may strike you how quiet this area is even though Buchanan Street is less than a mile away. Old maps show the long-lost St Enoch Burn ran through Townhead near here, turning south near St Enoch Square before flowing into the Clyde.

Medieval Glasgow, Townhead & Merchant City Walk

You soon pass the modern ㉘ **Townhead Village Hall**, which serves as a hub for the local community (it has a café). Townhead has a surprising son: Bobby Thomson (1923-2010) was born here before moving to the United State as a child. He became a baseball player known as 'the Staten Island Scot' and was immortalised for his 'shot heard 'round the world' when he helped the New York Giants win on 3rd October 1951, earning them the National League pennant.

Continue on, after a few minutes turning left into St James Road where you will see a classic ㉙ **Glasgow School Board** structure dating from 1906. It was initially called Canning Place Public School. When this area was more densely populated, 1,000 children attended here. Today, it is the only building in this immediate area that dates from before 1914. It later became an annexe to Allan Glen's School. Past pupils include actor Dirk Bogarde and Charles Rennie Mackintosh (when the school was at the junction of North Hanover and Cathedral Streets).

St James Road is home to St Mungo's student accommodation block, which opened in 2018. It is a sign of the times that in Glasgow, the primary source of new housing appears to be for students, and this has helped change Townhead. The Ensuite Bronze room option boasts a 'full-length mirror, ensuite bathroom with shower, toilet and basin and communal kitchen..'. At the time of writing, the city's waiting list for social housing stands at around 60,000.

Medieval Glasgow, Townhead & Merchant City Walk

Immediately after the old school, turn right down a narrow pedestrian lane, walking downhill to reach Cathedral Street. You get a good view of the rear of the school. Most of what you see now is dominated by the campus buildings of the University of Strathclyde and the City of Glasgow College. Together, they have around 40,000 students. Walk left along Cathedral Street, then right down Taylor Street.

After a short way take the first right and continue to reach ③⓪ **Callanish**, inspired by the ancient standing stones of Callanish in the Western Isles. Nicknamed Steelhenge, the 16 steel pillars were erected in 1974 and designed by artist and sculptor Gerald Laing (1936-2011). Laing served as an officer in the army before ending up in New York in the 1960's, where he became friends with Andy Warhol and was part of the Pop Art movement. Old maps show in 1890, this tranquil spot was much busier, surrounded by tenement streets, at least six pubs, a military drill hall, and a timber yard.

Follow the map through the University of Strathclyde campus into Rottenrow. You can now see how high up you are. Further along, look for remnants of the ③① **Glasgow Royal Maternity Hospital**, located here from 1860 until moving to its current location in 2001. This is where generations of Glaswegians emerged into the world.

This was also the site of Glasgow's guilty secret – the Lock Hospital – founded in 1805 and originally standing in the northeast corner of the site. It served

Medieval Glasgow, Townhead & Merchant City Walk

women, and sometimes their children, who had contracted venereal disease. Treatments were barbaric by today's standards, and many of the poorest and most desperate ended up here.

Admissions records from the 1870s show that the largest patient group was mill girls, followed by domestic servants, prostitutes, machinists and washerwomen. The name 'lock' may originate from an old word for leper house. Many patients came from the Magdalene Asylum for Fallen Women and Girls or Duke Street Jail.

Walk through the gardens, passing the **safety pin sculpture** known locally as the ㉜ **'Monument to Maternity'**, which commemorates the historical connections of the site. It is the work of Scottish artist George Wylie (1921-2012). Its official name is *Mhtothta* – Greek for maternity, it moved here when the Gardens opened in 2004.

Serial killer Ian Brady was born here on 2 January 1938 and lived in the Gorbals as a child. He moved south later on where he met Myra Hindley and together they murdered five children in the mid-1960s.

Medieval Glasgow, Townhead & Merchant City Walk

Rottenrow was one of the original eight streets that existed in the medieval city, where many clergy lived in manses. No one knows why it is called Rottenrow, and there are too many theories to mention here!

Follow the map down the hill to Montrose Street (passing the Channel 4 building) before reaching Ingram Street, named after merchant Archibald Ingram (1699-1770). As recently as 1780, there was only open ground between Rottenrow and this spot. Turn left along Ingram Street to reach the ㉝ **former Ramshorn Kirk**. If medieval Glasgow was dominated by the church and university, men such as Ingram transformed the city into a place of commerce during the 18th century.

After the political union of Scotland and England in 1707, local merchants benefitted from England's global trading network. Merchants such as Ingram imported vast amounts of tobacco and other commodities grown on slave plantations in the American colonies and the Caribbean. Their profits helped fund the construction of churches, canals, mansions, warehouses, factories, shipyards, and the foundation of banks.

Ingram, who served as Lord Provost, was just one of the so-called Tobacco Lords. Others included Andrew Buchanan, John Glassford, William Cunninghame, and Alexander Spiers. In recent years, controversy has raged about streets and other places named after those who profited from a trading system dependent on slavery. Ingram Street used to be called Canon Lane, a link to the area's ecclesiastical history.

Medieval Glasgow, Townhead & Merchant City Walk

The Ramshorn building was constructed in the 1820s on the site of an earlier church. If the gates are open, try to visit the graveyard at the rear. Many merchants and their families were buried here, evident if you read the inscriptions on the headstones. You will also see mortsafes – iron cages designed to let bodies rot so they were useless to the body snatchers who sold corpses to the medical schools.

Look down at the pavement in front of the former Kirk to see a slab referring to the Foulis brothers. You are standing over the burial place of Robert and Andrew Foulis, celebrated in the 18th century for their publishing house, which produced exceptional books to meet the demand from the nearby University.

They were important figures during the age of the Enlightenment when Edinburgh and Glasgow were internationally-respected centres of learning and new thinking, producing figures such as Adam Smith and David Hume. Glasgow's population was still small – around 32,000 in 1750 – and just beginning to spread out from the medieval district. The Foulis brothers met Dr Samuel Johnson when the latter visited Glasgow in 1773 and upset the great man by daring to argue back during a discussion.

The origins of the University of Strathclyde also stretch back to this period. John Anderson (1726-1796) was a professor of natural philosophy at the University of Glasgow. A true Enlightenment figure, he bequeathed money for the foundation of a progressive centre of learning named Anderson's Institution, which would later form the core of the University of Strathclyde. Anderson and his grandfather are buried in Ramshorn Kirk.

There are good cafés around here for a break, and opposite Ramshorn Kirk, by the car park, is an excellent mural featuring animals by street artist Smug, known as *Fellow Glasgow Residents*.

Walk down Candleriggs, opposite the Ramshorn, entering the heart of the Merchant City. As its name suggests, long ago candlemakers were established here, their works producing noxious smells that were kept far away from the residential streets lining the High Street. During the 18th century, the Tobacco Lords and other merchants founded warehouses here for tobacco, tea and sugar, as well as building new homes for themselves.

During the 20th century the area became run-down, but in recent years, it has been successfully revitalised under the new 'Merchant City' moniker. It contains some of the liveliest bars and restaurants in the city.

Fellow Glasgow Residents mural

Medieval Glasgow, Townhead & Merchant City Walk

Medieval Glasgow, Townhead & Merchant City Walk

Continue along, passing on the left **34** **Glasgow City Halls** – a concert venue founded in the 19th century and incorporating old market buildings. Next door is Merchant Square, now full of bars and restaurants but once the heart of the city's wholesale fruit, vegetable, and cheese markets. If you could stand here in 1810, you would see a bowling green, shortly to disappear as the Merchant City area became increasingly developed.

Continue down to Trongate. Turn right to reach the junction with **35** **Glassford Street** (with M&S just opposite). It is named after Lord John Glassford (1715-1783), a prominent Tobacco Lord who owned slave plantations in Virginia and Maryland. This was the site of Westport, the western entrance into the medieval burgh in the 16th century. To the south is Stockwell Street, originally Stockwellgait, which once led directly to the only medieval bridge over the Clyde.

Retrace your steps, walking on the south side of Trongate. The name reflects it was the way to the 'Tron' – a woodcen weighing beam – once situated here. The Tron was used to weigh goods to assess tolls and customs owed on merchandise brought into Glasgow.

You pass tiny passageways on the right, legacies of the medieval city: Old Wynd (where West Port also stood at a different time), and the New Wynd. The latter is home to the **36** **Britannia Panopticon** – a rare surviving Victorian music hall. With its origins in the 1850s, you can see regular

Medieval Glasgow, Townhead & Merchant City Walk

performances here that reflect how Glaswegians had fun before the arrival of cinema and television. This is where Stan Laurel made his debut. New Wynd is another thoroughfare medieval Glaswegians would have known, leading them to the Briggait area.

The ports (or gateways) into medieval Glasgow were rarely tested for their defensive properties. Still, they did allow the city authorities to control day-to-day life for travellers and residents. If there was an outbreak of the plague, the gates could be closed. They also provided a way to charge taxes on incoming goods and animals. As Glasgow expanded, the ports were demolished to help the follow of traffic.

Continue along Trongate, passing the ㊲ **Tron Kirk steeple**. This site was home to The Collegiate Church of Our Lady and St Anne, founded in 1525. After the Reformation, it remained a church, known as the 'Tron Church', and the steeple was added in 1628. The church was destroyed by a fire in 1793, and a new building was designed by Scottish architect James Adam. It incorporated the surviving steeple. In the 1980s, the church became home to the Tron Theatre and is reputedly haunted.

Ahead is Glasgow Cross and one of the city's oldest landmarks – the ㊳ **Tolbooth Steeple**. Dating from 1626, it is the only surviving part of the old tolbooth that once served as the administrative heart of Glasgow. It also contained a court and jail. The Tontine Hotel building stood next door, and in the 18th century, the coffee shop within it became the bustling heart of the city. Wealthy Tobacco Lords and other prominent figures would strut around here, making business plans and exchanging news. It was the commercial heart of Glasgow until the Royal Exchange opened on Queen Street.

Medieval Glasgow, Townhead & Merchant City Walk

Another key historical figure is remembered with a plaque above the guitar shop on the north side of Trongate. **㊴ James Watt** (1736-1819) occupied a workshop here in the early 1760s in what was then known as Buchanan's Land. A mathematical instrument maker, Watt would be forgotten today if Professor John Anderson had not asked him to repair a Newcomen steam engine. Watt realised he could improve the design, and his innovations helped kick-start the age of steam power and the Industrial Revolution. Watt arguably changed the world more than any other Scottish person before or since.

Tontine Lane

To the right of the guitar shop is Tontine Lane. By the 19th century, this area had a reputation for violence and vice. In and around Trongate there were 200 brothels and 150 drinking dens. Tontine Lane stands on the route of Tontine Close (there is a sign for the close too), and the latter was said to be the worst slum in Glasgow during the Victorian era. The close was home to around 2,000 people – many of whom were criminals or sex workers – who lived in squalor. In 1781, an ancient dug-out oak canoe was discovered during the excavation of foundations for the Tontine building.

The ㊵ **low-ribbed structure** in the middle of the road is a ventilation structure connected to Glasgow Cross station, which operated between 1895-1964. The octagonal ticket office was demolished long ago, and this is where the statue of King William (seen earlier) used to stand.

Medieval Glasgow, Townhead & Merchant City Walk

Cross over the busy junction to see ④ **a recreation of Glasgow's Mercat Cross** (the original was removed in 1659). The Mercat Cross was historically where proclamations were read, and a market was held. This version, dating from 1929, was designed by Edith Burnet Hughes (1888-1971), considered Britain's first practising female architect.

Medieval Glasgow, Townhead & Merchant City Walk

To the south is Saltmarket and then the Clyde. Glasgow received Burgh status in 1175, granting townspeople various trading rights, including the right to hold an annual fair and a weekly market. This led to the development of almost two parallel towns. The stretch north of Glasgow Cross was dominated by the church, while the southern strip towards the Clyde was the domain of commercial interests.

The name 'Saltmarket' dates from the mid-1600s when a market for salt, used to cure salmon, was established here. Medieval Glaswegians would have known it as Waulkergate, as it led to the neighbourhood near the river where the cloth waulkers lived.

Head past the Tolbooth Steeple, passing Gallowgate on the right. As its name suggests, this road led to the public gallows, and the East Port stood a little further along the route.

Continue up the High Street, stopping at Bell Street on the right. It contains ㊷ **old bonded warehouses** built by the Glasgow and South Western Railway for its College Goods Station (named for the university – or 'Old College'). In the late 19th century, Glasgow was a key site for blended whisky producers. Malt whisky would arrive by train and be stored there. The College Goods Yard operated between the 1880s and 1962.

Walk on, passing Blackfriars Street on your left, named after the Dominican Friary of the Black Friars, located further up on the right. The current ㊸ **Andrew Ure Hall** stands approximately where the friary was located, and retains parts of the wall of the railway complex. The Dominican Black Friars established a presence here in the 13th century. A papal bull of 1246 refers to a church and buildings belonging to the 'Friars Preachers of Glasgow'. By 1560, the

Medieval Glasgow, Townhead & Merchant City Walk

Reformation forced the Blackfriars to flee. The university used the old friary church as a place of worship for many years.

Andrew Ure Hall, and Parsonage Square behind it, occupy what was once the platforms of the College Goods Station mentioned earlier.

When you reach the corner with Blackfriars Road on the right, look up at the ㊹ **scowling face and memorial plaque**. This was donated by the University of Glasgow to commemorate its presence in this area for over 400 years. Walk on to reach High Street station and the end of this walk.

VISIT

Tennent's Wellpark Brewery
161 Duke St, G31 1JD
tennents.co.uk

Glasgow Necropolis
Castle St, G4 0UZ
glasgownecropolis.org

St Mungo Museum of Religious Life & Art
2 Castle St, G4 0RH
glasgowlife.org.uk

Britannia Panopticon
117 Trongate, G1 5HD
britanniapanopticon.org

EAT & DRINK

Drygate Brewing Co.
85 Drygate, G4 0UT
drygate.com

Celentano's
28-32 Cathedral Square, G4 0XA
celentanosglasgow.com

Copperbox Coffee
Cathedral Sq, G4 0QZ

Spitfire Espresso
127 Candleriggs, G1 1NP
spitfireespresso.com

Café Gandolfi
64 Albion St, G1 1NY
cafegandolfi.com

Glasgow Athenaeum, p.258

8 City Centre Architecture Walk

City Centre Architecture Walk

1. Grosvenor Building
2. Former Forsyth Store
3. Cast-iron Ca d'Oro Building
4. The Egyptian Halls
5. Caledonian Chambers
6. The Lighthouse
7. *The Herald* newspaper building
8. 98 Buchanan Street
9. Gallery of Modern Art
10. 205-17 Ingram Street
11. The Corinthian Club
12. Former Glasgow Savings Bank
13. Trades Hall of Glasgow
14. Hutchesons' Hall
15. City Chambers
16. No 9 George Square
17. John Burnet design
18. James Miller design
19. Merchants' House
20. 24 George Square
21. Anchor Line Building
22. Clydesdale Bank Headquarters
23. Former Western Club
24. Former Glasgow Stock Exchange
25. Royal Faculty of Procurators in Glasgow
26. 92 West George Street
27. Former Glasgow Athenaeum
28. Former Athenaeum Theatre
29. Alexander Thomson's design
30. Former Paramount/Odeon
31. Castle Chambers
32. 134-136 West George Street

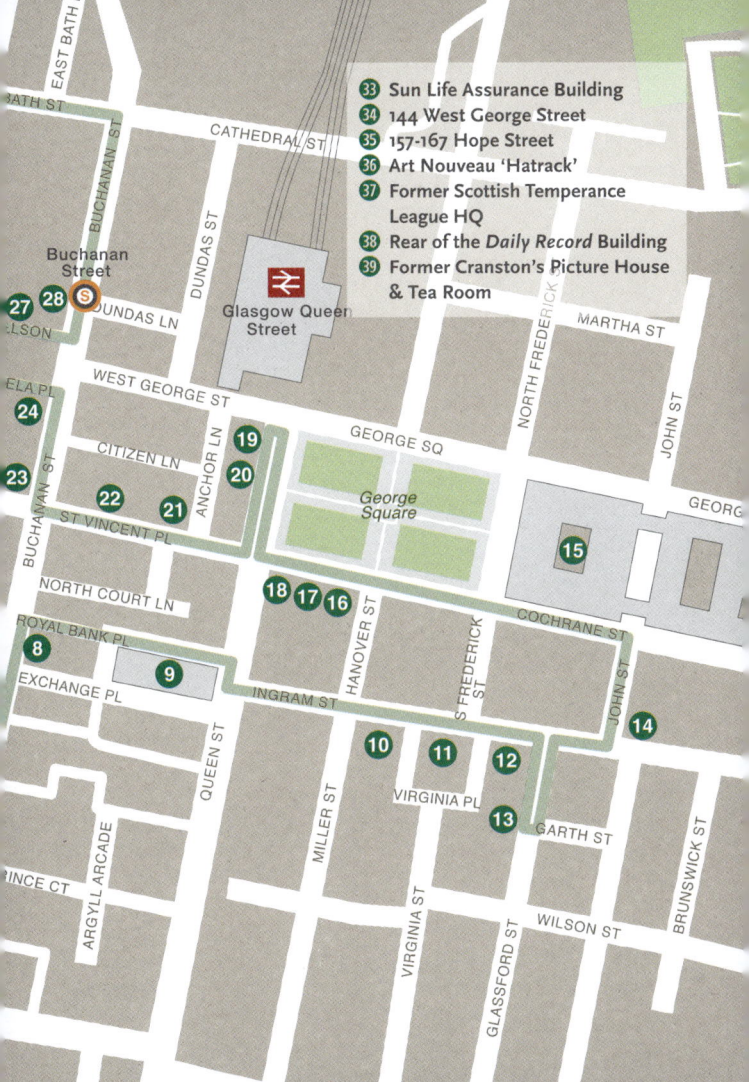

City Centre Architecture Walk

Start/Finish: Outside Central Station on Gordon Street
Distance: 2 miles

The centre of Glasgow boasts some of the finest buildings in the country. Along this walk, you will see the evolution of architecture from the late 18th century to the early 20th century, as Glasgow expanded rapidly. You will learn about certain key architects who shaped much of the city during this period.

Most residents and visitors to Glasgow are aware of Charles Rennie Mackintosh or perhaps Alexander 'Greek' Thomson, but architects with less familiar names – Wilson, Hamilton, Miller, Burnet, Salmon and Sellars – produced fine buildings that we walk past every day. Their work influences how we see Glasgow in the 21st century, and this walk seeks to focus on their surviving buildings. Since these architects worked on numerous commissions, this walk is only a taster and should not be taken as a comprehensive guide to the best buildings on the route.

The walk begins outside Central Station on Gordon Street, which features two significant buildings. The first is the ❶ **Grosvenor Building** (no. 72-80), designed by Alexander 'Greek' Thomson (1817-1875). He worked in Glasgow for over a quarter of a century, drawing inspiration from architectural styles favoured in ancient civilisations, not just Greek but Roman, Egyptian, and elsewhere.

Thomson never left Britain, learning much from printed sources. The next generation of architects began to travel abroad more, broadening their horizons. Some studied at the *École des Beaux-Arts* in Paris (inspiring Beaux-Art style buildings) or to see groundbreaking architectural styles being developed in places such as Chicago. You will see this progress as you follow the walk.

Thomson co-owned this warehouse when completed in 1861 (it was rebuilt in the same style after a fire). Everything above the first four floors was added by another architect, J.H. Craigie, in 1907 – look closely to see the different styles. The Greek motifs

City Centre Architects Walk

and other details on the façade are typical of Thomson. The Charles Rennie Mackintosh tourist industry has ensured CRM is the best-known local architect, but many regard Thomson as the greater talent. He definitely obtained more commissions than CRM.

Further along, on the corner with Renfield Street (now a Greggs), is the second most important building on the street, the ❷ **former Forsyth Store** remodelled by Sir John James (or J.J.) Burnet and completed by 1902. J.J. Burnet (1857-1938) was the son

and working partner of John Burnet Senior (1814-1901). Their family practice was one of the most respected in Glasgow. John Burnet Senior was active from the mid-1840s, while his son continued into the late 1930s. For nearly a century, when Glasgow was expanding at a great pace, this father and son had a remarkable and uninterrupted influence on the cityscape.

The Burnets were members of the architectural 'establishment' that emerged in Glasgow during the 19th century. Before then architects were not awarded titles or trained formally as architects. They often began as ordinary builders or masons, demonstrating their skills 'on the job' before winning commissions.

Things changed. The Royal Institute of British Architects (RIBA) was founded in 1834, and professional standards and associations in Glasgow and nationally developed. The Glasgow Institute of Architects traces its origins to the Glasgow Architectural Society founded in 1858, whose early members included several architects mentioned on this walk.

J.J. Burnet, born into a wealthy family, had a head start as his father had good connections with clients. He sent young J.J. to study at the *École des Beaux-Arts* in Paris

City Centre Architects Walk

in the 1870s. Unlike most Glasgow architects, Burnet also moved to London where he continued a successful career.

The influence of Burnet's studies is evident here. Designed for the upmarket outfitter R.W. Forsyth, the building would not look out of place in Paris. It was an innovative design, incorporating electric lighting, lifts, and central heating. Burnet transformed the original warehouse here into something more appealing, with a domed corner and sculpture by William Birnie Rhind, of Edinburgh.

In 1896, both Burnets travelled to the United States and were influenced by the emerging architectural styles there. J.J. Burnet became a member of the American Beaux-Arts Cosmos Club and the American Institute of Architects. As Glasgow became a globally important industrial centre, its architects began absorbing

City Centre Architects Walk

influences not just from the past – Greek, Roman, Gothic, Renaissance etc – but also further afield. A few, such as CRM, even created their own unique styles.

On the corner – now a Tesco – you'll see the striking ❸ **cast-iron Ca'd'Oro**, which began as a furniture warehouse. The windows were deliberately large so people could see the goods on offer in the days before electric lighting. This was designed by John Honeyman (1831-1914) and dates from 1872. He was not just an architect but also an inventor and writer. He took John Keppie (1862-1945) as a partner in 1889 (Keppie studied at the *École des Beaux-Arts*). Both men would hire the young CRM and advance his career considerably. Honeyman was active from the 1850s and continued even after his official retirement in 1901 when Keppie and Mackintosh bought him out of their practice.

The Ca' d'Oro is in the style of a Renaissance Venetian palace. The name means 'house of gold' and came from a restaurant housed in the building in the 1920s. The two end bays along Union Street are modern replicas of the original design.

Continue along Union Street and to your left, (third building down) you'll see ❹ **the Egyptian Halls** (completed by 1873). This is a late work by 'Greek' Thomson and is regarded as his best warehouse design. When it was constructed, Thomson was suffering from several long-term illnesses including bronchitis, that would lead to his death aged 57. The building is a mix of Renaissance and ancient styles with Egyptian columns and boasts a cast-iron framework – then an innovative technique.

Water damage has caused it to be shrouded in recent years, and it is a tragedy that one of Glasgow's best buildings is not able to be seen. Hopefully, it will avoid the Glasgow fate of being mysteriously burnt down one night and the site redeveloped.

Thomson served as president of the Glasgow Architectural Society and the Glasgow Institute of Architects. By his time, it had become difficult to become an architect without studying and learning the ropes as an assistant to a practising architect. Joining a professional body such as RIBA also required being proposed by other members, leading to a certain cliquishness.

City Centre Architects Walk

Just opposite is James Miller's ❺ **Caledonian Chambers**, dating from 1903. Miller (1860-1947) was one of the most prolific architects of his era, evident as you continue today. His early career involved working for the railway industry, particularly regular, large-scale commissions for the Caledonian Railway Company during the golden age of railway expansion. Miller worked on Central Station, and the Chambers contained a side entrance to the main concourse.

During this time, railway companies spent vast sums investing in new infrastructure. Lucky architects like Miller were among the biggest beneficiaries. He was solid, reliable, imaginative yet pragmatic. Miller was never as interesting as CRM, but his dependability led to commissions. Few project managers want to be obliged to explain to their financially minded bosses that a project was delayed or over budget ('yes, but look at the detail ...!').

Like the Burnets, Miller worked for several decades as he could adapt his style to fit new trends. He travelled in Europe, soaking up architectural influences, and later worked with assistants such as Richard M. Gunn, who brought their own experience of American architecture.

Miller worked from the late 1880s until 1941 – an incredibly long career. He undertook commissions all around Scotland, and the range of his work is remarkable, from rural railway stations and the North British Locomotive Building in Flemington Street to Glasgow's Royal Infirmary and the interiors for the doomed ocean liner RMS *Lusitania*.

Retrace your steps to Gordon Street, and then follow the map down Mitchell Street. Soon you'll reach the rear of the former **Glasgow *Herald* newspaper**

City Centre Architects Walk

building (1895), now known as ❻ **The Lighthouse**. CRM, working as an assistant for the practice of Honeyman & Keppie, had a major hand in this design. Its main feature is the Art Nouveau tower, which served as a water tank.

Compared to other architects mentioned on this walk, CRM's legacy in central Glasgow is modest. After leaving his partnership with Keppie in 1913, he failed to win enough commissions to sustain his career. Drinking too much and suffering from depression, CRM gained a reputation for being difficult to work with. Why would a risk-averse insurance company, bank or railway firm commission a maverick like CRM when Miller or Burnet were available? An embittered CRM left Glasgow with his wife, Margaret Macdonald, in 1914 and never returned to the city of his birth.

Today, the Lighthouse houses the Scottish Centre for Architecture and Design and is open to the public. There are regular exhibitions, and you can climb the staircase to the top of the tower to enjoy great views over Glasgow.

City Centre Architects Walk

Continue along Mitchell Lane to reach Buchanan Street, then turn right. The second building on the right-hand side (no. 69) is the ❼ **public-facing side of *The Herald* newspaper building**. John Baird designed the first building (1870), which was then remodelled in 1879 by James Sellars (1843-1888). Sellars was influenced by Thomson and was close friends with his assistant John Keppie. Look for the putti (figures of children/cherubs) holding newspapers, carved by Charles Grassby, and the statues of Caxton and Gutenberg higher up, by John Mossman.

Now walk the other way up Buchanan Street, stopping at a blonde sandstone building on the right at ❽ **number 98** (on the corner of Exchange Place). This three-storey construction was designed by Charles Wilson in an Italian Renaissance style and dates from around 1851. Wilson (1810-1863) was the leading architect of the mid-19th century in Glasgow, learning his trade first-hand from David Hamilton (more on Hamilton shortly). In turn, Wilson influenced the next generation of architects, and one of his pupils was John Burnet Senior. Wilson helped found both the Architectural Institute of Scotland and the Glasgow Architectural Society in the 1850s. He is best remembered for his design of the prestigious Park Circus development.

Take the next right down Royal Bank Place, and continue to the entrance of the ❾ **Gallery of Modern Art**. The original building dates from the late 1770s and was the mansion of tobacco merchant William

City Centre Architects Walk

Cunninghame. Much of what you see is the result of a later remodelling by David Hamilton (1768-1843) between 1827-32. The building was later used as the Royal Exchange. Hamilton is best known for his remaining buildings in Glasgow, such as Hutchesons' Hall (seen later) and the Nelson Monument on Glasgow Green.

Hamilton was one of the first Glasgow architects to be recognised nationally. He came third in the competition to design the Houses of Parliament in Westminster, a respectable position for a Scottish architect. He was definitely 'old school' – beginning as a mason before becoming an architect and learning on the job. He worked as an assistant to Robert and James Adam of the famous Adam architectural dynasty. As mentioned earlier, he also taught other important architects, including Charles Wilson. Hamilton is known as the father of the architectural profession in Glasgow and an important link between the past and future architects of the city.

City Centre Architects Walk

Walk down Ingram Street. On the right, on the corner with Miller Street at ⑩ **205-17 Ingram Street**, is another CRM connection. This was the third of the four tearooms opened by pioneering Victorian entrepreneur Miss Cranston. CRM was spotted by Cranston and put to work here on the interior. He was later given the commission to design the Willow Tea Rooms on Sauchiehall Street.

Continue along, and shortly on the right is the ⑪ **Corinthian Club**, worth a visit to the main bar to see one of the finest former banking halls in the city. The site was originally occupied by the Virginia Mansion, built in 1752. Few buildings in the city have had as many famous architects involved in their development as this one. David Hamilton designed it for the Union Bank in 1841, and you can see the locations of bank branches named on the exterior. There are also allegorical female figures representing Britannia, Wealth and other lofty ideals of the era, by John Mossman.

Yet another member of an architectural dynasty – James Salmon Senior (1805-1888) – was also involved in redesigning the

City Centre Architects Walk

interior in the 1850s. The Venetian-style frontage is largely by John Burnet Senior in 1876-9, and his son (J.J.).

Commissions for many civic buildings involved navigating a judging panel of other architects. Being elected to architectural bodies such as RIBA also required senior architects to propose you. If you were born into a family of established architects, attended the right church or masonic lodge, and behaved in the 'right way,' you were more likely to navigate these tricky waters, even if you were less talented than someone who lacked many of these advantages.

Next door is the ⓬ **former headquarters of the Glasgow Savings Bank**. The earliest part of this complex is a rather plain three-storey Italianate building set back from the pavement, designed by John Burnet Senior around 1866. His son, J.J., later designed the elaborate street-level extension dating from the mid-1890s. Reflecting the times, this design is more lavish, with impressive sculptures adorning the façade by Sir George Frampton. Look for the pair of Atlantes (a term for support columns in human form, named after Atlas who held up the sky on his shoulders).

One figure has a fine moustache that resembles J.J. Burnet himself – not the first time an architect has been immortalised on one of their own designs. There are also signs for 'frugality' and 'industry' – all values the Savings Bank wanted to promote to passers-by.

City Centre Architects Walk

City Centre Architects Walk

Take the immediate right onto Glassford Street. From this side you can see Burnet Senior's original bank building.

Next door on the right is the ⑬ **Trades Hall of Glasgow**, completed in 1794. The frontage was designed by Robert Adam (1728-1792). Robert and his brother James were sons of the prominent architect William Adam. The brothers would go on to develop their own interpretation of the Palladian Neoclassical style that made them arguably the finest British architects in the late 18th century.

Their work became influential in Britain and the wider empire. Robert travelled through Europe as a young man, influenced by the Roman ruins he visited in Italy. This all had a bearing on his later work, and with his brother, he helped design four buildings in Glasgow in the 1790s. The Trades Hall is the only substantive survivor, so it holds an important place in the city's architectural history.

David Hamilton was responsible for extensions in 1828 and 1838, while John Keppie did further work on the façade in the early 20th century. It remains the home of the Trades Hall, where the city's Trades House and 14 Incorporated Crafts are based. The institution dates back to 1604.

Follow the map onto Ingram Street where ⑭ **Hutchesons' Hall** stands on the corner. It was built as Hutchesons' Hospital by 'father of the profession' David Hamilton and completed in 1805. It was Hamilton's first major work in Glasgow, remarkably assured for a young man still in his 30s.

George and Thomas Hutcheson were wealthy brothers who died during the first half of the 1600s and left a legacy for a school (which continues today as Hutchesons' Grammar School) and a 'hospital' to house poor, ageing men (providing them with hospitality rather than medical care). Hamilton's Corinthian columns are flanked by statues of the brothers. These are the oldest portrait monuments in the city and came from the original 17th-century hall that stood on Trongate.

City Centre Architects Walk

Walk up John Street, turn left into Cochrane Street, and then continue to George Square. The ⓯ **City Chambers** complex, which dominates the east side of the square, was largely the work of London-based Scot, William Young (1843-1900). Italian Renaissance in style, it was already considered to be somewhat architecturally old-fashioned at the time of its completion in 1890.

Young was awarded the commission after winning the design competition in 1881. There were actually two competitions and each attracted around 100 entries from the UK. The rules of the competition stipulated that plans were to be submitted anonymously and marked with a symbol or motto to deter favouritism or fraud in the judges' selection. It was only after the winning designs were chosen that the architects were identified via a separate envelope with the same identifying mark. Esteemed local architects such as the Burnets, Salmons, William Leiper and John Baird II were among those who lost out to Young.

City Centre Architects Walk

On the left side at ⓰ **number 9 George Square** is a confident, mercantile building designed by James Miller and dating from 1924. It was originally called the McLaren Warehouse.

Miller was then working with Richard Gunn (1889-1933), who had gained experience in America before coming to Glasgow, and whose influence can be seen here. Gunn studied at the Glasgow School of Art from the age of 11, and served in World War I, being badly gassed during the fighting. His love of American commercial classicism positively impacted his boss, James Miller, and other city architects. It was also regarded as a turning point in the development of Glasgow's architecture at the time.

Stylistically, the building would fit into Chicago or any other big American city from the same era. This explains why Glasgow regularly stands in for America cities in Hollywood films (including *Indiana Jones and the Dial of Destiny* and *World War Z*).

On the right of this building is another ⓱ **John Burnet design**, this one from 1863. Not to be outdone, the one next door is also by ⓲ **James Miller**, and dates from 1905. In these three buildings, you can see architectural evolution taking place, gaining in height, as they move away from a more European-influenced style to reflect American trends.

Follow the map to the northwest side of the Square to admire the ⓳ **Merchants' House**, designed by John Burnet and dating from 1874. His son, J.J. Burnet, carried out additional work around 1908, adding two storeys and an attic. Founded in 1605, the Merchants' House institution represented the city's mercantile interests. Like the Trade's House, it wielded considerable political power, maintaining a presence on the town council until 1975.

City Centre Architects Walk

The history of this building is a reminder that it was not uncommon for a family of architects to work on the same site over several decades. This nepotism made it difficult for outsiders like Mackintosh to enter the close-knit architectural establishment that developed in the 19th century.

Next door at ⑳ **24 George Square** is another building by James Sellars, dating from 1874. Sellars died in his mid-forties from blood poisoning after standing on a rusty nail at the construction site of his Glasgow International Exhibition buildings in Kelvingrove in 1888. He was a major talent, and no doubt had he lived longer, he would have produced many large-scale buildings in the city.

Now follow the map and exit George Square from the southwest corner along St Vincent Place.

The first stopping point here is on the right – the steel-framed former ㉑ **Anchor Line building** designed by James Miller. Dating from 1907, it has been described as Edwardian Renaissance in style. This was the headquarters of the Anchor Line transatlantic shipping company. If you go inside (it is currently a restaurant), you can see the original signage recording the names of ocean liners high up on the walls. First-class passengers waited here to travel by carriage to board their liners on the Clyde before sailing on to exotic destinations.

The elaborate frontage features white Doulton Carrara tiles and maritime-theme sculptures by H.H. Martyn & Co. The tiles were designed to resist the pollution in the city that blackened many sandstone buildings.

The Anchor Line had a major influence on day-to-day life in Glasgow for decades, commissioning ships and buildings, transporting thousands of Scots to new lives abroad, as well as employing hundreds of people in shipbuilding yards and ticket offices.

Next door is the old *Citizen's* newspaper building (still bearing the sign) built in the 1880s. Next door, at **number 30**, is John Burnet's ㉒ **Clydesdale Bank headquarters** from the early 1870s.

City Centre Architects Walk

It is an example of a Venetian Renaissance design that was popular when the building was constructed. However, the building's florid style led one architectural critic at the time to describe it as resembling more a casino than a bank.

Look for the figure of Father Clyde above the entrance, carved by Charles Grassby. The allegorical figures and coats of arms were produced by John Mossman (1817-90) – known as the 'father of Glasgow sculpture' and a key member of the Mossman dynasty, which produced dozens of fine sculptures still seen today in Glasgow. They were employed by the best architects of the era to help adorn their buildings.

Continue and turn right into Buchanan Street. On the corner, at number 147, is the ㉓ **former Western Club**, dating from 1842. It is the third design by David Hamilton seen on this walk (in collaboration with his brother James). The Western Club still operates at another location and is the oldest gentlemen's club in the city, founded in 1825. The influence of the Italian palazzo is evident here.

Turn right along Buchanan Street, where on the left is the ㉔ **former Glasgow Stock Exchange** (1877). This was designed by John Burnet Senior in a Gothic style then popular in Britain. It features Mossman's roundels depicting far-flung regions of the world and various trades. Burnet was influenced by the Royal Courts of Justice building on The Strand in London.

His son, J.J., Burnet later worked on alterations to the Exchange. This is a rare

City Centre Architects Walk

reminder of a time when Glasgow and other cities had their own stock exchanges. These days, exchange activity is centred in capital cities like London, New York and Shanghai.

Continue along Buchanan Street and turn left into Nelson Mandela Place.

Around the bend at number 12 is the ㉕ **Royal Faculty of Procurators in Glasgow**. The building dates from 1854 and is another Venetian Renaissance design by Charles Wilson. The home of the city's lawyers, it contains a beautiful library if you can arrange a visit. There are fine keystone portraits here of real-life lawyers. A keystone is a piece of stone or other material at the apex of an arch. In the 19th century it was common to have sculpted faces incorporated into keystones.

Walk further to the junction with West Nile Street. Over on the opposite corner at ㉖ **92 West George Street** is a **modern classical-style former bank** designed by James Miller and dating from 1930. It features Portland Stone and bronze reliefs. Notice how the

City Centre Architects Walk

exterior decorations reflect the changing tastes of the time, much more subtle than the Beaux-Arts era features seen earlier.

Retrace your steps to the Faculty. Next door is the ㉗ **former Glasgow Athenaeum**, dating from 1886. The Athenaeum was a private college designed by J.J. Burnet. Founded in 1847, its school of music later evolved into the Royal Conservatoire of Scotland. Look for John Mossman's statues of Purcell, Reynolds, Wren, and Flaxman outside. At its peak, two thousand students crowded through its entrance.

Re-join Buchanan Street where, on the left at number 179 (now Hard Rock Café), is the ㉘ **former Athenaeum Theatre**. Dating from 1893, it was designed by J.J. Burnet and John Archibald Campbell and is regarded as a pioneering 'elevator' building that showed how new materials and techniques could build a large building on a small plot. Drama students studied here, and it contained a billiard room, dining room, gymnasium and theatre. You can make out the theatre's interior shape if you go inside.

Follow the map, up Buchanan Street, then left along Bath Street, before turning left again into West Nile Street. Further down on the right (at number 99-105 West Nile St, at the junction with Bath Lane) is one of ㉙ **Alexander Thomson's designs**. Dating from 1858, it is one of his lesser-known works. Look for similarities between this and the grander Grosvenor building seen at the start of the walk (imagine the latter with the top floors removed). It

City Centre Architects Walk

contains the decorative border known as a 'meander' or 'Greek key', which Thomson employed in many of his designs, inspired by buildings in the classical tradition.

Continue along Bath Lane to reach Renfield Street. Turn left and stop on the corner of West Regent Street outside the ③⓪ **former Paramount/Odeon art deco cinema**. Dating from 1934, this is the newest building you will visit on this walk.

Designed by Frank Verity and son-in-law Samuel Beverley, it originally occupied half a block and could seat 2,800 people. It symbolises the golden age of cinema building in the city. Within a couple of decades, the television revolution would kill off many cinemas (just as the latter helped kill off the music hall). Verity (1864-1937) was a prominent cinema architect of his era, working primarily for Paramount. The architectural practice of Verity & Beverley continues to this day.

Opposite is ③① **Castle Chambers**. It was designed in a Baronial-Baroque style by the firm of Frank Burnet and Boston, and completed by 1902 with fine sculptures by William Kellock Brown. This was originally the headquarters of the distillers and brewers McLachan & Co.

Keep walking down Renfield Street where, two doors along from Castle Chambers, you will find ③② **no 134-136 West George Street**, a simpler three-storey structure designed by John Burnet in 1867. If you compare this building to the previous one, you get a sense of how architectural tastes changed over time.

City Centre Architects Walk

Continue to the junction with West George Street. On the corner is William Leiper's ㉝ **Sun Life Assurance Building** of 1894. Leiper (1839-1916) was a well-regarded watercolourist who took a career break from architecture to pursue painting. Like CRM, one suspects if finances permitted, he would have preferred an artist's life, rather than competing for commissions in the architectural world.

Leiper is best known in Glasgow for Templeton's Carpet Factory on Glasgow Green, Dowanhill Church, Partick Burgh Hall, and the banqueting hall of Glasgow City Chambers. Most of his work consisted of houses in Helensburgh, and it seems a shame that an architect of his calibre did not design more buildings in Glasgow. He was the equal of his better-known contemporaries.

Designed in a French Renaissance style, this building won international recognition, earning a silver medal at the Paris International Exhibition of 1900. The allegorical figures on the exterior include copies of works by Michelangelo and were designed by William Birnie Rhind (1853-1933), one of the finest architectural sculptors of his generation.

Now turn right into West George Street, where on the right at ㉞ **number 144** is another gargantuan structure by James Sellars, dating from 1879 and now called James Sellars House. The building was home to the New Club and its French Classical style structure is complemented by numerous sculptures by William Mossman Junior. The reclining female figures above the entrance arch represent Summer and Autumn.

When finished, continue along West George Street, then turn left into Hope Street. On the corner at ㉟ **157-167 Hope Street** is a magnificent red sandstone building designed by John Archibald Campbell (1859-1909) and dating from 1902. Campbell (mentioned earlier, see point ㉘), worked as an apprentice for the Burnet architectural practice from 1877.

Like J.J. Burnet, he studied at the *École des Beaux-Arts* in Paris and returned to rejoin the Burnet family practice, becoming a partner in the firm in 1886. Campbell and J.J. Burnet worked well together for a decade, but it seems Campbell's fondness for a drink annoyed

City Centre Architects Walk

33

34

34

35

City Centre Architects Walk

his partner, leading them to go their separate ways. However, this building shows Campbell was the equal of J.J. Burnet and resembles a Spanish-style Alcázar (or fortress). Being an architect in Glasgow was demanding, often requiring long hours and great pressure to win commissions. A fair few developed a dependency on drink.

Continue walking, turning onto St Vincent Street. On the right, at number 144, is the famous ㊱ **Art Nouveau 'Hatrack'**, dating from 1902. It is regarded as the best work of James Salmon Junior (1873-1924) and John Gaff Gillespie (1870-1926). This tall (10-storey) structure is squeezed into a narrow plot and got its nickname due to the projecting features at the top.

James was the third member of his family to practice architecture in Glasgow. His grandfather, James Salmon (1805-1888), designed the new suburb of Dennistoun. His father was William Forrest Salmon (1843-1911). The elder James Salmon began working on building designs in Glasgow in the 1840s, his son William Forrest got involved in the family profession from the 1860s. The younger James and J.G. Gillespie, joined them in 1895, and are credited with designs right up to 1922. Like the Burnets, the Salmon dynasty shaped the city continuously over several decades.

James Salmon and Gillespie were part of a new breed of Glasgow architects who studied at the Glasgow School of Art. Salmon, whose nickname (on account of his size) was the 'Wee Troot', was a close friend of GSA student CRM. Gillespie also had a connection with CRM, as they jointly won the Glasgow Institute of Architects prize in 1889. Would Mackintosh have traded his *Herald* and *Daily Record* buildings (the latter seen shortly), tucked away down dark streets, for the more visible Hatrack building designed by his better-connected friend? I suspect so.

Retrace your steps and continue down Hope Street, to Renfield Lane. On the corner is the ㊲ **former headquarters of Scottish Temperance League** dating from 1894. It

City Centre Architects Walk

was designed by the architectural firm Salmon, Son and Gillespie, with J.Gaff Gillespie taking the lead. Look for the sculptures of Faith, Fortitude and Temperance.

Continue down Renfield Lane. On the left-hand side is the ❸⓼ **rear of the *Daily Record* building** (1904), designed by Mackintosh. This narrow, dark lane was not a prime spot for an ambitious architect like Mackintosh, but he did his best using glazed white tiles to help reflect the light. Mackintosh, along with Herbert McNair, Frances, and Margaret Macdonald, became known as 'The Four' – contributing to the so-called Glasgow Style.

Walk to the end of Renfield Lane, where – at the end on the left – you will find 13-17 Renfield Street, the ❸⓽ **former Cranston's Picture House and Tea Room** (1916), designed in a Beaux-Arts style by James Miller with Richard Gunn.

This was a huge establishment that could accommodate 847 diners and featured a cinema. Miller was commissioned by the catering business founded by tea-room pioneer Stuart Cranston, elder brother of the better-known Kate Cranston.

From here, head down Renfield Street to return to Central Station, marking the end of this walk.

VISIT...

Grosvenor Building
72-80 Gordon St, G1 3RS

The Lighthouse
11 Mitchell Lane, G1 3NU
thelighthouse.co.uk

Gallery of Modern Art
111 Queen St, Royal Exchange Square, G1 3AH
glasgowlife.org.uk

Gallery of Modern Art
111 Queen St, Royal Exchange Square, G1 3AH
glasgowlife.org.uk

EAT/DRINK...

TABAC
10 Mitchell Lane, G1 3NU
tabacbar.com

Sugo
70 Mitchell St, G1 3LX
sugopasta.co.uk

The Corinthian Club
191 Ingram St, G1 1DA
thecorinthianclub.co.uk

Mosob Bar & Restaurant
56 Dundas St, G1 2AQ
mosob.com

Paesano Pizza
94 Miller Street, G1 1DT
paesanopizza.co.uk

Kaffateria
5-7 Dundas St, G1 2AH

Lansdowne Crescent, see p.272

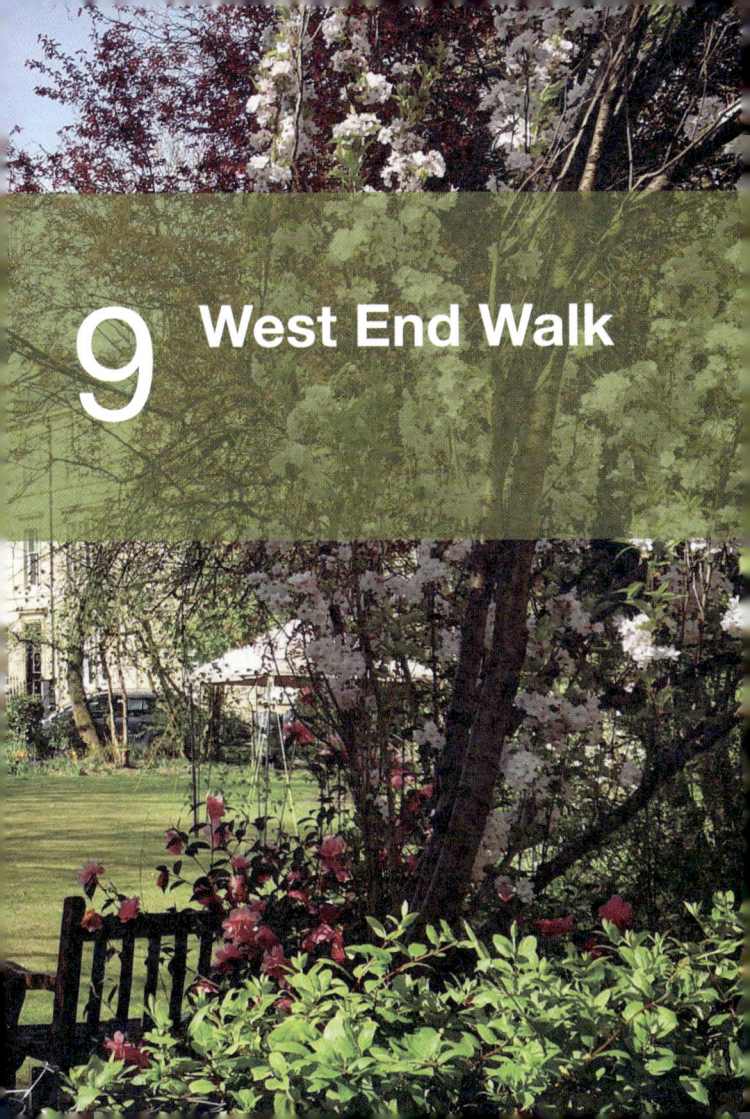

9 West End Walk

West End Walk

1. Kelvinbridge
2. Former Lansdowne Parish Church
3. Lansdowne Crescent
4. St Mary's Scottish Episcopal Cathedral
5. Holyrood Quadrant
6. Junction with Woodlands Drive
7. Former Burnbank Park
8. Al-Furqan Mosque
9. Statue of St George & the Dragon
10. Egyptian-style columns
11. 5 Melrose Street
12. Queen's Crescent
13. 14 Queen's Crescent
14. 4 Queen's Crescent
15. Birthplace of Sir William Ramsay
16. 49 West Prince's Street
17. Woodlands Community Garden
18. Glasgow Lodge of the Theosophical Society
19. Former Albany Academy
20. The Arlington Baths Club
21. Postcard Records
22. The Arlington Bar
23. Free Presbyterian Church of Scotland
24. Blonde sandstone villas
25. Lynedoch Crescent
26. 11 Woodside Terrace
27. 6 Park Gardens
28. Park Gardens Lane
29. Lord Roberts Monument
30. 22 Park Circus
31. Park Church Tower
33. Statue of Lobey Dosser & Rank Bajin
34. Former Willowbank Public School
35. Willowbank Community Garden
36. Burnbank Bowling Club
37. Former Woodside Public School
38. Shish Mahal
39. St Silas Church
40. Single-storey café
41. Staircase

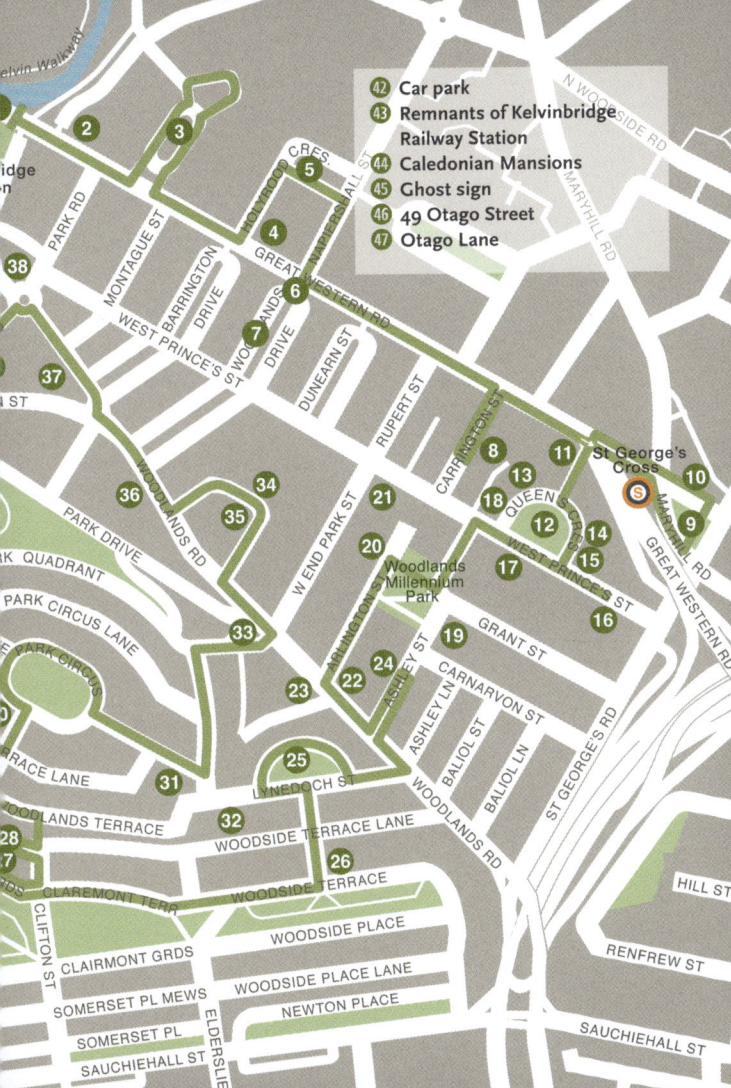

West End Walk

Start/Finish: Kelvinbridge subway station
Distance: 3 miles

This walk begins at ❶ **Kelvinbridge** (or Great Western Bridge). The third bridge on this site, completed in 1891, spans the River Kelvin near the historic ford that was used for centuries. The river originates near the village of Banton, 22 miles away. The renowned Glasgow firm Walter Macfarlane & Co supplied the cast iron railings and other decorative features. There is another Macfarlane connection later on. The iron and steel components were supplied by the Sir William Arrol & Co., best known for work on the Forth Bridge and London's Tower Bridge.

Walk eastwards down Great Western Road. This was originally a toll road after being established in 1840 by an Act of Parliament. Before then, this district was semi-rural, and an early 19th-century map of Glasgow doesn't even include it. The road's construction was part of the relentless expansion of the city as the 19th century progressed.

Kelvinbridge is now a popular area, filled with cafés, restaurants, and bars that attract a diverse crowd. In recent years, it even featured in one of *Time Out's* 'coolest neighbourhood' lists.

The first point of interest along Glasgow's 'Boulevard' is the ❷ **former Lansdowne Parish Church**, now home to Webster's theatre and bar. Dating from 1863, the church was designed by John Honeyman (1831-1914) in the Gothic revival style. Honeyman, one of the city's finest architects, later partnered with John Keppie, and both are best known today for recruiting Charles Rennie Mackintosh.

This building is celebrated for its stained glass, made by Al Webster in 1913. Webster tragically died of wounds inflicted at Ypres during World War I, but his name lives on through the theatre.

West End Walk

Turn left into ❸ **Lansdowne Crescent**, a charming street lined with elegant villas and upscale houses built for the city's wealthier residents during the 19th century. On an 1857 map, the crescent stands alone, surrounded by open land. As you walk along it clockwise, you'll notice that most of the buildings date from the mid-1850s. The lovely private gardens you pass hint at the exclusivity of the area—there are no community gardens here, unfortunately. The top end of the Crescent, with its absence of cars, could easily serve as a location in a Victorian period drama.

Back on the Great Western Road, walk towards the spire of ❹ **St Mary's Scottish Episcopal Cathedral**. It dates back to 1871, with the spire finally completed in 1891. It was designed by George Gilbert Scott (1811-1878), known for his Gothic Revival style and responsible for over 800 buildings. Many of his finest works are in London, including the Albert Memorial, though Glasgow also boasts several examples, such as the University of Glasgow building. The Scottish Episcopal Church is the third-largest Christian denomination in Scotland.

While at the cathedral, take a moment to admire the gargoyles. Many represent the stonemasons, builders, and clergymen who restored the cathedral a few decades ago. In 2001, one of those immortalised in stone, the Right Rev. Idris Jones, remarked: 'The stonemasons have been very generous—I look like a cheerful cherub'.

Follow the map up Holyrood Crescent, then right into ❺ **Holyrood Quadrant**,

West End Walk

passing a pleasant private garden. In the 1850s, two quarries lay a stone's throw north of here providing some of the sandstone used in tenements and villas built in that era. Within a few years, the old quarries disappeared and were replace by residential streets.

After the garden, turn right down Napiershall Road to rejoin Great Western Road. This was once a significant tram route. If you look opposite the Cathedral, towards the ❻ **junction with Woodlands Drive**, you can spot the old hooks (or 'rosettes') on the first floor, which once held the cross-street wires that supplied power to trams. These hooks serve as a reminder of Glasgow's tram system – once the largest in Europe before it closed in 1962. Look out for more as you continue along – there are many scattered throughout the area.

Down Woodlands Drive is the former site of ❼ **Burnbank Park**, which was founded in the late 19th century. This open space was initially a drill ground for the 1st Lanarkshire Rifle Volunteers and was later leased to sports clubs, including Rangers FC, who played here during the 1875-76 season. The park was also used by cricket, football, and rugby clubs, including Glasgow Academicals RFC.

Continue along Great Western Road, observing the varying colours of sandstone used in the tenement buildings. As a rule of thumb, cream sandstone was used from the mid-19th century, often sourced from local quarries. The red sandstone, so typical of Victorian Glasgow, became popular from the 1890s and into the early 20th century. This shift occurred as local quarries were exhausted, and new railway lines made it easier to transport the more durable red sandstone from quarries in Dumfries and Ayrshire. Look for colourful mosaic bollards designed by local people.

Bollards

West End Walk

Next, turn down Carrington Street to see ⑧ **the Al-Furqan Mosque**. A sign of Glasgow's evolving cultural landscape, this mosque, dating from 1984, is the second purpose-built mosque in the city. Unlike traditional mosques, it is multi-denominational, meaning it does not adhere to a specific school of thought within the Muslim faith. In Victorian times, the Burnbank U.P Church and hall stood on this site, accommodating up to 1,000 worshippers.

Follow the map to St George's Cross subway station and onwards to the green space containing the ⑨ **statue of St George and the Dragon**. Unfortunately, much of the impressive 19th-century development at St George's Cross was demolished to make way for the M8 motorway, leaving the area dominated by traffic with little appeal. The statue, dating from 1897, was designed by the well-known Mossman family of sculptors. It used to be found on the St George's Cross Co-operative Society building that stood nearby but moved here after the building was demolished.

West End Walk

Just opposite, look for ❿ **Egyptian-style columns** of a building constructed in the 1830s. It is the only remaining element of what was planned as a circus-shaped development and a rare reminder of how charming this area was before the arrival of modern roads. The building was home to Massey's grocery store, just one of several founded by Alexander Massey. His business began in the Gorbals in 1872 and became a Glasgow institution until he sold up in 1930 (this area was called Massey's Corner).

Retrace your steps up Great Western Road, then turn left into Melrose Street. In the early 19th century slavery was finally abolished in the British Empire, and as part of the compromise with vested interests, slave owners were compensated for their loss. At that time ⓫ **Number 5 Melrose Street** was home to Elizabeth Muirhead, who was born in Kingston Jamaica. Contemporary records describe her mother as a 'free mulatto,' and Elizabeth partly 'owned' five slaves in Jamaica. She received £109 2s 7d in compensation when they were freed (the former slaves received nothing).

Continue on to ⓬ **Queen's Crescent**. This is part of Woodlands, a residential district constructed in the 19th century. In 1795, this area was part of the Blythswood Estate, primarily consisting of open fields dotted with country houses, mines, and quarries. The opening of Great Western Road helped transform the area, attracting developers and property speculators keen to attract the city's wealthier citizens. Where you are standing was

West End Walk

Queen's Crescent

developed in the 1840s, and principally designed by John Bryce (1805-51). However, development was slow, and the crescent stood alone for years before the surrounding residential streets were laid out.

The fountain in the middle of the private garden stands over the entrance to a mine. The legacy of mines has caused structural problems for some local buildings, which in the past negatively affected property prices.

Walk right to arrive at ⑬ **14 Queen's Crescent**, where slave owner William Kirkland lived. In the mid-1830s he received several thousand pounds in compensation from the British government for the hundreds of slaves living on the 'Dumfries Estate' in Grenada.

Now walk in the other direction around Queen's Crescent stopping at ⑭ **Number 4**. This was home to Glasgow's first official gay nightclub – The Club. Founded by the Scottish Homosexual Rights Group, it opened in 1980 with three discos every week. Since homosexuality was not decriminalised in Scotland until 1980, The Club faced considerable controversy, particularly from some of the neighbours. It closed in 1982.

Number 2 was the ⑮ **birthplace of Sir William Ramsay** (1852-1916), who was awarded the Nobel Prize for Chemistry in 1904. Ramsay discovered argon, helium, neon, krypton, and xenon.

Educated at the nearby Glasgow Academy, he almost pursued a career in shipbuilding.

When you reach West Prince's Street, head to ⓰ **number 49**. This was where on 21st December 1908, an 82-year-old woman named Marion Gilchrist was brutally murdered. A German immigrant named Oscar Slater was convicted of the murder, but a high-profile campaign to prove his innocence was supported by Sherlock-creator Sir Arthur Conan Doyle. Slater was later released from prison, and his conviction was quashed in 1928. Conan Doyle, who involved himself in other real-crime cases, wrote a book about Slater. Gilchrist's murder remains unsolved and is featured in Jack House's classic 1961 book *The Square Mile of Murder*.

Look down the street to see the M8. Before it was built, you could have walked directly along here and then Shamrock Street to reach Cowcaddens.

Follow the map to ⓱ **Woodlands Community Garden**, an inspiring local space founded by residents on a derelict site after some houses were burnt down. The garden connects local people and produces a considerable harvest of vegetables and fruit.

Opposite is the ⓲ **Glasgow Lodge of the Theosophical Society** at 17 Queen's Crescent. The society espouses various New Age and esoteric beliefs, tracing its origins mainly to Russian Helena Petrovna Blavatsky, who founded the society with others in New York in 1875.

West End Walk

19

20

20

22

West End Walk

Walk down Ashley Street, where on the left you'll find a striking building designed in the Renaissance villa style, dating from around 1875. Originally known as **19** **Albany Academy**, it is believed to be the work of H&D Barclay, a distinguished architectural practice of its time. Hugh and David Barclay together designed more than forty schools in Glasgow. The figures on the front are Dante (on the left) and Homer (on the right). This was later home to the **Glasgow Gaelic School.**

Cross through Woodlands Millenium Park to visit **20** **The Arlington Baths Club** – one of the oldest institutions in Woodlands, dating from 1871. Like the Albany Academy, the construction of baths, churches, schools, drill halls, bowling greens, and other institutions in this new suburb was intended to serve the educational, spiritual, and physical needs of residents.

The baths were designed by John Burnet (1814-1901), an esteemed architect and father of the equally gifted Sir J.J. Burnet. This Victorian gem claims to be the oldest club of its kind in the world. It features a unique Turkish relaxation suite, a steam room, a sauna, and a swimming pool with acrobatic equipment. The original club was frequented by many middle-class locals who would often visit each morning and evening to exercise. One can only speculate what they would have thought of the nude swimming and yoga sessions held here more recently.

Behind the baths is the location of **21** **Postcard Records**, founded in a flat at 185 West Princes Street by Alan Horne in 1980. Its acts included bands such as Orange Juice, Aztec Camera, Josef K and The Go-Betweens.

Now walk down Arlington Street, where on the corner with Woodlands Road is **22** **Arlington Bar**. A true locals' pub, it claims to be home to the Stone of Destiny. The story goes that Jacob – from the Old Testament – had a pillow made of stone that somehow made its way to Scotland. For centuries, the Stone of Destiny sat beneath the coronation chair used for Scottish monarchs in Scone. It was then stolen by the English and used for the same purpose in Westminster Abbey. In 1950, Glasgow University students liberated the Stone and brought it back to Scotland, apparently celebrating in the bar.

West End Walk

They were obliged to return it, but provided a replica, with the original allegedly discovered in the bar. The official Stone of Destiny was returned to Scotland in 1996 and is now kept in Edinburgh Castle. However, the Arlington's version of the story is far more enjoyable.

Nearly opposite the bar is the French Gothic-styled ㉓ **Free Presbyterian Church**, originally named St Jude's. It dates from around 1875 and was also designed by John Burnet Senior. Walk along Woodlands Road (the Arlington on your left) and turn left down Ashley Street. A short way down on the left, you'll see some ㉔ **blonde sandstone villas** built in a classical style in the 1850s.

The Shia Asna Ashri Islamic Centre at number 19 reflects how ethnically diverse this area has become in recent decades. The centre made the news in 2019 when it was reported that it was being investigated by the charity watchdog. It was also picketed by exiles from Iran who, according to *The Times*, regarded it as 'Tehran's unofficial consulate in Scotland,' a claim denied by officials and the Iranian embassy in London. Though far from the Middle East, Woodlands is not immune to global politics.

Retrace your steps to Woodlands Road and cross over, heading up Lynedoch Street and into the Park Circus district, one of the most exclusive areas in Glasgow. You are ascending both geographically and socially. Many of the older buildings are from the 1840s, including those on Lynedoch Crescent, to your right.

Bear right around ㉕ **Lynedoch Crescent**. When it was built, it was popular with wealthy industrialists, merchants and professionals who sought more exclusive residences in the west side of Glasgow, safely isolated from the working classes, pollution and heavy industries.

West End Walk

A map of 1844 shows this area still being sketched out: a few buildings stood amongst empty streets yet to be developed. By 1857, however, it was a very different story. Most of what you see today had been built – a monumental effort by developers, architects, builders, and labourers. The new Park District, carved out of a hilltop, would be crowned by Park Circus (seen shortly).

The view up the hill is dominated by the towers of the old theological college, which you will learn more about later. Turn left down Lynedoch Terrace to reach Woodside Terrace. On the corner is ㉖ **number 11**, which was home in the 19th century to a lawyer named Andrew Bannatyne. He became embroiled in a dispute over who was entitled to compensation for 144 slaves on the Good Hope plantation in British Guiana in 1835. Bannatyne's client held a mortgage over the slaves, much like a bank holds a mortgage over a house, and disputed the slave owners' right to compensation of £7,168 15s 6d.

Many houses here were built in the early 1840s and designed by architect George

25

26

West End Walk

Smith (1793-1877). Smith was once dismissed by an employer who called him 'ignorant and useless'. Despite this setback, he recovered to design several houses in the Park District and was responsible for other buildings across Scotland from the 1820s until his death.

Turn right down Woodside Terrace, which becomes Claremont Terrace. Several buildings along here are attributed to John Baird I (1798-1859) and date from the mid-1840s. Baird was a leading architect, though never as famous as his first apprentice – Alexander 'Greek' Thomson. Baird nearly won the commission to design the Necropolis cemetery.

Soon you reach Park Gardens, and if you thought the list of notable 19th-century architects involved in the development of this area could not get any longer, you'd be mistaken. The houses here were designed by Charles Wilson (1810-63), who was also responsible for a substantial part of the original plan for the Park District, regarded by many as the finest example of Victorian town planning in Britain.

Retrace your steps, stopping outside ㉗ **number 6 Park Gardens**. While the Park Circus district can feel like it exists in its own bubble, this was not the case on 24 July 1913. Members of the Suffragette movement carried out several violent protests in Glasgow, ranging from arson attacks on post boxes to an attempt to set fire to this building. Ethel Moorhead (1869-1955) and Dr Dorothea Chalmers Smith (1874-1944) were arrested at the scene, carrying a card that stated their action was 'A protest against Mrs Pankhurst's re-arrest'. Both women ended up in the infamous Duke Street Prison, where Moorhead became the first suffragette to be force-fed.

West End Walk

Retrace your steps, turning uphill along Clifton Street. Take a detour on the left into ㉘ **Park Gardens Lane** – a charming mews built under a grass-covered terrace. This is one of the most hidden residential spots in the city, and numbers 1-2 were remodeled by Sir J.J. Burnet in 1906.

Continue up the steps to reach Woodlands Terrace. In front of you are more houses by Charles Wilson and John Baird I, dating from the mid-1800s. Turn left, continuing along with Kelvingrove Park to your left. You soon pass the Youth Hostel at number 7-8, one of the most impressive hostel locations in Britain. Look for the carriage stones opposite the entrance to several houses. These stones were used by people getting in and out of horse-drawn carriages.

Soon you'll reach an entrance into Kelvingrove Park. Turn in to find the ㉙ **Lord Roberts Monument**, dating from 1916. Eton-educated Lord Frederick Sleigh Roberts (1832-1914) symbolised the zenith of the British Empire. Nearly as famous in his day as Wellington had been before him, Roberts led a charmed life, serving in campaigns all over the world. He won a Victoria Cross during the Indian Mutiny and led the armed forces during the Boer War and World War I.

The figures on the monument recall these key moments, although to modern eyes they can appear as unsettling reminders of Britain's past. This is a copy of a memorial that once stood in The Maiden,

Carriage Stone

a park in Kolkata (previously Calcutta). It was designed by Harry Bates (1850-99), who studied in Paris and knew Rodin.

This site was also the location of Russian cannons from the Crimean War, described as 'Russian Trophies' on old maps. The nearby bench is worth a stop for tea and a sandwich, offering one of the best views in Glasgow. Kelvingrove Park, originally called the West End Park when created in 1852, provided a place for the new residents of the Park District to enjoy.

In Bill Forsyth's Glasgow-set film *That Sinking Feeling* (1979), Ronnie (Ronald Buchanan) has a conversation with the statue after reading the inscription describing Lord Roberts' many achievements:

> Kandahar, eh?
> Nicely done, Earl.
> Oh, wait a minute here.
> I don't see too many 'O' levels there,
> Earl old son.
> How did you do it?
> And why the bloody hell
> don't I have a job?

Ronnie's speech disturbs a man sleeping on the bench who shouts 'Oi! Go on your bike! I'm trying to sleep here'. Retrace your steps out of the park. Walk along Park Gate, then take Park Terrace Lane on the right. Continue on this quiet lane, passing little cottages that feel a world away from busy Glasgow. This lane was once home to stables and coach houses serving wealthy residents in the neighbouring large houses.

On the left, look for the back of one building with a cast-iron rear extension. This is ㉚ **22 Park Circus**, regarded as the finest residence in the area. It was built in the 1870s for industrialist Walter MacFarlane, and contained the most sumptuous interior of any city residence.

MacFarlane made his fortune from the Saracen Foundry, which produced ornamental metalwork exported worldwide. His firm supplied some of the metalwork for the Great Western Bridge. The building's interior is attributed to architect James Boucher, whose name can be found high up on the rear of the building. Boucher collaborated with MacFarlane on other projects.

At the end of the lane, turn left into Park Street South, and then on to reach oval-shaped Park Circus, the heart of Wilson's plan. Turn left to see the exterior of 22. From 1934, it was home to Casa D'Italia, a community centre for Scots-Italians. For decades, Scots-Italians came here for dances, dinners, language classes, and other social activities, with many meeting their future spouses at these events. It also served as the Italian consulate and later the city's register office.

This is one of the most desirable residential areas in Scotland, on par with anything in Edinburgh's Georgian New Town. However, as a visitor, it seems pretty soulless and quiet. You may spot a grand piano, but will you see anyone playing it?

In the late 18th century, the editor of the *Glasgow Herald*, James McNayr, built a house called 'Woodlands' on top of the hill. This Gothic construction was so remote from the city that it became known as 'McNayr's Folly'. Little did they know how things change.

This area could have been very different if history had taken a different course. In the 1840s, the summit of the hill was designated as the new site for Glasgow University (then situated by the High Street). The plans fell through, and the university moved to Gilmorehill instead.

Continue clockwise around Park Circus, passing more Wilson designs. Most of the buildings you pass were constructed between 1855-1863. The streets, often described as French in style, follow the

Park Circus

West End Walk

West End Walk

hill's contours. Over time, many of the houses became too large for even wealthy Glaswegians and were converted into offices. Institutions with international connections include the German *Goethe Institute* and the French *Alliance Française*. This is Range Rover country, along with many other luxury car brands you will no doubt spot in the area.

Walk down Park Circus Place. On the right is the ㉛ **tower of the old Park Church**, built in the 1850s. The rest of the church was demolished in 1968, and an office block built around the tower.

Cross to Lynedoch Street to see the magnificent ㉜ **former theological college** (or Trinity College) building. Its towers are more familiar to Glaswegians than the history of the College. In 1843, a great split occurred within the Church of Scotland, with many leaving to form the Free Church of Scotland. The latter developed its own colleges or seminaries, separate from the theology courses taught at the existing universities. This led to the opening of Glasgow College in 1856. When the United Free Church and Church of Scotland reunited in 1929, their teaching facilities were merged, resulting in the new name of Trinity College.

The college and adjacent church were designed by Charles Wilson. Trinity remained here until 1976 and continues as a Church of Scotland college at the University of Glasgow. The towers of the old college have been compared to the towers of San Gimignano in Tuscany.

Follow the map up Lynedoch Place to reach Woodlands Road again. On the corner is a ㉝ **statue of Lobey Dosser and Rank Bajin** on top of 'El Fideldo', a two-legged horse. The characters were created by Partick-born cartoonist William 'Bud' Neill (1911-1970). His work appeared in Glasgow newspapers from the 1940s to the 1960s. The statue was erected by public subscription in 1992.

Turn left into Woodlands Road, then right and down Willowbank Street. At the end is the ㉞ **former Willowbank Public School**, erected in 1900 by The School Board of Glasgow. It was designed by Alexander Petrie (1842-1905), now an obscure architect but who, over 30 years, built dozens of schools and churches.

West End Walk

This was one of many schools constructed by the Board after free state education was introduced by the Education (Scotland) Act of 1872. The school closed in 2010 and is now used for student accommodation. Before the school, the site was occupied by Willowbank Bowling Green, with an army drill hall on the north side.

Opposite is ❸❺ **Willowbank Community Garden** – further evidence of how the local community is proactive in using scraps of land for new purposes.

Continue down Willowbank Crescent to rejoin Woodlands Road and turn right. On the other side is ❸❻ **Burnbank Bowling Club**, one of many founded when Glasgow began to spread westwards. It has been going since 1866, and if you pop in to say hello, one of the members may show you the old photographs of the club stretching back to the late 19th century. This club occupies the site of Herbert's Farm of Woodlands.

Stroll along Woodlands Road, passing the ❸❼ **former Woodside Public School** on the corner – now a pub fittingly called The Old Schoolhouse. This building was designed by Robert Dalglish and dates from 1882. Look up on the side to see the 'School Board of Glasgow' sign (the school closed in 1999).

The Stand Comedy Club occupies the basement of the next-door building, an extension to the original school. Many comedians developed their careers here, including Frankie Boyle and Kevin Bridges. There is less laughter upstairs, where the Scottish Trades Union Congress have offices.

West End Walk

If you had been walking here in the 1840s, the whole area to the right of what was then called South Woodside Road was occupied by Woodside Quarry.

Just ahead, over the mini roundabout, is the ❸❽ **Shish Mahal**, which has been serving Indian food to Glaswegians for decades. The famous dish tikka masala was invented in the 1970s by the owner and Glasgow's 'curry king' Ali Ahmed Aslam, after a customer complained his meal was too dry. Mr Ali added some tinned tomato soup and spices. His own father is credited with opening the city's first proper Indian restaurant in 1959 (on Bank Street). Back in the 1840s, the whole area from the restaurant to the River Kelvin to the west was occupied by Woodside Village.

Turn left and continue down Park Road, passing ❸❾ **St Silas Church** – the second on this walk designed by John Honeyman (this dates from 1864).

As you reach Eldon Street, look for a ❹⓪ **single-storey café** that used to be a public toilet. On the right is Eusebi Deli, a great Scots-Italian family-owned establishment founded in 1954 – worth a visit if you are in need of a break.

Immediately after the deli, head down a ❹❶ **staircase** leading to the path by the River Kelvin. To the left, along the path you can see a closed-off tunnel. By the 1850s, the old village had largely disappeared, replaced by Woodside Paper Mills and a cotton power loom factory on the land just south of today's ❹❷ car park. Soon after, the Glasgow

West End Walk

Closed off tunnel

44

44

Central Line railway would run right by the river here. To your left, the railway line ran through the tunnel, under Kelvingrove Park, and to the next station at Stobcross. To your right, the line ran by the river's edge to Kelvinbridge station, then under Great Western Road to the next station at Botanic Gardens.

Follow the map, passing the car park, and crossing to the other side of the river. Continue on to see the ㊸ remains of **Kelvinbridge railway station**, which operated between 1892-1964. It was the work of James Miller (1860-1947), one of the most prolific architects of his time, best known for his many designs for the Caledonian Railway Company. The company operated the Glasgow Central Railway line, and a goods station occupied approximately the site of the current car park beside the subway. The Glasgow Central Railway opened in 1894 and was closed in stages until the mid-1960s.

Walk up the stairs just before the bridge and look for ㊹ **Caledonian Mansions**, a James Miller Arts & Crafts design from 1895. Look for the 'C' and 'R' under the sign for Caledonian Crescent, standing for the Caledonian Railway that owned the building. It was intended to accommodate guests who could not get into the Central Station Hotel.

Walk down the Crescent, and (with due care and attention) look over the wall on the right to see a stretch of the old railway line and tunnel. The Glasgow Central Railway line was an impressive feat of engineering, made even more so because public pressure

43 Remains of Kelvinbridge Railway Station & 44 Caledonian Mansions

West End Walk

forced the Caledonian Railway to construct five of the seven miles of track underground through tunnels.

Soon you reach Otago Street, with The National Piping Centre directly in front. On your left is the Guru Nanak Sikh Temple. Look at the ㊺ **ghost sign** above number 37, a late 19th-century building. This sign advertised Red Hackle whisky, founded in 1920 by two veterans of the World War I who had served in the Black Watch regiment. The Red Hackle refers to the red feather worn in the caps of the Black Watch soldiers.

Walk down to number ㊻ **49 Otago Street**, where you'll find the two-storey Janefield Cottage, dating from c.1840. There are few examples of this style of cottage left in Glasgow, and it is one of the oldest buildings in Hillhead – the district you have entered on the other side of the Kelvin. Why Otago Street? No one is entirely sure, but it's likely because Otago in New Zealand had become a destination for many Scots, and a shipping line ran a service there.

Continue to ㊼ **Otago Lane**, one of the coolest small streets in Glasgow. You can browse books in the Voltaire & Rousseau bookshop, vinyl in Mixed Up Records, or relax in the Tchai-Ovna tea room. In recent years, these local institutions have been fighting back against redevelopment plans for the area.

You can now retrace your steps to Great Western Road, where this walk ends. You can turn right here to reach Kelvinbridge subway station.

VISIT

Websters Theatre
416 Great Western Rd, G4 9HZ
webstersglasgow.com

Kelvingrove Park
Park Terrace, G3 6BY
kelvingrovepark.com

The Stand Comedy Club
333 Woodlands Rd, G3 6NG
thestand.co.uk

EAT & DRINK

Cottonrake Bakery
497 Great Western Rd,
G12 8HL
cottonrake.com

Sonny & Vito's Deli Café
52 Park Road, G4 9JG
0141 357 0640

Bananamoon
360 Great Western Rd,
G4 9HT
Bananamoonbar.com

The Hug and Pint
171 Great Western Rd, G4 9AW
thehugandpint.com

The Arlington
130 Woodlands Rd, G3 6HB
arlingtonbar.co.uk

Mrs Falafel
1 Ashley St, G3 6DR

Eusebi Deli
152 Park Rd, G4 9HB
eusebideli.com

Tchai-Ovna Tea Room
33 Otago St, G12 8JJ
Tchaiovna.com

Stravaigin
28 Gibson St, G12 8NX
stravaigin.co.uk

'Buffalo Bill' statue, see p.310

10 Dennistoun Walk

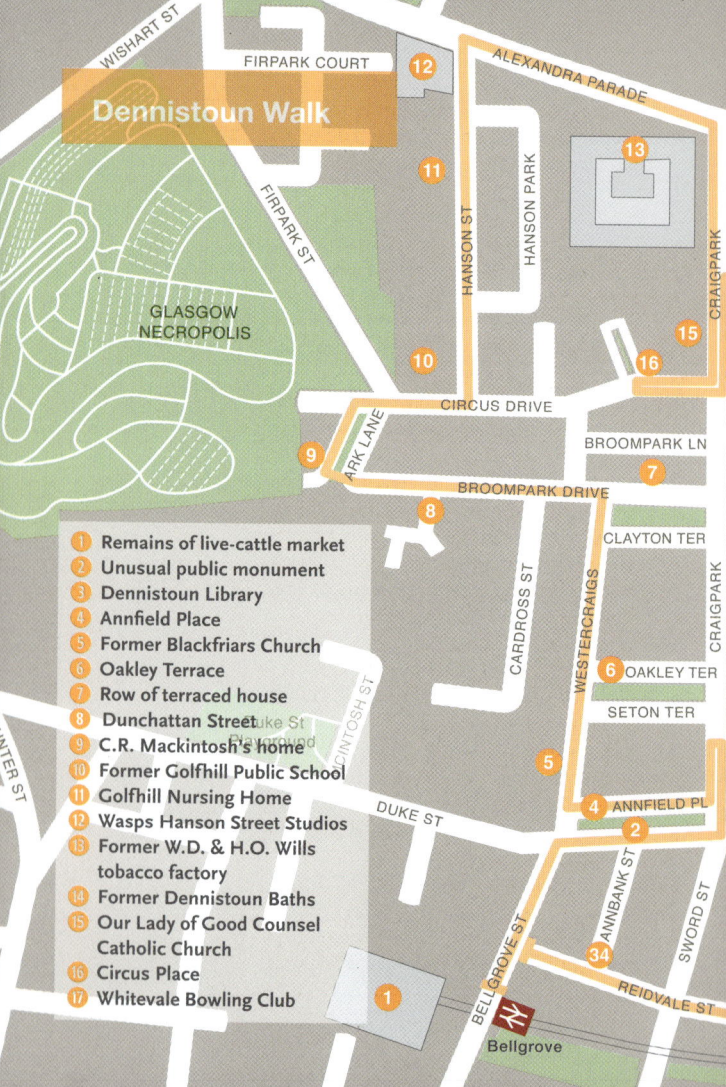

Dennistoun Walk

Start/Finish: Bellgrove railway station
Length 3.5 miles

The east-end suburb of Dennistoun is the main focus of this walk. In recent years, the area has become considerably gentrified and was featured in *Time Out's* list of the world's coolest neighbourhoods. However, as you will see today, much of it remains a quiet suburb with some fine houses and many tenement-lined streets.

Walk north up Bellgrove Street (with the station to your right). The ❶ **derelict land and buildings** on your left are remnants of the city's live-cattle and dead meat market. The first buildings for the live cattle market were constructed over the existing Graham Square after 1817, and it was later extended. By 1911, the complex was vast, extending up to Duke Street.

Originally, animals were brought here along streets, but later, many arrived by train at the Bellgrove Cattle Market station. The main market was on the east side, the meat market to the southwest, and the abattoir to the northwest. The site closed in the late 1960s and was subsequently used as a car auction site. By the time you do this walk the site may have been redeveloped.

In the 18th century, there used to be a street here called Witch Loan, which later became the north side of Bellgrove. The name 'Belle' comes from the English and Scots given name 'Bel,' derived from the Old French 'beu' or 'bel' meaning 'handsome'. Bellgrove was once a narrow road, with a row of trees on each side and a small ditch running from Duke Street to Gallowgate.

Continue to the junction and turn right onto Duke Street – said to be the longest street in Britain, though this claim remains uncertain. The creation of Duke Street in the 1790s is linked to the Industrial Revolution. The Carron Company of Falkirk promoted the street's development to improve the connection between Glasgow and Cumbernauld and further on to Carron.

Cross to the other side of Duke Street (opposite Annbank Street) and look for an ❷ **unusual public monument**. Unveiled in 1991, it was created as part of a series of seven milestones in the city to celebrate Glasgow's status as European City of Culture in 1990. It was sponsored by WD & HO Wills, the tobacco company then situated on Alexandra Parade, and designed by Jim Buckley of Glasgow Sculpture Studios. The monument was intended as a time capsule, containing an image of the Glasgow skyline and some mementoes behind glass.

Head up Craigpark Street and stop at ❸ **Dennistoun Library**. It opened in 1905 and was funded by a donation from Andrew Carnegie, the Scottish-American multi-millionaire who, despite being notorious for his maltreatment of employees, did fund many libraries around the world, including several in Glasgow. This enabled generations of working-class people to access information that would otherwise have been out of their reach. The library was designed in an Edwardian Baroque style by James R. Rhind (1853-1918), who also designed six other Carnegie libraries in Glasgow.

Sculptor William Kellock Brown produced the Glasgow coat of arms above the entrance, and figures representing Literature and Geography. The winged female on the dome is known as 'The Dennistoun Angel'. If it is open, the lobby contains old photographs of many places in Dennistoun.

Dennistoun Walk

Dennistoun Walk

Walk down ❹ **Annfield Place**. You will learn more about the creation of Dennistoun shortly, but initially, Annfield Place was all that existed here. In 1838, merchant John Reid began buying up land here and feuing it to developers. He died in 1851, just as Annfield Place was being completed. It remains the only part of his plan to survive. Had Reid not died so early, this district may have been named after him. On a map of the mid-1850s, Annfield Place stands alone, surrounded by open land, with only the odd building between here and what is now Alexandra Parade, over half a mile to the north.

Follow the map up Westercraigs, looking for the stone-gate pillars (by Duke Street) that indicate this was originally a gated community. Turn right up Westercraigs. Before proceeding further, it is worth reading a little about the beginning of the Dennistoun story.

In the mid-17th century, the powerful Merchant's House acquired much of the land here, which later divided into Easter Craigs and Wester Craigs.

Wester Craigs was further divided into distinct fields or parks, such as Craigs Park, Broom Park, and Golfhill. The Merchant's House sold off land to wealthy people who wanted to create estates outside of Glasgow (then centred around a dozen or so streets to the west of here). Throughout this walk, you will encounter streets named after these country estates and houses.

One wealthy man who acquired land here was James Dennistoun (1758-1835). He made his money through a transatlantic trading company with interests in tobacco, cotton, and banking. Golfhill House was built by James shortly after he bought the estate in 1802. His son, Alexander Dennistoun (1789-1874), grew up in Golfhill House and decided to create a new East End suburb from nothing.

Cross to the ❺ **former Blackfriars Church**, dating from 1877. It housed five bells, a rare complete set made by the Gorbals Bell and Brass Foundry. This replaced the original Blackfriars church, which stood within the Dominican friary by the High Street (later incorporated as a church within the old University of Glasgow campus). The Dominicans (or 'Blackfriars' due to the colour of their habits) founded a friary in Glasgow in 1246.

Dennistoun Walk

Continue up Westercraigs, which is lined with many superb 19th-century villas. In 1854, Alexander Dennistoun employed architect James Salmon (1805-1888) to plan the new suburb. The result was an architect's dream – a 200-acre site of grand villas, boulevards, avenues, and parks. It promised a new community in a part of Glasgow traditionally seen as beyond the pale by much of respectable society.

Adverts referred to 'New Suburb Proposed to be Added to Glasgow...self-contained houses, the lands of Golfhill, Craigpark, Meadowpark, Whitehill, Wester Craigs and Broompark...'. They also spoke of the desire of the 'middle class of Glasgow to reside in self-contained houses of moderate rent and price in preference to the present system of common stairs and common flats'. The suburb was envisioned with 'streets.....of unusual width, and being planned on the best continental models, will present in squares, boulevards, fountains etc, a style of beauty not hitherto followed out in this country.' Furthermore, as 'no shops or trading of any kind (were)permitted in its principal thoroughfares', the suburb promised 'a quiet, select and well classified neighbourhood'.

Unfortunately, the grand plans were not attractive enough. By the early 1870s, most of Salmon's original plan had been abandoned. It was too ambitious, and the middle-class Glaswegians targeted by Alexander Dennistoun were not persuaded to move here in sufficient numbers. Four of the originally planned terraces did appear – Seton, Oakley, Broompark, and Clayton. Villas were also constructed in Circus Drive, Craigpark, and Westercraigs. However, after this, the rest of the district was filled in with Victorian-era tenement buildings, as will become evident.

As you head up the hill, turn round and take in the view to the south of Glasgow. You can see why houses so high up, away from pollution, would have been attractive to those who could afford them.

On the right, you pass **Seton Terrace** and then ❻ **Oakley Terrace**, both sought-after residential streets dating from the mid-19th century. Number 10 Oakley Terrace was the home of Sir William Arrol (1839-1913), the civil engineer known for his bridges,

Dennistoun Walk

particularly the Forth Bridge. He moved here in 1880, conveniently close to his Dalmarnock Iron Works.

Oakley Terrace is named after the Oakley family, one of whom was the wife of Alexander Dennistoun's son. Other streets named after spouses of family members include Finlay, Ingleby, Wood, and Onslow Streets. The Dennistoun family's other residences also give their names to Armadale, Roselea and Garthland.

If Salmon's grand plan had been fully realised, Dennistoun might have been the finest Victorian suburb in Scotland and as well-known as Edinburgh's New Town. However, even though Dennistoun's development was more modest than originally intended, its tenements attracted aspirational working-class people, who felt they had 'made it' by moving here from less salubrious parts of the East End.

You soon reach Broompark Drive. On the opposite side to your right is ❼ **a row of two-storey late 19th-century terrace houses**. Turn left along the Drive, passing ❽ **Dunchattan Street** on the left. The Dennistoun suburb was largely built on open land and estates acquired from wealthy owners. However, there was some industry on the site of what is now an estate. George MacIntosh (d.1807) founded a factory in the 1770s that produced a dye called cudbear, which was used by textile manufacturers.

The factory was located on the Dunchattan estate, which contained Dunchattan House and a model village

Bluebells blooming, Clayton Terrace

Dennistoun Walk

for workers. To protect his trade secrets, MacIntosh employed Gaelic-speaking Highlanders who were sworn to secrecy. These workers were isolated within the factory grounds, enclosed by a ten-foot-high wall. Every morning, a roll call was conducted in Gaelic to maintain confidentiality. Dunchattan House, where MacIntosh lived, stood west of what is now Cardross Street, leading up to Broompark Drive. MacIntosh's son, Charles, carried on the family's innovative spirit. In the early 19th century, Charles found a way to dissolve India rubber and use it to waterproof textiles – the result being the 'Mackintosh' coat.

Continue right around the bend into Ark Lane. On the left is Firpark Terrace, a tenement street where – at number 2 – **Charles Rennie Mackintosh** moved into a flat with his family in 1872. At that time, the family name was spelled 'McIntosh', a name that was later altered to 'Mackintosh.' Charles's father, William McIntosh, was a policeman and a member of a world championship tug-of-war team. He would never have imagined his shy son would later become a renowned artist and architect. In 1875, young Charles began attending John Reid's Public School in Dennistoun. The Mackintosh family remained in Dennistoun until 1892, when they relocated to Strathbungo.

The back of the flat looks out onto the Necropolis and this is where Charles's first public work is located (a Celtic cross gravestone for his father's boss, Chief Constable Alexander McCall in 1890).

Dennistoun Walk

As you continue up Ark Lane, stop at the corner with Circus Drive to observe the ⑩ **former Golfhill Public School** and the adjoining janitor's lodge. These buildings date from 1902 and were designed by Alexander Nisbet Paterson (1862-1947). Paterson, like many Glasgow architects of his era, was heavily influenced by his studies at the École des Beaux-Arts in Paris. He entered the competition to design the Glasgow School of Art, but was bested by the firm Honeyman & Keppie, where Charles Rennie Mackintosh played a starring role. The Golfhill Public School building is slated for conversion into flats, threatening some of Paterson's original design.

Turn left up Hanson Street. On the left is ⑪ **Golfhill Nursing Home** which stands on the grounds of the Dennistoun family's estate that had Golfhill House at its centre. Golfhill house survived until the 1920s.

On the opposite side of Hanson Street, a large walled garden once stood, followed by a quarry that played a significant role in Glasgow's construction. Much of the stone used to build the city was extracted from local quarries like this one.

As you reach Alexandra Parade, you will find yourself at the northern boundary of Dennistoun (Duke Street marks the southern boundary). On your left is ⑫ **Wasps Hanson Street Studios**, housed in a former tobacco factory.

The tobacco industry was a major economic driver in Glasgow during the 19th and early 20th centuries. Thousands of people were employed in sorting, drying, and cutting the casks of tobacco, which were then made into cigarettes and cigars sold at home and abroad. This stretch of Alexandra Parade was called 'Tobacco Road'.

Dennistoun Walk

Dennistoun Walk

Across the road lies the unloved M8. If you had walked here in the 1890s there were hardly any buildings on either side of Alexandra Parade, and beyond the site of the M8 you would have reached the 12 mile long Monkland Canal constructed in 1771. The canal was a vital transportation route bringing coal into the city from the Monklands coal pits. The canal was closed in 1942, unable to compete with the railways and road traffic. The M8 was constructed over its path in the late 1960s. A relative of mine who lived here in the 1950s recalled fishing in the canal as a youngster.

Turn right along Alexandra Parade – a pretty soulless stretch of garages and commercial buildings. It is named after Princess Alexandra, wife of the future King Edward VII, who opened nearby Alexandra Park in the 1870s. The mythical Molendinar Burn, a waterway crucial to the founding of the village of Glasgow, runs underground roughly along the route of the Parade (there is a short stretch visible above ground just off Duke Street).

On the right you pass the **⓭ former W.D. & H.O. Wills tobacco factory**, part of the Imperial Tobacco Company. It was designed in around 1946 although not completed until 1953. At its peak, the factory produced 260 million cigarettes a week and employed 3,500 people. The factory closed in 1983, and the building was later used as the production office for the makers of the film *Trainspotting*.

This building was once lit up at night with neon signs for Woodbine, Golden Virginia and other brands. The loss of jobs along Tobacco Road had a big impact on the local community – another milestone in the de-industrialisation of Glasgow.

Turn right into Craigpark, named after another large estate house that once stood to the east. It was one of many such properties that disappeared as the Dennistoun family and others acquired land for tenement housing.

On the left, you'll see the former **⓮ Dennistoun Baths**, which operated as a private swimming club from 1883 until 1993. The building contained a Turkish Bath, and members could join affiliated clubs dedicated to activities such as cross-country running and water polo. In the 1890s, this spot was surrounded by open fields and grazing land, earning it the local nickname 'The Sheepy'.

Dennistoun Walk

Continue down Craigpark, passing the angular ⑮ **Our Lady of Good Counsel Catholic Church**. The church, a classic mid-1960s design, was created by the architectural firm Gillespie, Kidd & Coia. Jack Coia (1898-1981), a leading architect of his era in Glasgow, was part of the firm, which traced its history back to the Salmon family. James Salmon designed the plan for Dennistoun.

After the church, turn right up Circus Drive to reach ⑯ **Broompark Circus** up the hill on the right. The highlight here is the huge Adams Family style corner house (number 7). Originally Broompark Nursery, this Franco-Gothic building dates from c.1867 and may have been designed by James Salmon himself, though this is not certain.

James Salmon (1805-1888) lived at 3 Broompark Circus from the 1870s to late 1880s. His son and architect William Forrest Salmon (1843-1911) is also listed as living here from 1881 to 1891.

Retrace your steps, passing the church again then turning right into Golfhill Drive (central Dennistoun is known as 'the Drives'). Further along on the right is ⑰ **Whitevale Bowling Club**. Many suburbs created in 19th-century Glasgow saw the construction of churches, baths, parks, and bowling greens – all designed to serve the needs of Victorian ladies and gentlemen. Bowling was popular, with more clubs per head of the population than perhaps anywhere else in Scotland. Founded in 1836, this club is the second-oldest private club in Glasgow. In the early 1800s, Craigpark

Dennistoun Walk

Quarry operated on the site where the club stands today.

Turn onto Whitehill Street, walking briefly before turning right into ⑱ **Whitehill Place and Whitehill Court**. Walk into the Court and look on the right-hand side for **Dennistoun Masonic Hall**, home to Lodge Scotia No. 178. Many such lodges are tucked away in residential streets in the city. In the past, this area was the location of three other notable institutions.

Dennistoun Masonic Hall

In the mid-19th century, a reformatory and house of refuge stood here. Founded in 1836, its location was then on the outskirts of Glasgow. The nearest residential street was Annfield Place (visited earlier). This gives a sense of how undeveloped this area was. The reformatory was then transformed into the heart of the Glasgow East End Exhibition. The Exhibition opened in 1890 and continued up until April 1891.

Its aim was 'to establish a People's Palace in the East End of Glasgow'. The complex included a 3,000-seater hall which over 700,000 people visited. It was a showcase for the city's industrial might, and the choice of Dennistoun over other parts of the East End underscored its growing prominence.

Look for the statue of 'Buffalo Bill' in the tiny park. William Frederick Cody (1846-1917) was one of the famous figures to emerge from the legendary American 'Wild West'. As a teenager, he rode for the Pony Express, later distinguishing himself on the Union side during the Civil War, and served as a skilled army scout throughout the Indian Wars.

Dennistoun Walk

In the latter half of the 19th century, global fascination with the Wild West surged, driven by newspaper coverage, dime novels, and comics. This encouraged Cody and several other well-known figures to try and cash in. He founded Buffalo Bill's Wild West Travelling Show and included several Native Americans whom he had freed from prison following the Indian Wars. Sharpshooter Annie Oakley, famed for *Annie Get Your Gun*, also toured with Cody.

Buffalo Bill's show ran from November 1891 to February 1892. It must have been exciting for locals to see Native Americans such as Kicking Bear, Short Bull and One Bull, from the Lakota tribe, walking down Duke Street and visiting local pubs.

Cody returned to Glasgow in 1904, but by then he wasn't the only Wild West act in town. Other veterans and entertainers from the era were also touring Glasgow at that time. Cody's company arrived in Glasgow on three specially commissioned trains. Hundreds of horses, buffalo, cows and other animals were herded down Duke Street by real cowboys.

The garden where the statue stands is roughly on the site of Whitehill School, which dates from the 1890s. Near the hedge, you can still see the remaining stone gates of the school. Several notable people were educated there including journalist and author Jack House, artist and author Alasdair Gray, actors Rikki Fulton and Bill Paterson, and comedian Dorothy Paul. The old school was demolished after the current Whitehill School opened in 1977 on Onslow Drive.

Continue down Whitehill Street. On the right is Finlay Drive and a short distance along on the left (now covered by flats) is the approximate site of ⓳ **Dennistoun Palais**. The Palais first opened its doors in 1922 but tragically burnt down just fourteen years later. Fortunately for Dennistoun residents, it was rebuilt in 1938 in the Art Deco style. With a capacity for up to 1,800 dancers, it became the largest dance hall in the city.

In an age when many went out dancing several times a week, the 'Denny Pally' was likely the busiest place in the East End, if not Glasgow. One man recalled in a newspaper how 'The lassies would stand at one side, us idiots on the other, and you'd go up and ask for a dance. Sometimes, it was good to walk in with a lassie though, because you could smuggle your carry-out in to the hall in her handbag. There was no drink served in the dance hall, just Kia-Ora and milk!'. The Palais closed in 1962, later becoming a supermarket before being eventually demolished.

Walk down the other side of Finlay Drive (east of Whitehill Street), passing the site of ⓴ **Whitehill House** on your left. Old photographs reveal a substantial mansion that once stood here. John Reid, who first developed houses in the area, lived in Whitehill House and passed away there in 1852. The name 'Finlay' comes from May Finlay, the wife of James Dennistoun.

A few minutes further on the right is ㉑ **Christadelphian Hall**. This close-knit Christian group, which originated in the 19th

Dennistoun Walk

century, seeks to follow the teachings of Christianity as they believe it was practiced in the 1st Century AD. Members are pacifists. This street has a strong religious presence, with a Baptist church and the Christian Friendship Centre located next door.

Continue to reach Meadowpark Street, named after Meadowpark House, which once stood to the north of Finlay Street. On the other side is ㉒ **St Denis' Primary School**, originally the Dennistoun Public School (look for the original signage). It was designed by James Salmon & Son, the architectural practice begun by James Salmon and continued by his son and grandson. A typically sturdy School Board of Glasgow building, it dates from 1883.

Turn right down Meadowpark Street to reach Duke Street. Turn left and continue along, passing Duke Street railway station, opened in 1881 as part of the City of Glasgow Union Railway. Transport links like this and the tramline that once ran down Duke Street were key to the development of the suburb.

It is a bit grim along here: scrap merchants and run-down tenement blocks. Continue to ㉓ **The Louden Tavern**, which proclaims itself as 'The Greatest Pub in the World'. If you are a Rangers fan, you may agree. If you are a Celtic fan...perhaps not.

Tensions between rival fans can get heated. When Celtic won the treble in 2018, someone daubed graffiti on the Louden's walls referring to 'Rangers Scum' and 'Celtic CFC' – something the bar described as 'predictable as it is pathetic'.

Dennistoun Walk

Continue walking. On the left is the ㉔ **Hovis bakery** – a rare survivor of the industrial enterprises once prominent in the East End. In the 1890s, the site was occupied by the Lucifer Match Works. 'Lucifer' matches were sold all around Britain and used white or yellow phosphorus. This was toxic, and many workers – usually poorly-paid women – became sick. Some were disfigured, developing 'phossy jaw'. It took years of action by workers, the Salvation Army, and others to force manufacturers to switch to safer red phosphorus.

You are now in the neighbouring area of Haghill. If you want to start a long debate with locals, ask if it is true that Cumbernauld Road is the eastern border of Dennistoun.

Continue on to see another Rangers-supporting institution, ㉕ **the Bristol Bar**. On their 45th anniversary in 2018, the Dennistoun Rangers Flute Band played 'God Save the Queen' outside the Bristol in front of hundreds of supporters.

Now turn and retrace your steps along Duke Street into Dennistoun. The junction of Duke Street and Cumbernauld

Dennistoun Walk

Road is shown on old maps as Alexandra Cross. On the left side, look for ㉖ **the Alexandra Bar**, a classic Duke Street boozer first licensed in 1870. You may have noticed there are no pubs in the heart of Dennistoun north of Duke Street. The morally upright Dennistoun family made sure their planned suburb was 'dry'.

Turn left onto Whitevale Street and you'll see the ㉗ **Reidvale Neighbourhood Centre**. Founded in 1977, originally it was called the South Dennistoun Neighbourhood Centre. It continues to be a shining example of what local 'people power' can do, offering everything from Tai Chi, to services for young people and has a cosy café.

Outside the centre is a sculpture from 1981 designed by Stan Bonnar (b.1948) entitled *The Community*. His son, actor Mark Bonnar (b.1968), has appeared in *Unforgotten*, *Shetland*, *Line of Duty* and many other dramas.

㉘ **St Anne's RC Church** (next door) dates from c.1933, and was designed by Jack Coia (1898-1981) of Gillespie Kidd and Coia. Coia was apprentice for John Gaff Gillespie, who had worked with James Salmon Jr. Coia took evening classes at nearby Whitehill School and is best known for designing dozens of Roman Catholic churches.

Whitevale Street was the location of Reid's School (then numbered 13), where Charles Rennie Mackintosh attended as a child living in Dennistoun. He later went to Allan Glen's School and became great friends with James Salmon Jnr., the grandson of James Salmon, who mapped out Dennistoun's design.

'White Vale' was a street shown on a map of 1807 when no other buildings or streets had yet been built in the area. It must have felt cut off, surrounded by fields. Return

Dennistoun Walk

to Duke Street, and continue, taking the next left onto ㉙ **Bathgate Street**. Walk down this street to read about the saving of this neighbourhood in the 1970s.

The Duke Street area, and streets like this on the south side, were at the centre of a battle between the local community and urban planners in the 1970s. The creation of Comprehensive Development Areas in the post-war period saw many districts such as the Gorbals, Anderston and Townhead completely transformed. The old tenement streets, regarded as unhealthy slums, were knocked down. This displaced thousands of residents from Glasgow's working-class districts to newly developed areas like Easterhouse, Drumchapel, and Castlemilk.

In around 1975, there were around 1,500 tenement flats across nine streets on the south side of Duke Street, including Bathgate Street. These were scheduled for demolition by Glasgow Corporation.

However, at a public meeting at the nearby Thomson Street school, Bathgate Street

The Community by Stan Bonnar, Reidvale Neighbourhood Centre

Dennistoun Walk

resident John Butterly (1926-2001) declared he would never be moved to Easterhouse. He and others began a public campaign to take on the Corporation's demolition plans.

Against the odds, the so-called 'Bathgate Mafia' succeeded in forming Reidvale Housing Association, from the mid-1970s accessing public grants to modernise run-down tenements. Butterly, who lived at number 59, was later awarded an MBE in recognition of his work. The community's efforts not only preserved the character of the area but also inspired others to follow their example.

Continue along Duke Street, turning left into Garfield Street. Singer Lulu (b.1948) used to live in Bridgeton, but her family moved to ③ **29 Garfield Street**. She later recalled '...it was only a couple hundred yards, but mentally it was a lot further.... We had edged slightly up in the world, because we now lived closer to Duke Street and further away from the Gallowgate. There weren't so many poorly dressed kids or runny noses.'

Lulu's father worked at the meat market. She had a difficult life here, not helped by her abusive father who beat her mother. When she began to sing in the 1960s she dreamt of becoming a hairdresser, playing in a band at the weekend, having a family and a big Glasgow house with an indoor bathroom. However, fate had something else in store for her. She mixed with The Beatles, Elton John, the Stones, The Animals and The Kinks. She would marry a Bee Gee, act alongside Sidney Poitier in *To Sir With Love*, and become friends with David Bowie.

In 1964 she performed at a concert with several bands in the city, including The High Numbers. She brought the band back to meet her parents here. The band would later change their name to The Who. Imagine Keith Moon on Garfield Street drinking tea with Lulu's dad...

You might assume working-class Glaswegians went to the local public baths and washhouses because they had no hot

Dennistoun Walk

water or bath at home, but it was more complicated than that. Lulu would later recall: 'Not every family could afford the public baths, so the Scottish education authorities made sure all schoolchildren had mandatory showers. Once a week a mobile shower unit would arrive and park in the playground. It had a pipe system surrounded by heavy tarpaulin that created ten cubicles. Every class would have half an hour – fifteen minutes for the boys and fifteen minutes for the girls'.

Return to Duke Street, where there is a tenuous connection with David Bowie. After his death in 2016, a local petition was started to rename Duke Street as 'Thin White Duke Street' in his honour. It garnered 2,444 signatures but unfortunately wasn't successful.

Just up Whitehill Street on the right is the ㉛ **former Dennistoun United Presbyterian Church**, completed in 1870. Whilst Dennistoun now has a 'cool' hipsterish image, it faces the same problems as any other inner city area. At the time of writing a food bank operates in this church, one of perhaps fifty or more in Glasgow and the figure continues to grow.

Return to Duke Street and continue on, immediately on your right you'll see ㉜ **Coia's Café**, another local institution. A classic Scots-Italian café, it was founded in 1928 by Carmine and Amalia Coia, and is currently owned by the third generation of the Coia family – Alfredo and Antonia. They are related to architect Jack Coia.

Return to Duke Street and continue until you spot Thomson Street on the left. Walk down to reach the former ㉝ **former Thomson Street School** which opened in 1875. Initially charging high fees, the school

Dennistoun Walk

attracted pupils from the more affluent families in Dennistoun, particularly those living on the posher side of Duke Street.

Lulu later attended the school, and it was here, during a local meeting in 1975, that John Butterly famously declared, 'You go and live in Easterhouse if you like. I will not'. To learn more about this period in the city's history, watch the BBC documentary *The Secret History of Our Street – Duke Street* (2016).

In the mid-1980s, the Corporation decided to close about half the schools in the area, a reaction to reduced population density in East End. This triggered a spirited local campaign to save the school, but unfortunately, the effort was unsuccessful. However, the Reidvale Housing Association managed to save the building from demolition, and it has since been converted into flats.

At the end of Thomson Street turn right onto Reidvale Street, passing allotments on the south side. As you continue, you will pass ㉞ **Annbank Street**, named after Annfield House, which was built in the 1770s and stood here until 1870. The house, named for Ann, the wife of James Tennant who built it, was said to be haunted by a White Lady. The street is also home to John Butterly House, a retirement complex named in honour of the local activist.

Continue ahead to meet Bellgrove Street, turn left, and you'll reach the station, marking the end of the walk.

VISIT

Dennistoun Library
2A Craigpark, G31 2NA
glasgowlife.org.uk

The Glasgow Necropolis
Castle St, G4 0UZ
glasgownecropolis.org

EAT & DRINK

Redmond's
304 Duke St, G31 1RZ

The Louden Tavern
532 Duke St, G31 1NG

The Bristol Bar
600 Duke St, G31 1JX

The Alexandra Bar
468 Duke St, G31 1QJ

Coia's Café
473-477 Duke St, G31 1RD
coiascafe.co.uk

Dennistoun Bar-B-Que
585 Duke St, G31 1PY
dennistounbbq.com

Mesa Glasgow
567 Duke St, G31 1PY

Zennor
354 Duke St, G31 1RB
zennorcoffee.co.uk

11 Kelvin River & Canal Walk

Kelvin River & Canal Walk

- 23 Former Whitehouse Inn
- 24 Maryhill Library
- 25 Maryhill Burgh Halls
- 26 Maryhill Road Aqueduct
- 27 Hughes Memorial Orange Halls
- 28 Stockingfield Junction
- 29 Maryhill Iron Works
- 30 Ruchill Saw Mills
- 31 Church tower
- 32 Footbridge
- 33 Bridge
- 34 Mackintosh's Queen's Cross Church
- 35 Café D'Jaconelli
- 36 Firhill Basin
- 37 Firhill Stadium
- 38 Hamiltonhill Claypits
- 39 'Old Basin'
- 40 The Whisky Bond
- 41 Speirs Wharf
- 42 Canal House
- 43 Remains of Port Dundas Basin

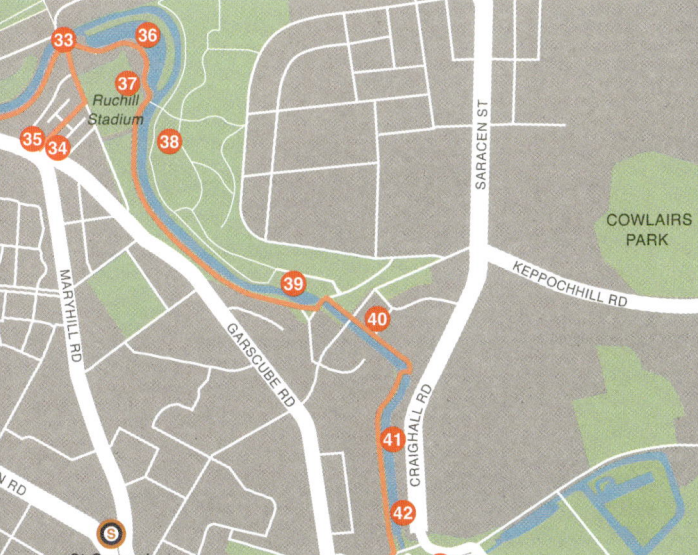

Kelvin River & Canal Walk

Kelvin River & Canal Walk
Start: Kelvinbridge subway
Finish: Cowcaddens subway
Distance: 5.25 miles

Kelvin River & Canal Walk

This walk takes you along the River Kelvin and the Forth & Clyde Canal, exploring relics of the city's past.

At ❶ **Kelvinbridge subway**, exit via the bottom exit (don't take the escalator up). Outside, you'll find a fine cast-iron staircase leading up to street level, which resembles something you might find in Manhattan. Look for the street art underneath. The 'squirrel poised on skull' is the work of Australian-born street artist Smug (real name Sam Bates). Smug has produced several striking pieces around the city, and his work is arguably more familiar to the average Glaswegian than anything created by a Turner-Prize winning graduate from the Glasgow School of Art.

Above is the Great Western Bridge – also known as the Kelvinbridge – which dates from 1891. It crosses the Kelvin River at a point where, for centuries, a ford was located. On the bridge itself, you can see the coats of arms of Glasgow, Lanarkshire and Hillhead.

Kelvinbridge

Walk through the arches and along the river path (with the Kelvin to your left). The river path is usually quiet, popular with dog walkers and joggers. For hundreds of years, the atmosphere would have been less peaceful, as the riverside was a place of work and industry. It was lined with railway stations, mills, factories, and other industries. Many were attracted to the river because it was a source of water power in the era before steam engines and electricity. The source of the river, a tributary of the Clyde, is 22 miles away in the village of Banton.

Kelvin River & Canal Walk

The path brings you up South Woodside Road. Follow the map into Tillie Street. The land on the right-hand side was the site of ❷ **North Woodside**, a substantial house surrounded by gardens and fields up until the 1860s. Within a few years, all was swept away, replaced by suburban residential streets built by developers seeking to attract the city's expanding middle-class population.

Take a left up Jardine Street and stop outside the ❸ **Territorial Army base**. This unusual Tudor-style building dates from 1894 and is a fine example of a Victorian-era drill hall. There are other examples around the city. In the late 1850s, there was concern about a possible invasion by the French, leading to dozens of volunteer army regiments being founded. One result was the building of over 340 drill halls all over the country – mainly between 1880-1910. This building is a reminder of the patriotic fervour felt by many during the zenith of the British Empire. Ironically, it would not be the French army that was the problem.

Regimental companies very often reflected class divisions. For example, some volunteer regiments were recruited from accountancy offices, others from the legal profession, or academics and students at Glasgow University. This was home to the 1st Lanarkshire Engineer Volunteers. You can see the initials of the regiment high up, and the hall was designed by a major in that regiment, Alexander Bryden.

Turn left into Garriochmill Road where you'll see the spire of ❹ **Kelvinbridge Parish Church** in the distance. Designed in the Scottish Gothic style, it was completed in 1902 by Glasgow-born architect John James Stevenson, who designed many other churches in Scotland and England. The church has a 'crown tower', similar to St Giles' Cathedral in Edinburgh. The street is named after Garrioch Mill, which stood a little further along the river.

Kelvin River & Canal Walk

Continue under ❺ **Belmont Bridge**, dating from around 1870. It was built for the City of Glasgow Bank, which owned land in the North Woodside area. The bank wanted to develop a residential suburb but needed to provide access for those moving to the north side of the river into central Glasgow. This is an example of a private bank-funded bridge and suburb – something hard to imagine today. The bank demolished the grand North Woodside House to make way for the new bridge.

On the south side of the river is ❻ **The Glasgow Academy**, founded in 1845, and one of the best schools in Scotland. Notable alumni include two founders of television channels (Sir Jeremy Issacs – Channel 4, John Reith – BBC), *Peter Pan* author J.M. Barrie, *Flashman* author George MacDonald Fraser, historian Niall Ferguson, politician and former First Minister of Scotland Donald Dewar, pop stars Andrew Innes (Primal Scream) and James Prime (Deacon Blue), and Nobel Prize winner Sir William Ramsay (discoverer of the noble gases). No pressure then for current pupils...

Kelvin River & Canal Walk

Continue on the Kelvin Walkway. On the left are the remains of ❼ **North Woodside Flint Mill and Lade**. A mill here is visible on a mid-17th-century map and was initially used for barley. During the Napoleonic Wars, it was used to grind gunpowder. In the 1840s, the old mill was replaced by one used for grinding flints (first burnt in the kiln), the remains of which are still visible. The product was used for glazing pottery by the Verreville Pottery in Finnieston (which closed in the early 20th century). This was still a working mill until the late 1950s, the last of its kind. Beside stood a separate flour mill and corn mill, and in recent years archaeologists have begun to explore the site (there are information boards with more details).

Look out for the deep channel – or 'lade' – used to funnel river water and concentrate its power before turning a water wheel. Turn on a tap and cover it with your hand, leaving a small space – you will then better understand the principle.

Continue along the riverside. Soon, you see the remains of one of Glasgow's 'lost' bridges – the original ❽ **Queen Margaret Bridge**. A wealthy horse-cab proprietor named John Ewing 'Hookey' Walker acquired 100 acres of wooded land in this area to develop a new suburb. To attract residents, he needed a bridge, particularly one allowing access to the Great Western Road. The result was the first Queen Margaret Bridge, built around 1870.

Known as 'Walker's Bridge', it was too low and had restricted access on the north side. Walker constructed a retaining wall on the north side, said to have been an attempt to make his new development more exclusive. The current Queen Margaret Bridge was completed in 1929, the original was closed and largely demolished in 1971.

Exit here to visit the retaining wall, punctured by the famous ❾ **'Sixty Steps'**. Most people believe this was designed in the early 1870s by one of the most renowned architects of the era, Alexander 'Greek' Thomson (1817-75). It is much easier to see the old bridge structures from the top of the steps. Built just before Thomson's death, the stairs include a mysterious 'door to nowhere' that may represent mortality or connections to a spiritual world.

Kelvin River & Canal Walk

Kelvin River & Canal Walk

There has been some debate as to whether Thomson designed the steps. However, The Sixty Steps Preservation Trust seems convinced he did. They do good work and you can volunteer to help them (www.sixtysteps.org.uk).

Go back to the river path and continue. The area to your right is called North Kelvinside. Pass under the three-arched Queen Margaret Bridge, and then reach the ⑩ **'Humpback' footbridge** that dates from 1908. This connects you to the Glasgow Botanic Gardens on the other side. The gardens were founded in 1817.

Further on is the ⑪ **site of the Garrioch flour and flint mill**, nothing of which remains today. Flint was brought to Glasgow as the ballast in ships, removed and then brought to mills for grinding. Nineteenth-century maps show a coal pit was located a hundred yards or so further ahead.

Soon you pass the ⑫ **Kirklee Footbridge**, or 'Ha'Penny Bridge'. There have been other bridges on this site, the original known as the Three Trees Well bridge, standing at the site of a Ford. One bridge was swept away by the river in 1994, and this replacement dates from 2002.

Kelvin River & Canal Walk

The 'Ha'Penny' name refers to a toll charged by the owner of Kelvinside House. It is said he imposed the sum because he wanted to discourage working-class residents of Maryhill from using the bridge.

Cross the footbridge for a slight detour to see an old 'ghost' train station (this is optional). Walk up Ford Road (named after the old ford). The railway platforms of ⓑ **Kirklee Station** once ran over Ford Road. The station opened in 1896 as part of the Glasgow Central Railway but ceased passenger services in 1939. The station building was demolished in 1971, and the railway bridge has now gone. The main site of the of the station is covered by modern flats. However, some remains can still be seen. If you walk up Ford Road and turn left into the Botanic Gardens, then bear immediately left through trees and hedges (be careful...), you can spot remnants of railway platforms and a tunnel behind a fence.

The railway tunnel led to the Botanic Gardens Station. King George V and Queen Mary slept for three nights in the tunnel by Kirklee Station when their Royal train was parked during their trip to the city in 1917. With the Russian Revolution taking place, and the continued carnage of the Great War, this was a time of radicalisation amongst the city's industrial workers. Those organising the Royal visit were worried about security, so the King and Queen were hidden away in the tunnel at night, guarded by local soldiers.

Return to the north side of the footbridge and continue along the river path, which bends to the right. Soon you will reach ⓮ **Kirklee Bridge**, one of the finest bridges in Glasgow. Dating from 1901, it resembles something from the Roman Empire, boasting pink granite Ionic columns and Glasgow's coat of arms. It was commissioned by the Corporation of Glasgow and modelled on the old Blackfriars Bridge in London (demolished in 1864). A ford once crossed the riverbank just to the south side of this site.

Continue along, passing the site of a ⓯ **long-lost cricket ground** (on the right) that stood here in 1900. You pass another footbridge (the Garrioch Drive footbridge, built in 1974), and then walk under the remaining structures of two former railway bridges known as the ⓰ **Garrioch Quadrant Viaducts**. These were built around 1896 and carried railways lines: the first by the Glasgow Central Railway, the second by the Lanarkshire and Dumbartonshire Railway. The lines have long since closed, but these relics remain, overgrown and forgotten.

As you continue on, you may see the ⓱ **Wyndford flats** to your right. In February 2023, residents of the Wyndford estate in Maryhill marched through north east Glasgow in protest against the demolition plans for the estate they called home. Their appeals were ignored and some of the towers may be gone by the time you walk due to redevelopment plans.

The Wyndford estate was built from the 1960s and was initially oversubscribed with people eager to move there. In later years it faced challenges typical of many housing schemes of that era and even featured as a gritty location in episodes of the TV detective series *Taggart*.

The estate stands on the site of the former Maryhill Barracks, which were constructed in the 1870s. The barracks were home to regiments such as the Highland Light Infantry and the Scots Greys. In 1942, President Charles de Gaulle visited French troops here, and Nazi Rudolf Hess – Hitler's friend and deputy – was held in the barracks after his bizarre 'peace mission' to Scotland in 1941. Most of the land to the east of the river was used as an exercise ground, whilst the rest of the site comprised a hospital, cavalry and artillery parade ground, and barracks. In the past you would have seen hundreds of soldiers, but today the estate is a relatively quiet place.

The barracks covered around 30 acres, and soldiers and their families played a significant role in the day-to-day life of Maryhill until the barracks closed in the 1960s. (You can see some remains of the old walls and gatehouse along Kelvindale Road). Charlie Nicholas (b.1961) who played for Celtic, Arsenal and Scotland, once lived on the estate. Maryhill Shopping Centre occupies the site where Maryhill Barracks Station once stood, located in the south east corner of the barracks.

Look out for ⑱ **the remains of an old railway bridge** stranded in the water. Follow the path which takes you across Kelvindale Road, joining the path on the other side. You are now walking along the route of the Glasgow Central Line. Over to the left, the other bank (approximately where Fortinghall Place is today) was once dominated by ⑲ **Kelvindale Paper Mills**, powered by the river and surrounded by several large reservoirs and filter beds that supplied clean water for paper production. The first mill was founded on this site in the 18th century and also produced snuff.

You pass obsolete railway bridge structures in the river, and soon on the right is the site of another 'ghost' railway station – ⑳ **Dawsholm Station**, a terminus on the Glasgow Central Railway. It opened in 1896 and closed in 1908. Tucked away under trees are remnants of supporting walls.

Kelvin River & Canal Walk

21

Maryhill Locks

22

Take the path leading right, away from the river, just before what looks like another bridge (follow the sign for Maryhill Locks). As you get level with the structure, you will realise that it is actually the 400ft-long ㉑ **Kelvin Aqueduct**, one of the most extraordinary structures in Scotland. This aqueduct carries the Forth & Clyde Canal, which you will follow for the remainder of your walk.

The canal opened in 1790, connecting the Firth of Clyde on the west coast with the Firth of Forth on the east. It stretches for 35 miles, from the River Clyde at Bowling to the River Carron at Grangemouth, with a branch line running south to Dundas Basin in central Glasgow – a key feature of this walk.

The construction of the canal was a monumental effort, the largest project of its kind in Scotland since the Romans built the Antonine Wall (with much of the canal following the same route). The aqueduct was also the largest in the world since Roman times. It was designed by engineer Robert Whitworth and was so expensive it almost bankrupted the canal company. The canal has since become a tourist attraction and a symbol of Scotland's transition into the modern age.

Turn right to begin walking towards Maryhill Locks. The five locks with basins on either side mark the highest point of the canal. On the north side is the ㉒ **Kelvin Graving Dock and Boatyard**, where canal boats were repaired, and where Swan & Co. constructed landing craft used on D-Day. The yard remained open until the 1960s.

Kelvin River & Canal Walk

Past the footbridge is the ㉓ **former Whitehouse Inn**, a white rubble sandstone building dating from around 1810 and originally a pub. It would have been thronged with thirsty workers on the canal just after it opened. The surrounding Maryhill area began to develop as a village in the 1770s due to the canal's construction. The land the canal passed through was owned by Robert Graham and Mary Hill. It saved their finances as the couple had struggled to generate revenue from their landholdings. Robert Graham stipulated that the developing residential area be named after his wife, and Mary Hill's gravestone can still be seen in Glasgow Cathedral's old cemetery.

Continue along the path, passing a sign leading off the canal for Maryhill Burgh Halls. If you have time, take a detour into Maryhill to visit two local institutions – ㉔ **Maryhill Library** and the former ㉕ **Maryhill Burgh Halls, washhouse and public baths** (now a community centre).

The library opened in 1905 and was one of several designed by James R. Rhind and funded by Scots-American industrialist and philanthropist Andrew Carnegie.

The Burgh Halls date from 1878, when Maryhill was separate from Glasgow, and they were a symbol of local civic pride and independence. This independence lasted from 1856 until Maryhill was annexed by Glasgow in 1891. When it was still a burgh, Maryhill had its own coat of arms featuring a steamship crossing the Kelvin Aqueduct, and other symbols of local industry such as a circular saw, spur wheel, and iron furnace.

Kelvin River & Canal Walk

Whether you take the detour or not, continue along the canal path, crossing over the ㉖ **Maryhill Road Aqueduct (1881)**. Look down to see the heart of Maryhill below. Shortly after, look out to the left side of the canal for ㉗ **Hughes Memorial Orange Halls** (a Union Jack flag may be flying). Founded in 1970, it is home to the LOL (Loyal Orange Lodge) Maryhill Orange & Purple District 46, and like many such halls resembles a fortified block house.

The Orange Order emerged in Ireland in 1795, but soon spread to Scotland, particularly after Protestant Irish people came to Glasgow in the 19th century seeking employment. Today's lodges remain, by and large, bastions of working-class, Protestant, Rangers-supporting locals, loyal to the British Crown. The Grand Orange Lodge of Scotland has around 50,000 members and is named after William III, Prince of Orange, who won the Battle of the Boyne in 1690 against the deposed Catholic, James II. The biggest Orange Walk in Glasgow is on the Saturday before the 12th July each year, to commemorate William's victory.

Carry on. By 1900, this area was heavily industrialised, and on the right, you would have once seen Maryhill engine works and a major paraffin works. However, there were still some remnants of the area's rural past – Gilshochill Farm stood near the Orange Hall site. It is hard to imagine how busy the canal once was – in the mid-19th century over 200,000 passengers travelled back and forth along the route and three million tonnes

Kelvin River & Canal Walk

of goods were transported. This gave rise to thousands of jobs – navvies digging the canal, basins, locks and offshoots; lock-keepers, those working in boatyards, inns, stables, in factories located by the canal – the list is almost endless.

After a few minutes, the canal path turns to the right and you reach ㉘ **Stockingfield Junction**. Above you is a recently installed pedestrian walkway that connects the communities of neighbouring Ruchill, Gilshochill and central Maryhill. Over the other side, look for the huge artwork depicting a mythological Scottish serpent: *'Bella' the Beithir*. It is part of Stockingfield Bridge Art Park, which is worth a detour if you have the time. Bella is the work of local artist Nichol Wheatley, who worked for many years with the celebrated writer and artist Alasdair Gray.

If you look to your left, the Forth & Clyde Canal continues on its main route for another 26 miles to Grangemouth on the east coast. There is also a connection at Falkirk between the Forth & Clyde Canal, and the Union Canal that leads into Edinburgh. The creation of canals linking across Scotland was once incredibly important for trade.

From its beginning in 1768, it took 22 years to finish the Forth & Clyde Canal, with work suspended for several years due to funding problems. Commercial interests also forced through a plan to build a southern offshoot of the main canal running three miles down into central Glasgow, and this extension began in 1791. It is this Glasgow branch you will walk beside for the remainder of the route after Stockingfield Junction.

In the past, a floating bridge operated here, allowing horses to be transported between the paths on the main route of the canal, and the Glasgow branch.

'Bella' the Beithir

Kelvin River & Canal Walk

Continue along the Glasgow branch (right hand path). The land on either side was once heavily industrialised – one such example being ㉙ **Maryhill Iron Works**, behind which ran the Possil Burn, still then running above ground. In the 1890s, on the other side of the canal, after about a mile, you would pass the ㉚ **Ruchill Saw Mills**, followed by a nail and rivet works, Ruchill Iron Works, Glasgow Lead and Colour Works, Ruchill Chemical Works, Glasgow Rubber Works, a gold extracting works, and the Caledonia Iron Foundry. This concentration of heavy industry was repeated on both sides of the canal right into central Glasgow on a scale difficult to fathom in today's post-industrial age. Now you will pass a ragbag assortment of gyms, car repair firms, print companies, and other enterprises.

You pass under Ruchill Bridge. If you are interested in Charles Rennie Mackintosh, you can take a detour here. Go up to Ruchill Bridge which runs over the canal. Look on the right for a ㉛ **church tower**. Head along the path towards it, entering Shakespeare Street where Mackintosh's Ruchill Church Hall stands beside the church. It dates from 1899. Return to the canal path when finished. There are information signs about the long-lost Glasgow Rubber Works that stood nearby, and you can see some 19th-century industrial buildings by the bridge.

31

After about five minutes, you reach a ㉜ **footbridge** to the Murano Street Student Village that serves the University of Glasgow. This stands on the site of Ruchill Oil Works, the scene of a vast blaze in 1884 that saw burning oil spread across the canal. Further along stood Caledonian Glass Bottle Works. The student accommodation is a reminder of how student money has driven the construction of flats in parts of the city that has changed local demographics considerably. Ruchill Park is located to the north of the student site.

Kelvin River & Canal Walk

The canal bends, and amidst the post-industrial landscape is a rare architectural delight if you wish a detour – this time to see Charles Rennie Mackintosh's Queen's Cross Church. At a ❸❸ **bridge** over the canal, take the path on the right and follow Firhill Road. Continue along until you reach Springbank Street, then turn right (across from the main entrance to Partick Thistle Football Club). At the end, you'll find ❸❹ **Mackintosh's Queen's Cross Church**, completed in 1899 while he was working for Honeyman & Keppie. It's the only church he ever designed that was built. Today it is home to the Charles Rennie Mackintosh Society and you can visit (see mackintoshchurch.com).

A few doors up is the famous ❸❺ **Café D'Jaconelli**, worth a stop for a well deserved break or just to admire the authentic Art Deco interior. It was founded by Italian Mario Jaconelli in 1924. Its vintage 1950s interior has meant it is regularly used as a filming location, including *Trainspotting* (Spud has a milkshake here before a job interview), *Carla's Song* (with Robert Carlye), and *Tutti Frutti* (with Robbie Coltrane). James Evans took over the café from Mario Jaconelli in the late 80s and recalled one famous visitor, singer Lulu, who he recalled starting singing 'WEEEEEEELL', (from her song *Shout*). 'You couldnae believe it, you could feel it off the walls'. After enjoying your break, retrace your steps back to the canal path.

Kelvin River & Canal Walk

Carry on along the canal path, reaching the kidney-shaped ㊱ **Firhill Basin**. This vast basin was used to transport timber, and was surrounded by saw mills. In Victorian times, the northeast side of the current basin was home to an iron works, the Western Saw Mills, and another basin that has since been filled in.

Walk on, passing ㊲ **Firhill Stadium**, home to Partick Thistle Football Club. As the name suggests, the club did originate in Partick in 1876 but came to Maryhill in 1909. If you stand here on match day, you can get a pretty good view of the game.

The area on the other side of the canal is the former site of ㊳ **Hamiltonhill Claypits**. The clay extracted here helped line the canal walls to reduce leakage. The site has since been transformed into the Claypits Nature Reserve, the only such reserve in central Glasgow. It is incredible to think you are less than two miles from bustling Buchanan Street. The Claypits are home to a range of bird species, such as whitethroat warblers and peregrine falcons. You may even spot a roe deer.

Continue until you see a pedestrian bridge that leads into Claypits Nature Reserve. You may wish to cross over and visit part of the reserve at this point, where there are benches for picnic stops.

Otherwise, continue along the canal path to reach the Applecross Basin, lined with buildings. Known as the ㊴ **'old basin'**, this dates from 1777 and was the original endpoint of the canal's Glasgow

Kelvin River & Canal Walk

branch. The branch was later extended down to Dundas Basin. The whitewashed canal buildings date from the late 18th century and were initially used as warehouses for goods transported on the canal, before being converted into workshops for the company running the canal. Information boards tell you more about other businesses once based here, including the Great Canal Brewery.

Hugh Baird & Company owned a brewery and The Old Basin Tavern near here in the 19th century. This is where many canal workers would gather to relax, including those working on the 'Hoolets' – little ships – that travelled between Edinburgh and Glasgow.

None of the ambitious engineers, investors and politicians who backed the canal's construction in the late 18th century could have foreseen that within a few years of the canal being completed, a transport revolution would limit the canal's long-term future. The arrival of the railway and the dredging of the Clyde (which allowed larger ships to travel into the heart of Glasgow) contributed to the canal's decline. It was sold in the 1860s to a competitor, the Caledonian Railway. During the 20th century, the decline continued, with improvements in road transport dealing a final blow. The canal closed in 1963 – quite late if you consider it represented a transport solution of the 1790s.

Community Café

Cross over the pedestrian bridge to the site of the buildings just mentioned (at the sign for 'Bairds Brae'). Ahead is a fine 18th-century building that today houses a community café – a good place for a break. Otherwise, continue along the other bank, with a large red-brick

Kelvin River & Canal Walk

building ahead of you on the left. This is the ㊵ **the Whisky Bond**, built for a distillery firm in 1957 and now home to the Glasgow Sculpture Studios. In recent years, many arts organisations and creative businesses have moved to this area, including the Royal Conservatoire of Scotland and The National Theatre of Scotland. This has created an artistic hub in what has long been a post-industrial, neglected part of Glasgow. However, despite this, it remains a surprising quiet place, far removed from the glory days when the canal and surrounding industry made it vibrant and busy. It may feel like you are a long way from the walk's starting point, but Kelvinbridge station is less than a mile to the west of here.

Pass the Whisky Bond to reach a modern building next door, home to the National Theatre of Scotland. It contains four large rehearsal rooms inside. Keep going, bearing right even as you move slightly away from the canal. Soon you reach the start of Speirs Wharf. You cannot walk further along this side, but instead take the pedestrian bridge back onto the opposite bank, continuing along the path, (with the buildings of Speirs Wharf on the other side of the canal).

㊶ **Speirs Wharf** is the most impressive section of the canal. It was named after Alexander Speirs (1714-82), a so-called Tobacco Lord who made a fortune from slavery through his trade with America and ownership of plantations. The grand buildings date from 1851 onwards and were originally used as a sugar refinery, bonded warehouses and flour mills. This was also home to the Forth & Clyde Navigation Co. and the City of Glasgow Grain Mill and Stores. After the canal closed and industry left Glasgow in the second half of the 20th century, the old buildings were converted into flats and offices. You will see several canal boats, although none are engaged in the heavy industrial work of their predecessors when this was a working canal.

Kelvin River & Canal Walk

40

42

41

Kelvin River & Canal Walk

43

The two-storey building at the end is ㊷ **Canal House**, dating from around 1812 and built for the Forth & Clyde Canal Company. This immediate area around Dundas Basin was the most heavily industrialised along the canal, home to distilleries, chemical works, foundries, timber yards, and cotton mills, all surrounded by reservoirs, storehouses, and wharves where canal boats were moored.

Continue along to see an isolated basin of water – the ㊸ **remains of Port Dundas Basin**, the terminus of the Glasgow branch of the canal. Completed by 1790, Port Dundas is named after Sir Lawrence Dundas (1710–81), a wealthy landowner, politician, and businessman who was a major investor in the canal. This was one of the most industrialised areas of the city, and a 138-metre chimney – the tallest in the world – was constructed here in 1859 and demolished in 1928. The name of the wharves that once lay on either side of Dundas Basin reflected their trading connections: Carron Wharf, Hamburg Wharf, Rotterdam Wharf, Leith Wharf etc.

The walk ends here, although the canal continues a little further to the Pinkston Watersports Centre. In the past, the canal went further, linking up with the 12-mile-long Monkland Canal. The latter was built in the late 18th century to allow the transport of coal from the mines of the Monklands district. Sadly, the end of the canal age saw most of the original canal system east of here filled in. Today, the M8 motorway stands over much of the old route.

Head down the footpath leading downhill (away from Dundas Basin). This path takes you under the M8 motorway, then down Garscube Road to Cowcaddens subway station.

VISIT

Glasgow Botanic Gardens
730 Great Western Rd, G12 0UE
glasgowbotanicgardens.com

Mackintosh Queen's Cross
870 Garscube Rd, G20 7EL
mackintoshchurch.com

The Claypits Nature Reserve
250 Ellesmere St, G22 5LZ

Glasgow Sculpture Studios
2 Dawson Rd, G4 9SS
glasgowsculpturestudios.org

The National Theatre of Scotland
125 Craighall Rd, G4 9TL
nationaltheatrescotland.com

EAT, DRINK...

Kelvin Pocket
72 South Woodside Rd,
G4 9HG
kelvinpocket.co.uk

Inn Deep
445 Great Western Rd,
G12 8HH
inndeep.com

Òran Mór
Byres Rd, Glasgow G12 8QX
oran-mor.co.uk

The Nolly Café
Maryhill Burgh Halls,
10-24 Gairbraid Ave, G20 8YE
maryhillburghhalls.org.uk

Café D'Jaconelli
570 Maryhill Rd, G20 7EE

Gathering Ground Café
Old Basin House,
5-7 Applecross St, G4 9SP
gatheringground.org

Aitken Memorial Fountain, see p.360

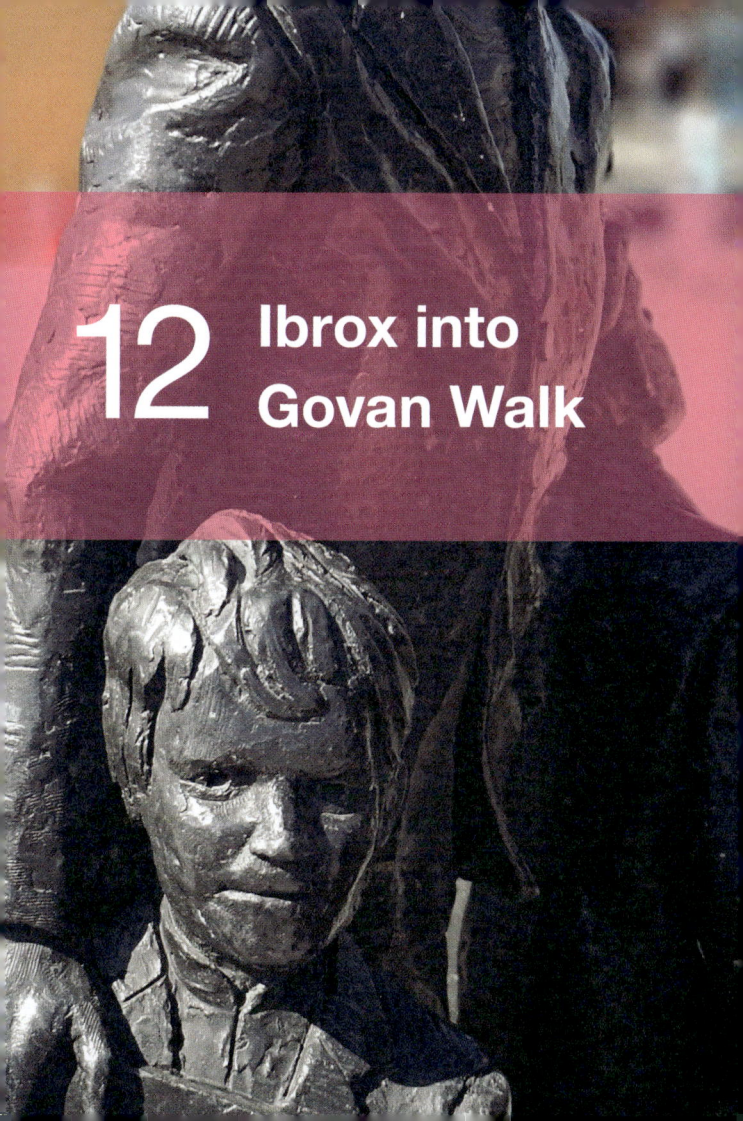

12 Ibrox into Govan Walk

Ibrox into Govan Walk

Start: Ibrox subway
Finish: Govan subway
Distance: 3 miles

This walk begins at Ibrox subway station. You are in Rangers territory. If you have any doubt, opposite is ❶ **The Louden Tavern**, a windowless fortification as inviting as Barlinnie prison (unless you support Rangers). The pub has made the news, often for being trolled by Celtic fans or being at the centre of controversy. Old Firm tensions are seen by many as a bad thing, but as a landlord of The Louden once said, 'if Glasgow didn't have Rangers and Celtic, it wouldn't be Glasgow. It'd be Edinburgh... without the castle.'

In 2012, Peter Ross, writing in *The Scotsman* described the significance of Rangers: 'Football is not just about skills on a pitch, it is an opportunity to say who you are and by extension, who you are not; it offers a feeling of belonging, community and family tradition in a city which increasingly lacks these things. For Rangers fans, support for the team can be an expression of cultural identity; defined for me in the Louden as being to do with Britishness, Unionism, the Kirk, and to a lesser extent the Monarchy'.

Walk up the residential side of Copland Road, passing beige and grey houses. Continue straight on until you reach a junction, following the sharp turn to the right to stop at the ❷ **former Govan Town Hall** on the left. The building has seen better days but is a reminder of the importance of Govan when it was an independent burgh outside of Glasgow between 1864-1912. It had its own civic administration, fire, police, and other services. The hall was opened in 1901, when Govan was at its zenith as an industrial powerhouse.

By 1914, Govan's shipyards employed around 70,000 workers. Today, roughly 180,000 people work across all manufacturing sectors in the whole of Scotland, giving some sense of how times have changed. Post-industrial Govan is a lot quieter today than it used to be.

The Town Hall was designed by architects Thomson & Sandilands in a Beaux-Arts style, no doubt influenced by John Sandilands' studies at the *École des Beaux-Arts* in Paris. John Thomson was the son of the famous Alexander 'Greek' Thomson.

Look for the old entrance to a concert hall, explaining the words 'Music' and 'Drama' up above. Directly below, you will see Govan's heraldic arms, reflecting the area's industrial importance. The arms depict a ship on the stocks, the shield supported by an engineer and a ship carpenter. Above is a salmon and a wheat sheaf, symbolising the area's past connections to fishing and agriculture, as well as (through the salmon) links to Glasgow. Look up and you will see the motto 'Nihil Sine Labore' – 'Nothing without work', a sentiment the people of Govan knew only too well.

Continue to Govan Road and observe the exterior of the building, including the Govan arms outside the entrance. Before Govan was annexed by Glasgow in 1912, these arms were visible throughout the area. Today, the building serves as a base for Film City Glasgow, described as the heart and soul of Scotland's film and television industry and home to around 25 media companies.

Look for two roundels displaying the faces of burgh officials, Provost James Kirkwood and Baillie John Marr.

Glasgow Science Centre and Glasgow Tower viewed from the Prince's Dock

It was largely from the 1840s that Govan village was transformed as new shipyards were founded here. Shipbuilding was not the only industry in Govan, but it had the biggest impact.

By the 1860s, Govan was so economically significant that it was granted burgh status in 1864. It included districts such as Plantation, Cessnock, Ibrox, Craigton, Drumoyne, Linthouse and West Drumoyne. It had its own Lord Provost and was the fifth largest burgh in Scotland. By 1912, when Govan was annexed by Glasgow, the population had grown from a few thousand in the early 1800s to around 95,000.

Turn left along Govan Road, onto the pavement nearest the Clyde. To your right is ❸ **Prince's Dock**, originally Cessnock Dock, built in the 1890s for the Clyde Navigation Trust. The trust was formed in the 1850s, succeeding the River Improvement Trust. It was responsible for managing the Clyde, including dredging the riverbed (key to making the Clyde accessible to large ships).

In 1962, the trust produced a booklet illustrating activities taking place. Prince's Dock was associated with ships travelling to East Africa, West and South Africa, Pakistan, India, the Great Lakes, Canada, Sweden, and South America. Before the Prince's Dock was carved out of the land by thousands of labourers, its site was home to the Clyde Shipbuilding Yard, Cessnock House and nurseries, and the substantial Clyde Villa.

Continue along Govan Road, stopping at ❹ **Canting Way** to your right (if the gates are open) to look across the dock and Clyde. Look for the Glasgow Tower – standing 127 metres high, it is the tallest fully rotating freestanding structure in the world (when it works).

The dock initially covered 35 acres of water, with three basins surrounded by warehouse buildings, a hydraulic power station, an accumulator tower, and tall cranes. The basins were filled in for Glasgow's Garden Festival of 1988, and the area has since been redeveloped. It is now home to the Glasgow Science Centre, BBC, IMAX cinema, and other attractions.

Ibrox into Govan Walk

Continue along Govan Road, and on the right are three graving docks, also built by the Clyde Navigation Trust. The last (southern) one opened in 1898 and was mainly used for overhauls and refits of Clyde steamers (the passenger ships known as the 'Cluthas'). The docks were closed in 1988 and have listed status – 'An outstanding graving dock complex without parallel in Scotland'. 'Graving' is an old nautical word meaning scraping, painting, or tarring something underwater. It became used in conjunction with 'dock' to refer to an enclosed place where a ship is brought for cleaning or repair below the waterline.

Continue walking until you start seeing shops. Stop at the building of the usave store (number 581) and spot the sign for ❺ '**Press Buildings**' with sculpted faces staring down. This was home to the *Govan Press* newspaper, founded by John Cossar and his wife Jane. The Cossar Buildings date from 1890 and were designed by Frank Stirrat. John died aged just 49, a few months after his firm moved here. Jane took over, acquiring other newspapers and expanding operations. She remained involved up until her own death in 1926.

Ibrox into Govan Walk

The frontage features the faces of John and Jane (middle), flanked by Johannes Gutenberg (inventor of the moveable-type printing press), writers and poets Sir Walter Scott and Robert Burns, and another printing innovator – William Caxton.

The Cossar family invented their own printing press which was sold worldwide. The spelling of Gutenberg with two 'tt's suggests either John Cossar knew something we do not, or it is Govan's most public spelling mistake.

When this building was constructed, there were around 30 pubs on Govan Road. In those days, the Temperance movement and religious groups tried to prevent workers from spending their wages on the demon drink. One famous local character is Rab C. Nesbitt, an alcoholic, work-shy man played by Scottish comedian Gregor Fisher's in sketches since the late 1980s. Described as 'sensitive by Govan standards,' one of Rab's lines was, 'Some place Govan, eh? Where else can you get a fish supper at 9am? Simple, just steal it off a drunk that's been lyin' pished outside a close all night'.

Billy Connolly attended St Gerard's Secondary School on Vicarfield Street, to the south of here. He would travel from Drumchapel to Partick and then take the Govan ferry. He later worked at Alexander Stephen & Sons shipyard in Linthouse, about a 30-minute walk from here.

Retrace your steps to take the next left onto Stag Street. On your right are the ❻ **Govan Graving Docks**, and – sometimes – you can get through the fence and wander around (but be careful!). On one visit, local kids were perched on a wall fishing in the Clyde. They mentioned that their parents and grandparents had done the same.

Bear left along Clydebrae Street. It is difficult to imagine the effort it took labourers to excavate these docks, but also the impact it had on the area. For example, the third graving dock stands on the site of Southcroft House, a large dwelling surrounded by a big garden, once familiar to generations of Govanites.

Ibrox into Govan Walk

6

6

Ibrox into Govan Walk

The area to the left and right of here, right up to the Clyde, was once dominated by shipyards. Their history is complex, as yards were founded and later taken over several times by new owners, and their names changed. This vicinity was home to the central Govan yards, sometimes described as the East, Middleton, and Old yards.

The Old Yard was occupied by the family shipbuilding firm founded by pioneer Robert Napier from the 1840s. It was later owned by Randolph, Elder and Company,

Govan Wetlands

and the Mackie and Thomson firms. The Middleton Yard was also developed in the 1840s and taken over after 1912 by Belfast-based Harland & Wolff. As you follow the map along Clydebrae Street look for the entrance to Govan Wetlands, that is in the process of transforming this post-industrial wasteland into a nature reserve.

The ❼ **basin** was dug in the early 20th century. Previously it was home to shipbuilding firms (in the 1850s Govan East Iron Shipbuilding Yard). Continue walking. To the west of the basin stood the ❽ **Middleton yard**, that opened in the 1840s.

Harland & Wolff, best known for building the *Titanic*, opened their Govan site partly because of political instability in Ireland. In 1946, the firm employed 6,000 workers across Govan and three other sites in Glasgow. However, the Govan site was shut in 1963, one of many Glasgow yards to flounder in the face of international competition and poor labour relations between owners and workers.

Continue on and stop at the junction with Napier Street, named after the engineer Robert Napier (1791-1876), credited as the father of shipbuilding in Govan. He began making steam engines for steamers in the 1820s, and by 1841 had founded a shipbuilding company here. Many prominent shipbuilders, including John Elder (more on him shortly), learned their trade under him. All the ❾ **modern housing** was also once the site of shipyards. If you have time, walk through the estate to reach a quiet riverside path.

Ibrox into Govan Walk

Continue along the main route of this walk and turn left by ❿ **Riverside Garden**, with a fantastic mural (2022), by street artist Smug (Sam Bates) depicting a child picking a daffodil. It commemorates the 50th anniversary of the Govan Housing Association and is named 'Georgie' after Georgie Hay, a local member of the association. Politicians, including Jeremy Corbyn and Nicola Sturgeon, have visited the garden for photo opportunities.

Re-join Govan Road and turn right. Further along, near Neptune Street, at ⓫ **number 667** (the current fire station), once stood a tenement that was the childhood home of local legend Alex Ferguson (b.1941).

Ferguson played for leading clubs like Rangers but became famous as a manager of Aberdeen and Manchester United. Ferguson wrote, 'I read an article about me that said: 'Alex Ferguson has done really well in his life despite coming from Govan.' Spot the offending phrase. It's precisely because I started out in the shipbuilding district of Glasgow that I achieved what I did in football'. Ferguson used to own pubs, his first being at the junction of Govan Road and Paisley Road West, and popular with dockers. In the late 1950s, Ferguson went around Govan pubs with a collecting tin for the apprentices' strike fund, giving political speeches to drinkers.

Ibrox into Govan Walk

Turn left down Orkney Street, where on the right is the ⓬ **Orkney Street Enterprise Centre**. The building served as Govan's first burgh hall and dates from 1866. It was designed by John Burnet (1814-1901), one of Glasgow's finest architects and father of architect Sir John James Burnet.

Today, it houses several businesses and organisations, and if you can get inside (no harm in asking), the highlight is the Victorian police cells. Nazi, Rudolph Hess (1894-1987) was (allegedly) held here in May 1941 after parachuting from his plane and landing near Eaglesham, a few miles away. The deluded Hess believed he could negotiate a peace deal. The cells were used from 1867 until 1998 and could hold 120 prisoners. Rab C. Nesbitt was a regular 'guest' here.

Head down Orkney Street, turning right into ⓭ **Orkney Place**. This area contains the classic red sandstone tenement buildings (dating from 1898) that Glasgow is known for. Govan used to have many more streets like this, but concerns about slum conditions in the area led to many being demolished in the second half of the 20th century and replaced with modern housing.

Old police cells

In the late 19th century, urban planners were patriotically minded. Orkney Street was originally called Albert Street, while neighbouring Neptune and Vicarfield Streets were Victoria and Windsor Streets.

At the end of Orkney Place, look for ⓮ **Broomloan Subway Depot**, dating from 1896. When the subway opened in 1896, it was one of only three such systems

Ibrox into Govan Walk

worldwide. At the time, carriages were pulled by a cable system. The building here served as a maintenance depot for the subway carriages, where cranes would lift trains to place them on the running lines.

Walk right down Broomloan Road to join Govan Road. On the corner is a ⑮ **former branch of The Glasgow Savings Bank**, designed by Eric A. Sutherland and dating from 1907. It is a rare survivor from the Edwardian era and one of the finest buildings in Govan.

Turn left along Govan Road, stopping outside the ⑯ **subway station**. It opened in 1896 and was called Govan Cross. Outside is a statue of Mary Barbour (1875-1958), at the head of a group. Mary was a working-class Govan resident famous for her role in the rent strikes of 1915.

At the time, there was a housing shortage. Taking advantage of the fact many men were fighting in World War I, landlords kept increasing rents. Mary, along with other women in the Glasgow Women's Housing Association, fought back with a rent strike in Govan in May 1915.

Strikes began in other districts, and the government was forced to introduce rent controls. The statue by Andrew Brown captures a

day in November 1915 when Mary led a rent protest of 20,000 people through Glasgow. Mary lived on the other side of Elder Park (10 Hutton Drive – there is a plaque).

Continue to Govan Cross, the heart of Govan. Cross to the cast-iron ⑰ **Aitken Memorial Fountain**, dating from 1884. It commemorates Dr John Aitken (1838-1880), Govan's first medical officer. His care for the poor and sick was fondly remembered by Govanites, especially during an era when life expectancy rates were 40 for men and 44 for women. During Aitken's time, Govan's population grew from 8,000 to 46,000, and it is said he worked himself into an early grave.

Look for the arms of Govan, the Manchester Unity of Oddfellows, the Ancient Order of Foresters, and Masonic symbols. These 'secret' societies played a major role in Victorian society. The baby or cherub holding a paddle disappeared in the 1980s, only rediscovered when a man saw a media report about the 'lost baby' and realised he had it in his back garden. The 'Govan Baby' is once again a local landmark.

Turn into ⑱ **Water Row** and down to the end facing the Clyde. This is probably the oldest street in Govan, and 19th-century photos show it was lined by thatched cottages. Labour Party pioneer Keir Hardie may have lived here. In September 2024 a new pedestrian bridge opened linking Govan to Partick. This bridge, and good quality new residential buildings nearby, seem likely to help transform this part of Govan in coming years. Across the bridge you get a good view of the Riverside Museum on the other side.

For centuries, there was a ford here, illustrating how shallow the Clyde was (only 15 inches at low tide) before it was dredged from the late 1700s. There was also a ferry from medieval times up to the 1960s. The new bridge is therefore re-establishing historic links between the districts (both part of the old Govan parish) that were lost when the ferry service stopped. In recent years, a small summer passenger ferry service between the museum and Govan was introduced.

View of Riverside Museum & Partick Bridge from end of Water Row

Ibrox into Govan Walk

In the 19th century, there were ten or more ferry services on the Clyde, many transporting workers to shipyards. Why did ferries disappear? Competition from the subway, trams, buses, cars, and new bridges hastened the decline.

The area to the right of the water's edge by Water Row is the approximate site of an ancient hill about 17 feet high, known as a ⑲ **Moot or Doomster Hill**. It may have served as a ceremonial site, and public meeting place, where oaths of allegiance to rulers were made and judgements pronounced. Govan was a prominent ecclesiastical centre and village in the Dark Ages, with links to Dumbarton, the capital of the ancient Kingdom of Strathclyde.

The hill disappeared after the late 19th century when a dye works was built here, and for a while, it was used as a reservoir. The origin of 'Govan' is debated, but it may have been derived from an old word meaning small mound, so perhaps you are standing at the true heart of ancient Govan.

On the left is a ⑳ **site** used by the travelling community, although plans to redevelop the area have caused tensions. In the 1890s, there were shipyard buildings here all the way to the parish church (seen shortly), and later Harland & Wolff's framing sheds. Retrace your steps to Govan Cross.

On the corner is a ㉑ **red sandstone building**, an excellent example of the 'Glasgow Style', dating from 1900. Built for the British Linen Bank, it was designed by two of the city's great architects – James Salmon Jr. (1873-1924) and John Gaff Gillespie (1870-1926).

Ibrox into Govan Walk

Salmon, born into a distinguished architectural dynasty, studied with Charles Rennie Mackintosh and became one of Mackintosh's closest friends. Gillespie also knew Mackintosh, studying with him at the Glasgow School of Art and sharing the Glasgow Institute of Architects prize in 1889. Their shared journey explains why this building is not dissimilar to Mackintosh's own style.

Look for the standout feature – a ship above the entrance, blown by wind gods using shell trumpets. Also worth noting are the letters 'B L Co' (for the bank) visible in the ship's sail, the tiny figurehead on the front of the ship, and sculptures representing professions.

If you had stood here on a weekday in the early 1900s, when Govan had 95,000 residents, this place would have been packed. Today, the streets are much quieter, and the population is less than a fifth of that figure. In 2017, a report on the area stated, 'People in Govan have poorer life outcomes than the city average. The average number of years that local men are likely to spend in good health is 52, compared to the Glasgow average of 56. For local women, Healthy Life Expectancy is 53 years, compared to 58 across the city'.

Statue of William Pearce and Brechin's Bar

It remains an area still suffering from the economic decline resulting from the de-industrialisation of Glasgow.

Continue through the heart of Govan. On the right is the ㉒ **'P.I' or The Pearce Institute**. This community hub was named after Sir William Pearce (1833-1888).

Randolph, Elder & Co. was a successful engineering firm that founded a shipyard here in 1858. The driving force was John Elder (1824-1869), a brilliant engineer who had worked for Napier's yard in Govan before setting up independently. His work on the compound marine engine revolutionised the efficiency of steamships worldwide.

After he died, his widow, Isabella Elder, sold the business to a partnership that included Sir William Pearce. Alongside Napier and Elder, Pearce was a key figure in turning Govan into a world-leading shipbuilding centre. Pearce also served as an M.P, and his firm's name was changed to the Fairfield Shipbuilding & Engineering Co. in 1886. At its peak, the Fairfield yard would become one of the largest in the world.

The institute was a gift from Pearce's widow, Lady Dinah Pearce, to the working men and women of Govan. Completed in 1906, it was designed by Sir Rowand Anderson, best known for parts of Central Station and the University of Edinburgh. The institute offered a range of distractions for local people, from reading rooms to a gymnasium and workshops where lessons were held. It is said Lady Pearce's ghost haunts the balcony of the building.

It resembles a Scottish Renaissance palace. Look out for the ship's model at the top, produced by workers at Fairfield. The institute's future looked in doubt for many years, but recently it has been revitalised and is again serving the community. Generations of locals have met their partners here, socialised with friends and held important events at the P.I. There is also a café if you need a break (and toilet).

Opposite is a ㉓ **statue of Pearce**, unveiled in 1894 and primarily funded by local people who held Pearce in high regard, including the 5,000 men who worked at Fairfield. He holds a drawing plan for a ship (look carefully to see the outline). It is perhaps HMS *Achilles* (which Pearce oversaw the construction of aged just 27) or one of the fast ships his shipyard produced, known as *Ocean Greyhounds*.

Whilst Pearce was regarded as a genius in business and a significant figure in Govan's community, as a politician he opposed some reforms that would have benefitted his workers. Every week he received a reported salary of £3,700 whilst his workers had to make do with £1. The unveiling ceremony was a grand affair, and among the thousands attending was scientist Lord Kelvin. Sooty deposits gave rise to the statue's unofficial name (the 'Black Man'), but restoration efforts have cleaned up Edward Onslow Ford's design considerably.

Opposite is old-school boozer ㉔ **Brechins**. This building dates from 1894 and is often described as having been (ironically) a temperance hall, but that is now contested. Walk to the south side to spy a carving of a rat-catching cat up high, said to be inspired by the story of a local cat that made short work of an influx of rats coming into Govan on visiting ships.

Ibrox into Govan Walk

A surprising visitor in 1990 was Noam Chomsky (b.1928). One of the world's greatest thinkers, he visited the Pearce Institute when it was hosting a conference and is said to have had a pint in Brechins afterwards.

Next, turn right past the **war memorial**. The memorial dates from the early 1920s and is worth a look, just to see all the names of far-flung places worldwide where Govanites lost their lives. Men wounded in World War I helped in its construction. In the 1930s, unemployed shipyard workers helped create the landscape between the church and the memorial.

Continue to ㉕ **Govan Old Parish Church**, which occupies the most historically important site in the area. The first place of worship here dates back to the 5th or 6th century AD, and the church was dedicated to St Constantine of Strathclyde (c.570 AD-640 AD). There is little known about this saint, but he may have been the son of the King of Strathclyde and came here to Govan to found a monastery or church. His feast day is 11 March, and he may also have been buried here, so this could have become

Ibrox into Govan Walk

a pilgrimage site or even a place associated with the ancient Kings of Strathclyde.

The church building seen today is from 1888, and inside you can see the Govan Stones – burial markers dating from the 9th to 11th centuries AD. These include the Viking 'hog-back' stones, which are unlike anything else found in Scotland. The Govan Sarcophagus contains a carving of a horseman and animals. The stones, discovered in the graveyard over many years, have made the church one of Glasgow's most impressive visitor attractions.

The graveyard contains headstones that recall Govanites who lived here when it was just a village. The old Govan parish extended north and south of the Clyde, including areas such as Partick and the Gorbals, and was one of the largest parishes in Scotland. If you could travel to the old village in the early 1800s, you would find it dominated by two-storey thatched cottages. Many residents made their living from fishing, weaving, and agriculture. Some gravestones bear trade symbols, indicating the deceased's profession (there is a guide to the symbols inside the church). Behind the church is a path by the Clyde which offers good views to Partick and the north.

Govan, and the area around today's Glasgow Cathedral founded by St Mungo, developed as important ecclesiastical centres in the Dark Ages. Had history taken a slightly different course, we could be in a city called Govan and Glasgow would be just a district within it.

Channel Four's *Time Team* visited Govan in 1997, and a trench was dug in the graveyard and by the Moot Hill near Water Row, unearthing an ancient road used to link the two sites. A local man told me how, as a kid, he and his friends snuck down into the graves that had been uncovered.

Bond legend Sean Connery (1930-2020) came here in 1967 to direct a documentary titled *The Bowler and the Bunnet*. It focussed on an experiment between the government, industrialists and trade unions to save the Fairfield shipyard from bankruptcy. The film captures a pivotal moment in Govan's history. In 1950 there had been 28 shipyards on the Clyde, but by 1967 only a third remained. To save what was left, the privately owned shipyards were reorganised in the late 1960s into the Government-backed Upper Clyde Shipbuilders Limited.

The film shows Govan as it then was: many more tenements, smarter shops along Govan Road, and busy shipyards. However, there were ominous signs – vast, abandoned industrial buildings that would soon be swept away. In the film, Connery stands outside this church and then explores an abandoned shipyard.

Political activist, trade unionist, and writer Jimmy Reid (1932-2010) will always be associated with Govan and its shipyards. A service was held at the church after Reid's death, attended by figures such as Gordon Brown, Sir Alex Ferguson, and Billy Connolly. More on Reid later on.

Return to Govan Road, passing 26 **St Anthony's Roman Catholic Church**, designed in a Romanesque style by John Honeyman and dating from 1879. Honeyman (1831-1914) was a good architect who is now mainly remembered for being Charles Rennie Mackintosh's boss (alongside John Keppie).

Ibrox into Govan Walk

Since the mid-19th century, most working-class districts of Glasgow have been affected by sectarian tensions. Govan is no exception and is home to loyalist, pro-Rangers, flute bands such as The Pride of Govan Flute Band and The Govan Protestant Boys. Sectarianism was also prevalent in the shipyards. It was said that Belfast-founded Harland & Wolff had an unofficial hiring policy favouring Protestant workers. As skilled jobs required being hired as an apprentice, this had a significant impact on who did what. It is also said that Rangers' association with Protestantism and the Orange movement began when H&W moved Protestant workers from Belfast to Govan, and these workers began supporting their local team.

Sadly, sectarian tensions still exist. In August 2019, a street battle occurred between here and Elder Park, involving hundreds of Loyalists and Republicans. It was sparked when the James Connolly Republican Flute Band attempted to march through Govan. The BBC reported how 'riot police, mounted officers, a helicopter and dog units were called in following an Irish Unity march and counter-protest in Glasgow'.

Near this spot, a local named Jim told me his story. He had spent years working in a local shipyard before layoffs forced him to seek work elsewhere. His search for employment led him to the mines of England, then to the monumental task of digging out the Channel Tunnel, and finally to the construction of a remote refinery. The relentless pressures of these tough, transient jobs took a heavy toll on his personal life, ultimately leading to the breakdown of his marriage and his departure from Govan for many years. His story is not an uncommon one, and a reminder that it is Jim and others like him who created the infrastructure many of us take for granted.

Continue along, passing the former ㉗ **Lyceum Cinema** on the corner. This art deco cinema opened in 1938, built on the site of an earlier theatre and music hall dating from 1899. The cinema could hold 2,600 people

when Glasgow boasted around 130 cinemas. It is said Glasgow had more cinema seats per head of the population than any other city on earth, and Govan used to have four.

Cinema helped kill off the music hall, and in turn, from the 1950s, television forced many cinemas to close. The Lyceum was typical of this decline, forced to become a bingo hall. Today, it is an empty shell, awaiting redevelopment. In Sean Connery's film, hundreds of shipyard workers are shown inside the building voting on proposals about new work practices. Few of them could have guessed that soon all the yards would have shut except for one.

In the 19th century, ㉘ **Govandale House** stood behind the cinema site, surrounded by open land. In the 1890s, this area became home to the Linthouse Football Ground and Linthouse F.C. Ten thousand fans watched them play Celtic in September 1895. However, the club failed to thrive and disbanded in 1900. To the west of here stood the Govan Silk factory, a reminder that shipbuilding was just one industry in the area.

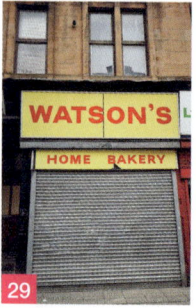

Continue along Govan Road, turning left down Shaw Street to stop at ㉙ **Watson's Home Bakery**, a local institution run for over 50 years by the McBean family. Known for its excellent Scotch pies, its most famous customer is Sir Alex Ferguson, who once stopped the team bus to get pies for his players.

㉚ **The Old Govan Arms** on the left is another well-known Govan pub, also visible in Connery's film. It had a high-profile visitor when Prime Minister Tony Blair came for a

Ibrox into Govan Walk

drink in 2007. Blair's father, Leo (1923-2012), was adopted by a Govan couple, and his adoptive father worked in the shipyards as a casual labourer. Leo grew up in a house on neighbouring Golspie Road.

During his visit, the Prime Minister (looking a little out of place) described his father's connections and one local asked: 'So you're here to pay his rent arrears then?'. The pub has a reputation for welcoming Celtic fans and used to be owned by Celtic player Thomas Colgan in 1916.

Leo attended Govan High School (as did Ferguson) and was influenced by the left-wing politics of Govan. He worked for a Communist Party newspaper before becoming an academic. By contrast, Blair went to Fettes College in Edinburgh, Scotland's answer to Eton and where the fictional James Bond went to school.

Blair said: 'I've never actually been here before, so I thought it would be nice to have a look. I remember for so much of my childhood hearing my dad talking about Golspie Street and being brought up here… He used to tell the story of how he used to save up the lemonade bottles to go to the cinema.'

Opposite the pub is ㉛ **Sunny Govan Community Radio**, as well as other premises used by creative groups including an artist in residence. Walk further along the high street and take a right onto Elder Street, then into Luath Street to stop outside ㉜ **number 10**.

A significant and unusual event in the city's social history took place here. In 1972, this was the home of John and Annie Gibbons. At the time, this street was one of many due to be demolished in the name of urban planning. Planners thought it too challenging to modernise old tenements to include an indoor bathroom. However, at number 10, architects managed to convert a space to create a bathroom and – hard to imagine now – it caused a sensation. The press reported that hundreds of (nosy) people flocked here to visit the toilet, suggesting few entertainment options were available in Govan in the early '70s.

Ibrox into Govan Walk

The modernisation here helped convince the authorities that tenements could be revived rather than pulled down. It also helped create the local housing association. The story is best told in Raymond Young's book *Annie's Loo*.

Return to Govan Road and on your right is the site of the famous ❸❸ **Fairfield Shipyard**. This is still a working shipyard, today owned by BAE Systems, which runs facilities here and at Scotstoun. The main office facing Govan Road has recently been transformed into the Fairfield Govan Heritage Centre and Workspace.

The site's history could fill a whole book, so the best way to learn about the place is to visit the heritage centre.

At its peak during World War I, Fairfield employed 10,000 workers. It survived for a few more decades before filing for bankruptcy in 1965. The government stepped in, and Fairfield was absorbed into the Upper Clyde Shipbuilders (UCS).

Sean Connery interviewed workers and management for *The Bowler and the Bunnet*. The title refers to the bowler hat worn by management and the bunnet – or flat cap – worn by working men. The documentary captures hundreds of men rushing out of these gates at the end of the day, often to the local pub where trays of whiskies would be laid out.

Some firms used to split pay packets so the men's wives got money separately. Even then, it was common for children to be sent to local pubs to try and stop their father's spending all their money on drink. Heavy drinking was a feature of life in many industrial trades in Govan (and elsewhere). One local told me how workers used to attend AA meetings held within Fairfield's offices.

Between 1971-1972 worker and management relations collapsed. The government threatened to pull funding from the Upper Clyde Shipbuilders (UCS) and close four Glasgow shipyards, including at Govan. This put 6,000 jobs at risk and led to an innovative response. Inspired by figures such as union

Ibrox into Govan Walk

Ibrox into Govan Walk

member and Govanite Jimmy Reid, a 'work-in' took place. Instead of going on strike, workers sought to complete existing ship orders. It forced the government's hand, embarrassed that the 'work-in' was being reported worldwide.

In a speech to workers, Reid declared: 'Nobody and nothing will come in and nothing will go out without our permission. And there will be no hooliganism, there will be no vandalism, there will be no bevvying because the world is watching us'. John Lennon and Yoko Ono were among the famous figures who lent support, donating £5,000.

When Reid announced Lennon's gift to assembled workers, one wit called out 'But, Lenin's deid!'. The couple sent red roses, and a card reading, 'Power to the People, with love from John and Yoko August 9th 1971'. The roses ended up at a nearby maternity ward.

Despite the work-in, the shipyards continued to close down, and now the only one left is BAE Systems.

The oldest part of the shipyard offices dates from 1890 and was designed by Honeyman & Keppie (who hired Charles Rennie Mackintosh). The striking figures at the entrance of an engineer and shipwright are similar to the figures on Govan's coat of arms seen earlier. This is the finest example of a Victorian-era shipbuilding office in Britain.

Monument

Outside the entrance is a sculpture of kissing cormorant birds created by Helen Denerly in 1994 using scrap materials from the shipyards.

Carry on to enter ㉞ **Elder Park**. In a classic act of Victorian philanthropy, the park was created by Isabella Elder as a monument to her shipbuilder husband John Elder, and to give local people 'healthful recreation by music and amusement'. It occupies 37 acres

Ibrox into Govan Walk

of land once belonging to the old Fairfield Farm (after which the shipyard was named). It was opened in 1885 by Lord Rosebery and designed by John Honeyman.

Near the entrance, look for a monument to those who died in the submarine K13 in 1917. Built at Fairfield, it sank during trials, killing 32 men, including six from the yard. The submarine was salvaged and renamed K22 (the unlucky number 13 was never used again for a Royal Navy submarine). There is another K13 memorial in Australia, where one of the survivors emigrated.

Continue along the perimeter of the park, built on the site of Fairfield Farm. Just past the pond between the path and the park railings is ㉟ **a run-down old building, once part of the farmhouse** and a rare survivor of the era before shipbuilding. The pond is used by the Elder Park Model Boat Club, and in the past retired ship workers would make models and come here to sail them. It is said that to be a true Govanite, you need to have fallen into the pond.

Elder Park pond

Ibrox into Govan Walk

Elder Park

Ibrox into Govan Walk

Near the pond is a classical-styled portico, the remains of ㊱ **Linthouse Mansion**. The mansion was built in 1791 and possibly designed by the famous architect Robert Adam. It became the office of local shipbuilder Alexander Stephen in 1869, and after that building was demolished in 1920, the remains were moved here.

Walk to the other side of the park to the ㊲ **statue of Isabella Elder**. Close by (near the railings) is a monument commemorating the SS *Daphne* disaster. On 3 July 1883, SS *Daphne* was launched from the Alexander Stephen and Sons shipyard but capsized with 200 workers on board as horrified spectators looked on. The death toll from the 'Linthouse Disaster' reached 124, including many children. There is a memorial in Craigton Cemetery where many bodies were buried. The ship was salvaged, renamed, and later returned to service.

Walk to the east side of the park to locate a ㊳ **statue of John Elder**, which stands alongside the innovative compound engine that made his fortune. It is the work of sculptor Sir J. E. Boehm, who was a favourite of the Royal family. When Boehm died of a heart attack at his studio in 1890, he is said to have been in the arms of his mistress and fellow sculptor, Princess Louise, daughter of Queen Victoria.

Walk towards the grand building on the corner of the park – ㊴ **Elder Park Library**. Isabella Elder supported many charitable causes in Govan, including the establishment of a School of Domestic Economy for local girls and this library. It was designed by Sir J.J Burnet. Jimmy Reid was one local kid who benefitted from the opportunities presented by the library, and he was regularly seen walking home with several books under his arm. By the age of

Monument to SS Daphne

Ibrox into Govan Walk

fourteen, he had read Karl Marx and many other influential writers, so the library shaped his life.

In 1972, Reid became Rector of Glasgow University and gave a famous speech to students on alienation 'A rat race is for rats. We're not rats. We're human beings'. The speech struck a chord worldwide, with *The New York Times* describing it as 'the greatest speech since President Lincoln's Gettysburg Address'. Not bad for a working-class kid who worked as a fitter at Fairfield and educated himself in this library.

Designed by Sir J.J. Burnet, the library opened in 1903 with Scots-born American industrialist Andrew Carnegie in attendance. Carnegie, known for his controversial stance on trade unions, later gained some redemption through his philanthropy, funding public libraries worldwide (though not this one). His presence at the opening would have been quite an event, akin to Elon Musk attending the launch of a public building in Govan today. Look for the Govan coat of arms at the entrance.

Exit the park near the library, walking along Langlands Road to view examples of modern residential developments. Continue straight until you reach the corner with Golspie Road, where you'll find the former ㊵ **Abraham Hill's Trust School**, built in 1874. An earlier version of the school was funded by a bequest from 18th century merchant Abraham Hill, hence the name. It was designed by James Thomson (1835-1905), a respected architect and partner in the firm Baird & Thomson.

From here, follow the map to rejoin Govan Road, then continue to the subway.

VISIT

The Glasgow Tower & Glasgow Science Centre
50 Pacific Quay, G51 1DA
glasgowsciencecentre.org

The Pearce Institute
840-860 Govan Rd, G51 3UU
govanpi.com

Govan Old Parish Church (The Govan Stones)
866 Govan Rd, G51 3UU
thegovanstones.org.uk

Elder Park
Govan Rd, G51 4XS
friendsofelderpark.wordpress.com

Fairfield Heritage Centre
1048 Govan Rd, G51 4XS
fairfieldgovan.co.uk

EAT & DRINK...

Louden Tavern
111 Copland Rd, G51 2SL
theloudentavern.co.uk

The Old Govan Arms
907 Govan Rd, G51 3DN

The Wee Dhaaba
17 Elder St, G51 3DY

Index

A

Adam, James 230, 247
Adam, Robert 251, 379
Adelphi Terrace School 110, 124
Aitken Memorial Fountain 348, 360
Albany Academy 268, 279
Albany Mansions 77, 105, 106
Alexander, Betty 86, 87, 88
Alexandra Bar 297, 314, 319
Al-Furqan Mosque 268, 274
Allison Street Murders 188
Anchor Line Building 238, 254
Anderson, John 11, 226, 232
Anderson family 43, 56, 62
Anderson's College Medical School 6, 11
Anderston footbridge 40, 47
Anderston Rice Mills 40, 53
Anderston Station 40, 50
Andrew Ure Hall 203, 234, 235
Annette St Primary School 169, 190
Argyll Arcade 147, 157, 158, 165
Arlington Bar 268, 279
Arlington Baths Club 268, 279
Arrol, Sir William 270, 302
Arthur, James 202, 217
Art Nouveau 'Hatrack' 239, 263
Athenaeum Theatre 238, 258

B

Baird, John 246, 252, 282, 283
Bajin, Rank 268, 287
Barony Church 202, 216, 217
Battle of Rottenrow 217
Battle of the Boyne 216, 336
Belmont Bridge 322, 327
Ben Nevis bar 41, 66
Berkeley Square 41, 72
Bishop Mills 6, 18
Bishop of Glasgow 21, 43, 204
Blackfriars Church 296, 301
Blessed John Duns Scotus 110, 123, 143
Blind Burn 124, 133, 195
Boer War 197, 283
Bon Accord 40, 44, 73
Bonnar, Stan 314, 315
Botanic Gardens 63, 290, 330-1, 345
Boyle, Jimmy 130, 131, 134
Brazen Head Pub, The 111, 139, 143
Brechin's Bar 348, 364, 367, 368
Bristol Bar 296, 313, 319
Britannia Panopticon 203, 229, 235
British Linen Bank 111, 141, 363
Broomloan Subway Depot 348, 359
Brown, William Kellock 259, 299
Bruce, Robert the 212, 232
Buffalo Bill 82, 309, 310
Bunhouse Flour Mills 6, 14
Burgh Hall 7, 28, 30, 183, 260
Burnbank Bowling Club 268, 288
Burnbank Park 268, 273
Burnet, J.J. 50, 105-6, 113 115, 217 241-2, 249, 253, 258, 260, 263, 279, 283, 359, 380
Burnet, John 113, 115, 186, 209, 238, 241, 246, 249, 253-4, 256, 259, 279, 280, 359
Butterly, John 316, 318

C

Ca' d'Oro 238, 243
Café D'Jaconelli 323, 339, 345
Caledonian Chambers 238, 244
Caledonian Mansions 269, 290
Caledonian Railway 113, 187, 244, 290, 341
Caledonia Road Church 111, 137
Campbell, John A. 217, 258, 260
Canal House 323, 342
Carlton Bingo building 7, 36

Index

Carnegie, Andrew 43, 48, 127, 192, 299, 335, 380
Castle Chambers 238, 259
Cathedral House Hotel 202, 215
Comprehensive Development Area 51, 57, 125-6, 132, 221, 315
Charing Cross Mansions 77, 105-6
Chivas Strathclyde Distillery 110, 125
Christadelphian Hall 296, 311
Church of St Simon 6, 16
Citizens Theatre 111, 129, 142, 143
City Chambers 153, 238, 252, 260
Claypits Nature Reserve 340, 345
Clifford, H.E. 51, 52
Clyde Navigation Trust 24, 54, 353, 354
Clydesdale Bank HQ 238, 254
Cochrane, John 155, 162
Coia, Jack 308, 314, 317
Coia's Café 297, 317, 319
Conan Doyle, Sir Arthur 277
Connery, Sean 370, 372, 374
Connolly, Billy 31-2, 72, 355, 370
Conrad, Joseph 19
Convent of Mercy 76, 88, 96
Convent of the Sisters of the Gospel of Life 168, 185
Corinthian Club 238, 248, 265
Cossar, John 354, 355
Cranston, Katie 7, 59, 146-165, 171, 239, 248, 264, 392
Cranston, Mary 162
Cranston, Robert 159
Cranston, Stuart 147, 150, 152, 158, 160, 264
Crosshill Station 168, 181
Crosshill Synagogue 185
Crown Flour Mills 40, 54
Crown Tea & Luncheon Rooms 149
Cumberland Street Station 111, 140
Cunninghame, William 225, 246
Cuthbertson Primary School 169, 197

D

Daily Record Building 147, 161, 239, 264
Dawsholm Station 322, 333
Deanside Well Garden 202, 207
Dennistoun, Alexander 301-3
Dennistoun, James 301, 311
Dennistoun Baths 296, 307
Dennistoun Library 296, 299, 319
Dennistoun Masonic Hall 309
Dennistoun Palais 296, 311
Dennistoun United Presbyterian Church 297, 317
Dixon, William 130, 183-4
Dixon Halls 168, 181, 183-5
Dolphin Pub, The 6, 9, 22
Doomster Hill 348, 363
Dosser, Lobey 268, 287
Dowanvale Free Church of Scotland 7, 34
Drill Hall 41, 72, 169, 196, 223, 288, 326
Drygate Brewing Co. 202, 211, 235
Duke St Prison 202, 210-11, 217, 283
Dundas Court 76, 80
Dundasvale Court 76, 78

E

Earl of Eglinton 112, 117
Education Act 51, 209
Education (Scotland) Act 34, 51, 105, 124, 209 288,
Edward VII 187, 307
Egyptian Halls 238, 243
Elder, Isabella 348, 365, 376, 379
Elder, John 348, 357, 365, 376, 379
Elder Park 348, 360, 371, 376-381
Elder Park Library 348, 379
Elmbank Iron Foundry 44

Index

F

Fairfield Shipyard 348, 374
Ferguson, Alex 358, 370, 372
Finnieston Bar 41, 67
Firhill Basin 323, 340
Firhill Stadium 24, 323, 340
Forrest, William 205, 263, 308
Forsyth Store 238, 241
Forth & Clyde Canal 78, 325, 334, 337, 342
Free Presbyterian Church 268, 280

G

Gaiety Theatre 40, 56
Gallery of Modern Art 238, 246, 265
Garnethill Community Garden 76, 77, 95, 100
Garnethill Park 77, 97, 107
Garnethill Primary School 77, 104
Garnethill Synagogue 76, 90
Garnethill Viewpoint 76, 90
Garrioch flour mill 322, 330
Garrioch Quadrant Viaducts 322, 332
George V 331
George VI 47
Gillespie, J.G. 58, 263, 264, 314, 363
Glasgow Academicals RFC 273
Glasgow Academy 276, 322, 327
Glasgow Athenaeum 238, 258
Glasgow Boys 215
Glasgow Cancer Hospital 76, 92
Glasgow Cathedral 217-8, 335, 369
Glasgow Central Gurdwara 41, 71, 73
Glasgow Central Mosque 110, 122, 143
Glasgow Central Railway 50, 63, 69, 290, 331-3
Glasgow City Halls 203, 229
Glasgow Empire Exhibition 115
Glasgow Evangelical Church 202, 215
Glasgow Film Theatre 77, 100, 107
Glasgow Gurdwara 169, 198, 199
Glasgow Herald 159, 161, 244, 285
Glasgow International Exhibition 152, 254
Glasgow Necropolis 212-3, 235, 319
Glasgow Reformed Presbyterian Church 7, 32
Glasgow Royal Maternity Hospital 203, 223
Glasgow Savings Bank 58, 76, 83, 110, 113, 238, 249, 348, 360
Glasgow School Board 51, 124, 197, 203, 222
Glasgow School of Art 58, 77, 85-6, 89, 95, 96, 99-103, 107, 141, 253, 263, 305, 325, 364
Glasgow Science Centre 352-3, 381
Glasgow Sculpture Studios 299, 342, 345
Glasgow Stock Exchange 238, 256
Glasgow Tower 352, 353, 381
Glasgow University 13, 15, 208, 279, 285, 326, 380
Glasser, Ralph 119, 137
Golfhill Public School 296, 305
Gorbals Art Project 141
Gorbals Boys statues 111, 131
Gorbals Cross 110, 121, 122, 123
Gorbals Parish Church 118
Gorbals Public Bath 111, 142
Gorbals Public Library 110, 120
Gorbals Rose Garden 111, 133, 143
Gorbals Sound recording studio 111, 139
Gorbals Station 111, 140
Gorbals Vampire 129
Govandale House 348, 372
Govan Graving Docks 348, 355
Govanhill Baths 169, 194, 199
Govanhill Free Church 168, 185

Index

Govanhill Library 169, 192
Govanhill Park 169, 195
Govanhill Picture House 169, 191
Govan Iron Works 183
Govan Old Parish Church 348, 368, 381
Govan-Partick Bridge 20
Govan Press 354
Govan Stones 369, 381
Govan subway station 348
Govan Town Hall 348, 350
Grassby, Charles 246, 256
Gray, Alasdair 185, 311, 337
Great Famine 22, 45, 137
Grosvenor Building 238, 240, 265
Grove Pub, The 41, 67
GSA Library 77
Gunn, Richard 253, 264

H

Haldane Building 77, 99
Hamilton, David 80, 93, 118, 212, 246, 247, 248, 251, 256
Hamiltonhill Claypits 323, 340
Hankinson, Molly 7, 30, 125
Harland & Wolff 19, 23, 357, 363, 371
Harley, William 84, 101, 105
Herald, The 81, 87, 88, 92, 127, 160, 191, 238, 246
Hidden Lane 41, 69, 73
Highland Clearances 36
Hill, Abraham 348, 380
Hive, The 41, 69
Holl, Steven 103
Holy Cross Catholic Church 168, 185
Holyrood High School 168, 183
Holyrood Quadrant 268, 272
Honeyman, John 71, 186, 215, 243, 270, 289, 370, 377
Honeyman & Keppie 103, 156, 159, 220, 245, 305, 339, 376
Hospital for Sick Children Dispensary 76
House, Jack 277, 311
Howgate 202, 220
Hughes Memorial Orange Halls 323, 336
Hume, David 226
Hutcheson, George & Thomas 124, 251
Hutcheson, Thomas 124, 251
Hutchesons' Hall 238, 247, 251
Hutcheson's Hospital School 136
Hutchesontown Library 111, 127

I

Iannucci, Armando 33, 97
Ignatian Spirituality Centre 76, 96

J

James II 216, 336
Jubilee Bridge 181

K

K13 Disaster 377
Kelvin Aqueduct 322, 334, 335
Kelvinbridge 268-70, 290, 292, 322, 324, 325, 327, 342
Kelvinbridge Railway Station 269, 290
Kelvindale Paper Mills 322, 333
Kelvin Dry Dock 21
Kelvin Graving Dock 323, 334
Kelvingrove Park 63, 283-4, 290, 293
Kelvin Hall 9, 13, 14, 16, 37
Kentigern House 40, 50
Keppie, John 11, 13, 103, 156, 159, 160, 220, 243-6, 251, 270, 305, 339, 370, 376
King Billy 202, 216, 217
Kingston Bridge 40, 55
Kirkland, Alexander 63, 66, 117

385

Index

Kirklee Bridge 322, 331
Kirklee Footbridge 322, 330
Kirklee Station 322, 331

L

Lady Well 202, 212
Laing, R.D. 169, 193, 197
Lanarkshire Rifle Volunteers 183, 196, 273
Langside Synagogue 168, 174
Lansdowne Crescent 268, 272
Lansdowne Parish Church 268, 270
Laurie brothers 117, 118, 133
Laurieston Bar 110, 112, 143
Laurieston House 110, 118
Leiper, William 28, 252, 260
Lighthouse, The 147, 159, 165, 238, 245, 265
Linthouse Mansion 348, 379
Lipton, Sir Thomas 129, 137
Lismore Pub, The 7, 34
Loch Katrine Distillery. 122
Louden Tavern, The 296, 312, 319, 348, 350, 381
Lucifer Match Works 313
Lulu 316, 317, 318, 339
Lyceum Cinema 348, 371
Lynch, Benny 111, 134

M

M8 43-48, 55, 79-80, 83, 90, 106, 220, 274, 277, 307, 344
Macdonald, Margaret 125, 153, 159, 245, 264
Macdonald, Mary 76, 89
MacIntosh, George 303
Mackintosh, Charles Rennie 13, 25, 40, 58, 61, 71, 77 89, 101, 103, 141, 149, 150, 153, 156, 157-165, 171, 173, 186, 215, 220, 222, 240-245, 248, 260, 263, 270, 296, 304, 305, 314, 338, 339, 345, 364, 370, 376
Mansfield Park 33, 34, 37
Marriott Hotel 40, 50
Martyrs' Public School 202, 220
Maryhill Barracks 332, 333
Maryhill Burgh Halls 323, 335, 345
Maryhill Iron Works 323, 338
Maryhill Library 323, 335
Maryhill Road Aqueduct 323, 336
Mary Macdonald House 76, 89
Marzaroli, Oscar 95, 131
McGregor, Ewan 16, 112
McGregor, John 21, 22
McLellan Galleries 77, 101
McNayr, James 285
McNeil Street Bakery 110, 126
Meadowside Shipyard 6, 20, 21
Mercat Cross 203, 233
Merchants' House 238, 253, 301
Miller, James 25, 113, 160, 197, 238, 244, 253-4, 257, 264, 290
Mitchell Library 40-4, 72, 73
Molendinar Burn 202, 204, 210, 211, 212, 218, 307
Monkland Canal 78, 221, 307, 344
Monument to Maternity 203, 224
Moorhead, Ethel 282
Morgan, J.P. 47-8
Morgan Stanley 40, 47, 48
Mossman, John 246, 248, 256, 258

N

National Trust for Scotland 90, 165
Nesbitt, Rab C. 355, 359
Nicholas, Charlie 332
Nisbet, James 215, 220
North British Station Hotel 147, 154, 163
North Woodside 322, 326-8
North Woodside Flint Mill 322, 328

Index

O

O'Connell, Daniel 30, 120
Old Govan Arms 348, 372, 381
Old Partick Bridge 6, 12, 13
'Old' Partick Parish Church 6
Old Savings Bank 40, 58
Orkney Street Enterprise Centre 348, 359
Our Lady of Good Counsel 296, 308

P

Park Bar, The 41, 67, 73
Park Church 268, 287
Partick Academy 10
Partick Bridge 6, 12, 13, 14, 362
Partick Castle 6, 14, 21
Partick Central Station 6, 16
Partick Cross 6, 9, 30
Partick Cross Mansions 6, 9
Partick Curling Club 28
Partick Fire Station 7, 25
Partick Methodist Church 7, 26
Partick Parish church 10
Partick Station 7, 26, 27
Partick Thistle 24, 104, 339, 340
Partick West Station 6, 25
Patrick Burgh Hall 7, 28
Pearce, Sir William 190, 365
Pearce Institute 348, 365, 368, 381
Peden, Liz 131, 133
Pentagon Centre 40, 52, 53
People's Palace 143, 309
Phoenix Foundry 79-80
Phoenix Recreation Park 76, 80
Pinkerton, Allan 122, 137
Pointhouse Shipyard 6, 19
Port Dundas Basin 323, 344
Prince's Dock 348, 352, 353
Provand's Lordship 202, 218
Pugin, Augustus 45, 185
Pyramid at Anderston 40, 57

Q

Quakers Burial Ground 7
Queen Margaret Bridge 322, 328, 330
Queen's Cross Church 323, 339
Queen's Park 168, 170, 173, 174, 176, 177, 179, 193, 199
Queen's Park Baptist Church 168, 173
Queen's Park Govanhill 168, 174
Queens Park Station 169, 187
Queen's Park United Presbyterian Church 179

R

Ramsay, Sir William 268, 276, 327
Ramshorn Kirk 203, 225, 227
Rangers FC 29, 273, 312-13, 336, 350, 358, 371
Reid, Jimmy 370, 376, 379, 380
Reid, John 301, 304, 311, 314
Reidvale Neighbourhood Centre 297, 314-5
Rhind, James R. 127, 192, 299, 335
Rhind, William Birnie 242, 260
River Kelvin 9, 13, 14, 63, 67, 270, 289, 325
Riverside Garden 348, 358
Riverside Museum 6, 19-20, 37, 361-2
Robert the Bruce 212, 232
Roberts, Lord 268, 283, 284
Rosevale Pub, The 7, 27
Royal Faculty of Procurators in Glasgow 238, 257
Royal Hospital for Sick Children 76, 88
Royal Samaritan Hospital for Women 169, 195
Ruchill Church Hall 338
Ruchill Saw Mills 323, 338
Ryan's Bar 169, 189

Index

S

Salmon, James 58, 141, 248, 263, 302, 308, 312, 314, 363
Salmon, William F. 205, 263, 308
Salvation Army centre 40, 59
School Board of Glasgow 169, 188, 312
Scotsman, The 32, 350
Scotstoun Grain Mills 6, 14
Scott, Andy 24, 61
Scott, Sir Walter 207, 355
Scottish Jewish Archives 92, 107
Scottish Temperance League 239, 263
Sellars, James 11, 86, 88, 246, 254, 260
Sick Children's Hospital Dispensary 76, 85
Spence, Sir Basil 132
Sixty Steps 322, 328, 330
Smiddy Bar 32, 37
Society of Friends (Quakers) Burial Ground 36
Southern Necropolis 111, 129, 143, 207
South Portland St Suspension Bridge 110, 117
South Portland St Synagogue 121
Speirs Wharf 323, 342
SS *Daphne* disaster 379
St Aloysius' Church 77, 100, 107
St Aloysius' College 89, 96, 97
St Andrew's Church 77, 104
St Andrew's Halls 40, 42, 43, 86
St Andrew's Suspension Bridge 110, 126
St Anne's RC Church 297, 314
St Anthony's Roman Catholic Church 348, 370
St Denis' Primary School 296, 312
St Enoch Burn 221

St George's Cross 84, 274
St Mark's Church 55
St Mary's Scottish Episcopal Cathedral 268, 272
St Mungo 50, 127, 202, 204, 207, 210, 218, 221, 222, 235, 369
St Mungo Museum of Religious Life & Art 202, 218
St Mungo's RC Church 202, 221
St Patrick's RC church 40, 45
St Peter's Boys School 7, 32
St Peter's Catholic Church 7, 33
St Peter's RC primary school 7, 34
St Silas Church 269, 289
St Vincent Bowling club 41, 65
Stephen, Alexander 355, 379
Steven Holl Architects 103
Stirrat, Frank 183, 354
Stobcross House 44, 55, 56
Stockingfield Bridge Art Park 337
Stone of Destiny 279, 280
Stow College 76, 84
Sturgeon, Nicola 61, 132, 358
Sun Life Assurance Building 238, 260
Sunny Govan Community Radio 348, 373
Sutherland, Eric A. 191, 360

T

Tennent's Wellpark Brewery 202, 211, 235
Theosophical Society 268, 277
Thomson, Alexander 'Greek' 122, 127, 129, 137, 171, 173, 178, 179, 190, 238, 240, 258, 282, 328, 351
Thomson, John 351
Thomson Street School 297, 317
Tod & McGregor 22, 23
Tolbooth Steeple 203, 230, 234
Townhead Martyrs 202, 215

Townhead Village Hall 202, 222
Trades Hall of Glasgow 238, 251
Trainspotting 7, 16, 32, 307, 339
Trams 9, 15, 69, 85, 121, 152, 169 181 190, 197, 199, 273, 312, 363
Tramway Arts Centre 166, 97
Tron Kirk Steeple 203, 230
Twomax Building 111, 133

U

University of Glasgow 13, 43, 202-4, 226, 235, 272, 287, 301, 338
Upper Clyde Shipbuilders 370, 374

V

Victoria, Queen 29, 53, 177, 187, 379
Victoria Bar 169, 189, 199
Victoria Pub, The 7, 29

W

Walker, John Ewing 'Hookey' 328
Wallace, William 212, 218
Walter Macfarlane & Co 270
Walton, George 150, 152, 153, 156, 158, 160, 162, 163
Washington Flour Mill 40, 54
Washington Street School 40, 51
Washington Temperance Hotel 147, 162
Wasps Hanson St Studios 296, 305
Water Row 348, 361, 362, 363, 370
Watson's Home Bakery 348, 372
Watt, James 54, 112, 203, 232
WD & HO Wills 296, 299, 307
Weavers Society Anderston 57
Websters Theatre 293
Wellcroft Bowling Club 168, 178
Western Club 238, 256
West of Scotland Cricket club 7, 29
Whisky Bond 323, 342
Whitehill House 296, 311

Whitehouse Inn 323, 335
Whitevale Bowling Club 296, 308
William III 120, 202, 216-7, 336
Willowbank Community Garden 268, 288
Willowbank Public School 268, 287
Willow Tea Rooms 147, 156, 162, 165, 248
Wilson, Charles 30, 93, 130, 210, 246-7, 257, 282-3, 287
Windsor Tavern 27, 37
Woodlands Community Garden 268, 277
Woodside Public School 268, 288
World War I 9, 31, 72, 99, 160, 197, 253, 270, 283, 292, 360, 368, 374
World War II 16, 79, 90, 125, 174
Wyndford Estate 332

Y

Yorkhill Station 6, 18
Young William 252

Z

Zique's 7, 33, 37

Image credits

Cover Image, Provand's Lordship © Jon Arnold Images Ltd / Alamy Stock Photo, p.144, p.163, p. 164 Mackintosh at the Willow © Rachel Keenan Photography, p.177, inside cover images: view from Queen's Park, Stockingfield Bridge © Visit Scotland/Kenny Lamb

About us:

Based in London, Metro is a small independent publishing company with a reputation for producing well-researched and beautifully-designed guides.

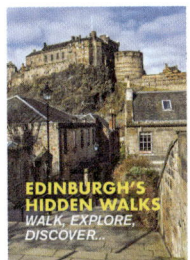

From narrow medieval 'wynd' to 21st-century thoroughfare, every Edinburgh street has a story to tell. Walk in the footsteps of great thinkers of the Scottish Enlightenment such as David Hume, find out where Robert Burns kissed his Nancy for the last time and shudder at the exploits of murderers Burke and Hare.

Edinburgh's Hidden Walks contains 14 detailed walks of the city, from the industrial docks of Leith to the grand Georgian squares of the New Town.

London's Hidden Walks Series

 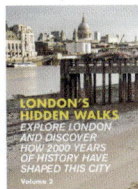 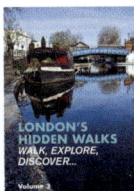 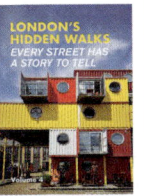

To find out more about Metro and order our guides, take a look at our website:

www.metropublications.com